Contemporary Women Writers of Spain

Twayne's World Authors Series

Spanish Literature

TWAS 798

Contemporary Women Writers of Spain

By Janet Pérez

Texas Tech University

Twayne Publishers
A Division of G. K. Hall & Co. • *Boston*

Contemporary Women Writers of Spain
Janet Pérez

Copyright 1988 by G.K. Hall & Co.
All rights reserved.
Published by Twayne Publishers
A Division of G.K. Hall & Co.
70 Lincoln Street
Boston, Massachusetts 02111

Copyediting supervised by Barbara Sutton
Book production by Gabrielle B. McDonald
Book design by Barbara Anderson

Typeset in 11 pt. Garamond
by Compset, Inc., Beverly, Massachusetts

Printed on permanent/durable acid-free paper
and bound in the United States of America

Library of Congress Cataloging in Publication Data

Pérez, Janet.
    Contemporary women writers of Spain / by Janet Pérez.
        p.   cm.—(Twayne's world authors series ; TWAS 798. Spanish
literature)
    Bibliography: p.
    Includes index.
    ISBN 0-8057-8229-X (alk. paper)
    1. Spanish literature—Women authors—History and criticism.
2. Spanish literature—20th century—History and criticism.
I. Title.   II. Series: Twayne's world authors series ; TWAS 798.
III. Series: Twayne's world authors series. Spanish literature.
PQ6055.P4   1988
860'.9'9287—dc19   87-34830
                                                                    CIP

For Genaro

Contents

About the Author

Janet Pérez obtained the M.A. and Ph.D. in Romance Languages at Duke University and has taught since 1977 at Texas Tech University where she is Paul Whitfield Horn Professor of Spanish and Associate Dean of the Graduate School. Previous teaching posts include Queens College, CUNY, and the University of North Carolina at Chapel Hill. She is the author of nearly one hundred articles and chapters in books, and has presented many papers at professional meetings, primarily in the areas of the twentieth-century Spanish novel, theater, poetry, and essay. Among her books are *The Major Themes of Existentialism in the Works of Ortega y Gasset,* and in the Twayne World Authors Series, *Ana María Matute, Miguel Delibes,* and *Gonzalo Torrente Ballester.* She edited *Novelistas femeninas de la postguerra española* and is a past or present member of some thirty editorial boards.

Preface

Spanish literature until quite recently has been less fortunate in attracting translators' attention than had literatures in French and German. The situation has improved in the second half of the century, but many classics from all periods of peninsular literature remain unknown outside of Spain. This is particularly true of contemporary works: with the exception of a few best-sellers, foreign publishers hesitate to risk the investment in writers who have not yet withstood the test of time and become incorporated in the literary canon. The novel, which requires the largest investment by translator and publisher, is most affected by such criteria. As a result, only a small percentage of this century's Spanish novels are known to an international reading public. Given the relative inaccessibility of peninsular fiction as a whole, it comes as no surprise that Spain's women novelists are still less known internationally.

Few general reference works are available to the English speaker; fewer yet include an adequate or representative number of women writers. Indeed, there are few up-to-date general references on Spanish women writers in any language (these are surveyed in chapter 1). Those women who write in other languages of the peninsula beside Castilian are often unknown even to the rest of Spain. Several bibliographical projects are currently under way, some concentrated upon the women writing in a given language and others limited by period or genre. Ambitious and complex undertakings, these projects will, when completed, add considerably to our knowledge of an undeservedly obscure literary corpus. Currently, however, the only relevant material in English requires a piecemeal approach to the subject of Spain's women narrators in this century. There is no general introduction or reference work on contemporary women narrators, only studies of specific individuals or a handful of such writers who share some common denominator. This book will therefore attempt to present a general overview and introduction for students of Spanish literature, for the monolingual reader of English, for the nonspecialized Hispanist, and for those with an interest in women's studies.

The quantity of writers and titles involved is surprisingly large, and often specific works have been unavailable for consultation or inclusion. The tradition of critical neglect combined with the small printings of works published in Spain (with the result that even relatively successful works are frequently soon out of print) has relegated a large number of works by women to oblivion or to the category of rare books. An often-unpropitious cultural context (wherein the female is viewed as intellectually incompetent) has contributed to unfavorable or patronizing criticism when neglect is not the norm. Even the expert on twentieth-century Spanish literature may be surprised by the frequency of unfamiliar names and titles. It is with full awareness of the inevitability of undeserved omissions and the necessarily provisional nature of the undertaking that this book is offered, not to fill the void but to begin to populate it.

Works by twentieth-century women writers in Spain comprise hundreds of authors and thousands of titles. Not all are equally meritorious or otherwise deserving of inclusion, and some prior evaluative selection has been made. As a rule, publications belonging to genres customarily perceived as subliterary have been excluded, as have authors of no more than three works (the reasoning here is that their contribution is limited, but not necessarily that the quality is subliterary). If exceptions occur, they are in the case of some of the most promising and most recent writers, who have had brief careers to date.

In the absence of powerful contravening factors, division by chronological groupings usually duplicates already-accepted schemes in use for male writers or the novel as a whole. When appropriate, factors uniting the women writers to established generational groupings are noted, and instances wherein women have anticipated developments in writings by male counterparts are indicated. Every effort is made in discussion of the works to give appropriate attention to aesthetic considerations, to recognize innovation and experimentation, and conversely, to take due notice of egregious shortcomings and failures. However, given the panoramic scope and introductory nature of the present volume, no in depth studies of individual writers or works are attempted. Without eschewing interpretation and evaluation, the text concentrates upon presentation and synthesis. Critical methodology is necessarily eclectic, including historical, biographical, sociological, cultural, symbolic, mythical, archetypal, feminist, rhetorical, and other hermeneutic components.

Treatment of writers bears little quantitative relationship to individual significance or artistic merit; rather, those writers whose importance has been recognized by critical studies in English are given relatively short shrift because of the availability of such reference works. Such writers are included, albeit briefly, however, because to exclude them would not only deform the total picture but give disproportionate visibility to others who have achieved less recognition. For the most part, I have consciously avoided attempts at definitive evaluation and have constructed no value hierarchies. To do so properly is a task that would require a separate volume. Nonetheless, some value judgments underlie the selections and inclusions in a work such as the present one, in which demands of space and limitations of length necessitate extreme selectivity in both primary and secondary sources. Primary works have been selected partially on the basis of relevance for women's studies; secondary works have been chosen with preference for accessibility and availability in English, or for the more recent and presumably more comprehensive, up-to-date coverage. Quotations in the text are minimal because of the impossibility of textual analysis of individual works, and most often such citations are extracts of critical works. In all cases, translations are my own. The Chronology has been severely pared, since it would be more confusing than useful if it were fully representative. Important prizes won by women are especially noted in the Chronology, and as many as possible of the important works by women in a given year. Even though some of the writers and works appearing in the Chronology may be currently unknown, their inclusion reflects significance at the time of appearance. Translations of the titles, contrary to usual practice, are not provided in the Chronology because of sheer numbers of works, but titles will be translated in the text.

The Notes contain specific references, so that secondary sources listed in the Selected Bibliography are limited to (1) works of a panoramic or general nature on contemporary women writers in Spain, (2) works of specific relevance for specialists in women's studies that include Spanish writers, and (3) studies of individual writers, with emphasis on books in English or otherwise of relatively easy access.

Very special thanks are due to the Dean and staff of the Graduate School at Texas Tech University for moral support and other more tangible support services, and to the Texas Tech Committee on State-Organized Research Funds for a grant permitting invaluable research opportunities in Spain.

Janet Pérez

Texas Tech University

Chronology

1902 Caterina Albert publishes *Drames rurales*.

1905 Albert, *Solitud*.

1906 Gregorio and María Martínez Sierra, *Tú eres la paz*.

1909 Carmen de Burgos, *Los inadaptados*. Concha Espina, *La niña de Luzmela*.

1910 Espina, *Despertar para morir*. María Martínez Sierra, *Todo es uno y lo mismo*.

1914 Espina, *La esfinge maragata*, winner of Fastenrath Prize.

1915 Burgos, *En la sima*.

1917 Burgos, *La rampa*.

1918 Espina's *El jayón* wins major theatrical prize.

1920 Espina, *El metal de los muertos*.

1926 Espina's *Altar mayor* wins National Prize for Literature.

1930 María Teresa León, *La bella del mal amor*. Rosa Chacel, *Estación, ida y vuelta*.

1931 Burgos, *Quiero vivir mi vida*.

1932 Carme Montoriol i Puig, *Teresa o la vida amorosa*. Mercè Rodoreda, *¿Sóc una dona honrada?*

1934 Rodoreda, *Del que hom no pot fugir*.

1936 Chacel, *A la orilla de un pozo*. Rodoreda's *Crim*.

1937 León, *Cuentos de la España actual*. Rodoreda's *Aloma* awarded Crexells Prize.

1938 Anna Murià i Romani, *La peixera*.

1941 León, *Contra viento y marea*. Chacel, *Teresa*.

1942 León, *Morirás lejos*. Elisabeth Mulder, *Crepúsculo de una ninfa*.

1944 Carmen Conde, *Vidas contra su espejo*.

1945 Carmen Laforet's *Nada* published; winner of first Nadal Prize. Chacel, *Memorias de Leticia Valle*.

1947 Eulalia Galvarriato's *Cinco sombras* wins Nadal Prize.

1948   Ana María Matute, *Los Abel.*

1950   León, *Las peregrinaciones de Teresa.* Conde, *En manos del silencio.*

1951   Elena Quiroga wins Nadal Prize with *Viento del norte.*

1952   Laforet, *La isla y los demonios.* Quiroga, *La sangre.* Matute, *Fiesta al noroeste.* Maria Aurèlia Capmany, *Necessitem morir.*

1953   Paulina Crusat, *Mundo pequeño y fingido.* Conde's *Las oscuras raíces* and *Cobre.* Dolores Medio's *Nosotros, los Rivero* wins Nadal Prize.

1954   Medio, *Compás de espera.* Quiroga, *Algo pasa en la calle.* Matute, *Pequeño teatro.* Carmen Martín Gaite, *El balneario.*

1955   Elena Soriano completes censored trilogy, "Mujer y hombre." Mercedes Fórmica, *A instancia de parte.* Mercedes Salisachs, *Primera mañana, última mañana.* Quiroga, *La enferma* and *La careta.* Matute, *En esta tierra.* Capmany, *L'altra ciutat.*

1956   Mercedes Ballesteros, *La cometa y el eco.* Salisachs, *Carretera intermedia* and *Una mujer llega al pueblo.* Medio, *Funcionario público.* Quiroga, *Plácida la joven.* Matute, *Los niños tontos.* Capmany, *Tana o la felicitat.*

1957   Rodoreda, *Vint-i-dos contes.* Martín Gaite wins Nadal Prize with *Entre visillos.*

1958   Medio, *El pez sigue flotando. Los hijos muertos* by Matute wins National Literary Prize after winning previous year's Critics' Prize.

1960   Chacel, *La sinrazón.* Ballesteros, *Taller.* Salisachs, *Vendimia interrumpida.* Quiroga, *Tristura.* Martín Gaite, *Las ataduras.* Matute, *Primera memoria,* awarded Nadal Prize.

1961   Medio, *Diario de una maestra.* Matute, *Tres y un sueño* and *Historias de la Artámila.*

1962   León, *Fábulas del tiempo amargo.* Rodoreda, *La Plaça del Diamant.* Martín Gaite, *Ritmo lento.*

1963   Conde's *Obra poética (1929–1962)* receives National Literary Prize. Concha Alós, *Los enanos* and *Los cien pájaros.* Medio, *Bibiana.*

1964   Matute, *Los soldados lloran de noche.*

1965   Alós, *Las hogueras.* Quiroga, *Escribo tu nombre.*

1966   Rodoreda, *El carrer de les Camèlies.* Alós, *El caballo rojo.*

1969 Matute, *La trampa*. Capmany, *Feliçment jo sóc una dona* and *Un lloc entre els morts*.

1970 Alós, *La madama*. Laforet, *La niña y otros relatos*. Ana María Moix, *Julia*. Montserrat Roig, *Molta roba i poc sabó*. . . . Maria Antònia Oliver, *Cròniques d'un mig estiu*.

1971 Matute, *La torre vigía*. Capmany, *Quim Quimà*. Moix, *Ese chico pelirrojo a quien veo cada día*. Antònia Vicens, *Material de fulletó*.

1972 Alós, *El rey de gatos*. Roig, *Ramona, adéu*. Oliver, *Croniques de la molt anomenada ciutat de Montcarrà*.

1973 Carmen Kurtz, *Al otro lado del mar*. Salisachs's *Adagio confidencial* a best-seller. Medio, *La otra circunstancia* and *Farsa de verano*. Quiroga, *Presente profundo*. Moix, *Walter, ¿por qué te fuiste?* Nùria Serrahima, *Mala guilla*.

1974 Rodoreda, *Mirall trencat*. Martín Gaite, *Retahilas*. Vicens, *La festa de tots els morts*.

1975 Salisachs' *La gangrena* tops best-seller lists. Alós, *Os habla Electra*. Oliver, *Coordenades espai-temps per guardar-hi les ensaimades*.

1976 *Barrio de Maravillas* by Chacel wins the Critics' Prize. Kurtz, *El regreso*. Martín Gaite, *Fragmentos de interior*. Lourdes Ortiz, *Luz de la memoria*.

1977 Conde, *La rambla*. Spanish edition of Chacel's *La sinrazón* wins a second Critics' Prize. Salisachs, *Viaje a Sodoma*. Helena Valentí, *L'amor adult*. Roig, *Els temps de les cireres*. Carme Riera, *Jo pos per testimoni les gavines*.

1978 Chacel and Conde nominated for Royal Spanish Academy; latter elected. Rodoreda, *Semblava de seda i altres contes*. Martín Gaite wins National Prize for Literature with *El cuarto de atrás*. Esther Tusquets, *El mismo mar de todos los veranos*.

1979 Tusquets, *El amor es un juego solitario*. Rosa Montero, *Crónica del desamor*. Ortiz, *Picadura mortal*.

1980 Rodoreda, *Quanta, quanta guerra*. Tusquets, *Varada tras el último naufragio*. Roig, *L'hora violeta*. Riera, *Una primavera per a Domenico Guarini*.

1981 Chacel, *Novelas antes de tiempo*. Tusquets, *Siete miradas en un mismo paisaje*. Montero, *La función Delta*. Ortiz, *En días como éstos*. Riera, *Epitelis tendríssims*. Valenti, *La solitud d'Anna*.

1982   Serrahima, *L'olor dels nostres cossos*. Roig, *L'òpera quotidiana*. Oliver, *Vegetal* and *Muller qui cerca espill*.

1983   Montero, *Te trataré como a una reina*. Josefina Aldecoa, *Los niños de la guerra*. Cristina Fernández Cubas, *Los altillos de Brumal*. Maria Angels Anglada, *Viola d'amore*.

1984   Aldecoa, *La enredadera*. Magdalena Guilló, *Entre el ayer y el mañana*.

1985   Chacel a contender for the Cervantes Prize. Moix, *Las virtudes peligrosas*. Tusquets, *Para no volver*. Fernández Cubas, *El año de Gracia*. Adelaida García Morales, *El Sur* and *Bene;* also, *El silencio de las sirenas*. Oliver, *Crineres de foc* and *Estudi en lila*.

1986   Alós, *El asesino de los sueños*. Ortiz, *Arcángeles*. Soledad Puértolas, *Burdeos*. Aldecoa, *Porque éramos jóvenes*. Guilló. *Un sambenito para el señor Santiago*. Valentí, *La dona errant*.

Chapter One
Introduction: Status of Women Writers in Spain

Women and women writers still face an uphill struggle in the relatively "liberated" societies of northern Europe and North America, yet their comparable freedom of movement, their access to education and to cultural opportunities, and their greater entrenchment in the job market may mislead the English-speaking reader into the assumption that similar situations prevail in Hispanic countries. Without orientation on the Spanish woman writer and her context, it is difficult to appreciate the effort required to produce fiction and the degree of innovation that specific works represent.

State of the Secondary Literature

Until recently, remarkably little scholarly treatment was accorded Spanish women writers, whether in Spain, the United States, or elsewhere. A survey in the late 1970s of doctoral dissertations in relevant fields completed in this country during a five-year period at the close of the Franco era (1972–76) revealed that only twenty-one of 1,145 dissertations, or 1.8 percent, had Spanish women writers as their subjects. Conditions were not too different on the postdoctoral level, as a review of five major professional periodicals for Hispanists edited or published in the United States (*Hispania, Hispanic Review, Hispanófila, Revista de estudios hispánicos, Revista hispánica moderna*) over a ten-year span disclosed that only twenty-six articles dealt with Spanish women writers (3 percent of the 850 articles published by these journals during the decade in question). Interest tends also to concentrate upon a few to the detriment of many. Of the twenty dissertations on postwar women novelists produced during the decade 1975–85, nine dealt with Ana María Matute, four with Elena Quiroga, and three with Carmen

Martín Gaite. The four with a multiple focus (considering more than one woman writer) all included at least two of the above. Thus, although interest in certain writers has intensified, it has by no means become generalized to the remainder of women writing.

Another symptom of generalized scholarly neglect of the majority of Spanish women writers is the limited space allotted them in literary histories and anthologies, where the few mentioned are exceptions that prove the rule that the woman writing in Spain is at considerable risk of being ignored. Of 215 twentieth-century Spanish writers listed in the *Columbia Dictionary of Modern European Writers* (2d ed., 1980), only nine are women, while the Revista de Occidente *Diccionario de literatura española* (4th ed., 1972) included only thirty women among more than 550 twentieth-century Spanish writers, a percentage of 1.8. Such statistics, while not exhaustive, are indicative, and even greater imbalance would result if earlier centuries were included in the sample.

Neglect by literary historians and professional Hispanists notwithstanding, Spain has produced a much larger number of worthy women writers than is generally known. The pioneering bibliographical works on Spanish women writers appeared in the latter part of the past century and early years of the present one, the first being Diego Ignacio Parada y Barreto's *Escritoras y eruditas españolas* (Madrid, 1881). Later in the same decade Juan Pedro Criado y Domínguez published his *Literatas españolas del siglo XIX: Apuntes bibliográficos* (Madrid: Pérez Dubrull, 1889), listing some 390 women in the categories of lyric poets, novelists, dramatists, and writers of unspecified genres, as well as writers of exclusively religious material (presumably nuns). Criado y Domínguez limits his focus to the nineteenth century, but a more ambitious bibliographer is Manuel Serrano y Sanz, easily the most significant compiler of women writers with his monumental effort, *Apuntes para una biblioteca de escritoras españolas desde el año 1401 al 1833* (Madrid, 1903–5; Notes for a Library of Spanish Women Writers from 1401 to 1833). This work made available the biographical and bibliographical or manuscript data for nearly 1,100 women writers, the majority of them authors whose works had remained buried in the archives of convents or languished out of print in libraries, seldom or never reissued. More recently, Margarita Nelken published another general work on the subject, *Escritoras españolas* (Barcelona: Labor, 1930) that is as much a political statement or denunciation of the biased treatment of women writers as a serious effort at comprehensive bibliography.

Nelken indicts the "rule" that in Spain there were/are no women writers.

Anthologies of women writers in this century have included Serrano y Sanz's specialized anthology of lyric poets, *Antología de poetisas líricas* (Madrid, 1915), as well as Carmen Conde's *Poesía femenina española (1939–1950)* (Barcelona: Bruguera, 1967) and *Poesía femenina española (1950–1960)* (Barcelona: Bruguera, 1971). The most comprehensive general anthology of women writers exclusive of poetry is that of Isabel Calvo de Aguilar, *Antología biográfica de escritoras españolas* (Madrid: Biblioteca Nueva, 1954), containing eighty-five contemporary writers, with a one-page biography/bibliography and short selection for each. In addition, three series of bibliographical articles on women writers that appeared during the late nineteenth and early twentieth centuries are worthy of note.[1]

Deserving mention as a symptomatic curiosity is the book *El feminismo en la literatura española* (1938; Feminism in Spanish Literature),[2] which begins with the image of women in the *Poem of Mio Cid* (ca. 1140) in which the wife and lady of royal family greets her husband (a lesser noble) by kneeling before him, weeping, and kissing his hands. The survey continues through some eight centuries of Spanish literature, with seldom a mention of female writers emphasis is upon the literary presentation of feminine figures. Of interest is the notion that the astute and malicious females who appear in medieval apologues (many of which came into Castilian literature by way of Oriental and Arabic sources) are skilled in all manner of tricks to deceive men, "the only defense of the serf. The woman who appears in these works is the natural product of Oriental feminine slavery." Later medieval works view women as objects of "utility or enjoyment," while the ideal of Don Juan Manuel (Castile's greatest medieval prose writer) is "absolute submission of the wife to the husband."[3]

So common was misogyny and so numerous the detractors of women that the liberal eighteenth-century encyclopedist, Benito Jerónimo Feijoo (1676–1764), a Benedictine friar who wrote his major work *Theatro crítico universal* (1726–1739, 8 vols.) to expose and combat serious common errors, devoted one of the longest discourses of his first volume to the "Defense of Women" (discourse 16). Feijoo observed that so frequently were women vilified that "hardly anything good about them is admitted." He further states that what is most emphasized is their limited understanding. "Therefore, after defending them briefly, I shall write at more length about their aptitude for all kinds of learning and sublime knowledge."[4] Noting that women's intellectual and artistic capacity had been a matter of sporadic debate from the Renaissance onward, Oñate points out that the situation of women in Spain "continued to be the same as in previous centuries. . . . *the only career for a woman was matrimony*" (220, italics in text).

Two recent works of relevance for the present discussion are Lucia Fox-Lockert's *Women Novelists in Spain and Spanish America* (Metuchen and London: Scarecrow Press, 1979) and Beth Miller, *Women in Hispanic Literature: Icons and Fallen Idols* (Berkeley, Los Angeles, and London: University of California Press, 1983). The former contains twenty-two essays on as many women narrators, most of them treating a single novel. Only nine of these women are from Spain; twentieth-century peninsular novelists include Espina, Laforet, Quiroga, Soriano, Medio, and Alós. Fox-Lockert's focus is upon family, social class, and sexuality, which may explain the disparity of quality and significance among the novels selected. The volume edited by Miller is relevant only marginally, emphasizing not women writers but the female characters portrayed in Hispanic literature of varied periods and countries. The theoretical considerations presented in the introduction (1–25) provide helpful cultural orientation, as does Linda Gould Levine's contribution, "The Censored Sex: Woman as Author and Character in Franco Spain" (289–315).

Amalia Martín-Gamero's *Antología del feminismo* (Madrid: Alianza Editorial, 1975) is sociological and international in focus, with translations from British, French, and American writers on the subject. A few early Spanish feminists—some of whom were also significant writers—are likewise included.[5]

The foregoing schematic review omits books and essays on individual women writers and biographical/bibliographical compilations related to an individual woman's writing in order to emphasize the scarcity of panoramic introductions, histories, and reference works. Almost nonexistent and seriously outdated for the most part, the few available sources are also of difficult access, which increases the significance of the newly published reference manual, *Women Writers of Spain: An Annotated Bio-Bibliographical Guide,* edited by Carolyn Galerstein (Westport, Conn.: Greenwood Press, 1986). This volume's focus is primarily upon the nineteenth and twentieth centuries. Without replicating unduly the efforts of Criado y Domínguez, the guide provides an expansion of available information on nineteenth-century women writers in Spain, and it offers the first general overview of women writing in the various creative genres in twentieth-century Spain, with entries on approximately two hundred figures.

Recalling that Serrano y Sanz ended his coverage (1401–1833) with some eleven hundred names, and that Criado y Domínguez listed some four hundred literary women of the nineteenth century who had achieved visibility prior to 1889, a ballpark estimate can be made of the total number of Spanish women writers. With approximately two hundred fifty figures listed in *Women Writers of Spain* whose birth dates (1865 or after) are sufficiently late that they would not have been included by Criado, the three bibliographies total some 1,750. Other names mentioned by Nelken, included in the articles cited in Note 1, or anthologized by Calvo would bring the total to around two thousand.

If only the top ten percent of these (i.e., two hundred) are worthy of remembering and reading, they comprise a number well in excess of the minimum necessary to establish a feminist canon and tradition. Yet, as Galerstein observes in her introduction, "The average reader of Spanish might have heard the names of Santa Teresa and Pardo Bazán but might not be familiar with their works. Those are about the only two women writers who would appear in histories of Spanish literature and anthologies which the average undergraduate major in Spanish would have studied." The chances of students' having read any others are minimal, for the majority of women novelists—even such world-class figures as Rosa Chacel and Mercè Rodoreda—are all but unknown, even in Spain.

For those who must rely on translations, the offerings are still more restricted. The list in *Women Writers in Translation: An Annotated Bibliography, 1945–1962* (New York and London: Garland Press, 1984) includes only twelve authors from Spain, with twenty individual titles plus two translations of Santa Teresa's collected works. Yet the prolific and distinguished accomplishments of Spain's women writers in the one hundred years just past are unparalleled in the country's history and frequently on a par with Europe's best.

Women who write in Catalan, Gallego, or Spain's other minority languages are "doubly minorities," essentially condemned to perpetual oblivion. Kathleen McNerney, editor of the non-Castilian materials in *Women Writers of Spain,* explains in her introduction that only one Catalan name was originally included in the list for annotating. Since no lists of Catalan women writers existed, she searched other bibliographies and dictionaries, histories of literature, and critical works for names that might be Catalan and female. The task was fraught with pitfalls, for example, the best-known Catalan writer of the turn-of-the-century years, Caterina Albert (1869–1966) used a male pseudonym, "Victor Català." Such practices were not uncommon: one of Spain's best-known writers in the nineteenth century, Cecilia Böhl von Faber, wrote under the male pseudonym "Fernán Caballero." Not only did women conceal their identities behind male pseudonyms and assumed female names, they also frequently hid behind first initials giving no clue as to gender, with the result that much work by women was in danger of being attributed to men. A case in point is that of María Lejárraga (María de Martínez Sierra) whose collaborations with her husband masked her authorship of many of "his" works (as shown by Patricia O'Connor in her study, *Gregorio and María Martínez Sierra* [Boston: Twayne, 1977]). Even María's *Cartas a las mujeres de España* (1916; Letters to the Women of Spain) are attributed to Gregorio in— of all things—the bibliography of *Antología del feminismo*.[6]

Spain's conservative, traditionalist society has long held rigid and narrow views concerning women's roles and proper activities. Critical distortion and ridicule, as Dale Spender shows in *Women of Ideas (and What Men Have Done to Them)* (London: Pandora Press, 1984), have combined with patriarchal scholarship to bury the works of many women or to devalue their ideas. Possibly some future feminist researcher will do for Spanish women novelists what Dale Spender has done for the English in her *Mothers of the Novel: 100 Good Women Writers Before Jane Austen* (London: Pandora Press, 1986). Such a work might well begin with María de Zayas, author of what has been called the "Spanish *Decameron*." The listing offered by Juan Ignacio Ferreras— who names eighty-three women novelists in his *Catálogo de novelas y novelistas españoles del siglo XIX* (1979; Catalogue of Spanish Novels and Novelists of the Ninteenth Century)—would provide ample basis. Women's contributions to fiction in the past century are summarized at the end of this section in order to situate the works by Spain's twentieth-century female writers within a specific tradition and canon.

A small number of additional sources dealing with multiple women writers have recently appeared, including a volume of interviews with Spanish feminists, *Feminismo ante el Franquismo,* edited by Linda Gould Levine and Gloria Waldman (Miami: Ediciones Universal, 1982), and a collection of critical articles that I edited, *Novelistas femeninas de la postguerra española* (Madrid: Porrúa, 1983). *Estreno,* the review of contemporary Spanish theater, devoted a volume (X, 2 [Fall 1984]) to Spain's women dramatists. And in addition to many individual studies, dissertations, and other works in progress, a more complete annotated bibliography of Catalan women writers is under way.

Condition of Women in Spain

Some notion of the sociological context in which Spanish women writers have had to work is an indispensable prerequisite to understanding their concerns, as well as for any hermeneutics of their fiction. The accelerated rate of change since 1975 necessitates some retrospective framework: visiting Spain today would give little notion of the conditions for women under Franco or those factors that contributed to their psychic formation. For several reasons 1975 is a watershed year for Spanish women. As UNESCO's International Women's Year, it began late in Spain and on a low key. Although feminists found end results disappointing, the observance did bring some attention to bear upon the anachronistic morass in which Spanish women dwelt. An unrelated but enormously significant event, the death of Franco in November 1975, marks the beginning of the transition to democracy. More on the enormous changes of the past decade can be found in Antonio Bar, "Spain: a Culture in Transition," in *Culture and Society in Contemporary Europe,* edited by Stanley Hoffman and Paschalis Kitromilides (Boston: Center for European Studies, Harvard University, 1981) and in Raymond Carr and Juan Pablo Fusi, *Spain: Dictatorship to Democracy* (2d ed.; London: Allen & Unwin, 1981).

A fairly detailed historical picture providing a sociopolitical context within which to place the contributions of some early feminist writers is offered by Concha Fagoaga, *La voz y el voto de las mujeres.*[7] This history of Spanish suffragism concentrates upon the early feminist movement from 1877 to 1931, which resulted in women's gaining the vote. Another essential source, a classic in its field and historically valid despite intervening change, is Margarita Nelken's *La condición social de la mujer en España* (1922?; The Social Condition of Women in Spain), written in 1919 and reprinted in 1975 with a prologue by Catalan feminist Maria Aurèlia Capmany.[8] Nelken's essay was highly controversial upon appearance because of the frank discussion of working conditions for women, such problems as prostitution, women's powerlessness in legal matters, and substandard maternity care.

Many advances gained during the Second Republic (1931–36) were promptly revoked by the Franco regime: divorce laws were repealed, and stringent, reactionary legislation enacted, severely curtailing women's right to work.[9] Under guise of protecting the family, married women were not allowed to work outside the home, except for those employed in domestic service. Such statutes resulted in extending the lengthy *noviazgo* (official engagement), averaging eight or nine years, so that women could work before marriage. The negative psychological effects of institutionalized extended engagement are presented in a study published at the end of the Franco era, *Noviazgo y matrimonio en la burguesía española* (1974; Engagement and Marriage in the Spanish Upper Middle Classes).[10] Under laws viewing her as a perpetual minor, the married woman became a ward of her husband, and one statute made him responsible for any crimes she committed. It was under this provision that the well-known leftist playwright Alfonso Sastre was imprisoned in 1974 along with his wife, psychiatrist Eva Forest, when she was implicated in the assassination of Prime Minister Carrero Blanco. The plight of internationally known novelist Ana María Matute, estranged from her husband in the 1950s, illustrates the married woman's dilemma in Franco Spain. During more than three years while the legal separation procedure dragged on, she was forced to live in limbo, residing with a sister, because as a married woman she could not have her own apartment without her husband's consent, nor could she have her own bank account. When awarded an international literary prize, she could not go to claim it: she was not permitted to leave the country without her husband's authorization. Nor was she allowed to travel with her son without the husband and father's documented permission. Her semi-incarceration attests more succinctly than any theoretical legal or sociological exposition to the situation in which Spanish women, writers included, found themselves under Franco.

Reform of the Spanish Civil Code in the early 1970s brought changes in the work laws affecting women and restored (on paper and in theory) certain civil rights. Socioeconomic realities do not change by fiat or overnight, however, and an article by María Victoria Abril and María Jesús Miranda in the liberal magazine *Triunfo* (April 1975) concluded that Spanish women with family responsibilities at that date continued to be "absolutely dependent," economically and otherwise, on the male "head of the family," not so much because of legal norms as social ones. A detailed picture of women's situation at the end of the Franco era appears in *Sexo, mujer y natalidad en España* (1974; Sex,

Women and the Birth Rate in Spain) by the controversial sociologist, Amando de Miguel.[11] In *El miedo a la igualdad* (1975; Fear of Equality),[12] Amando de Miguel analyzes Spanish sexual behavior, denouncing male attempts to dominate and control, ranging from masculine opposition to women's working to "macho" resistance to using contraceptives. As a complement to Miguel's essay, Nuria Beltrán's *¿Muerte civil de la española?* (1975; Civil Demise of the Spanish Woman?)[13] provides the perspective of a female lawyer on problems of women in marriage, separation, widowhood, and sexual questions.

Whatever the problems of the married woman, those of the spinster in patriarchal Spanish society of the recent past were such that only a woman of rare courage would opt for the single life. Throughout most of the country's history women were prepared only for marriage or the convent, and the Republic's incipient reforms were swept away with the return to traditional norms.[14] The almost nonexistent "career woman" was suspect, and prejudice against the spinster was so strong that she was little short of a pariah. So ingrained were/are these discriminatory attitudes in Spanish society and so pervasive the negative stereotyping that even female writers tend to portray the unmarried woman as an object either of pity or of scorn.[15] More detailed information on the situation of unmarried women in the Franco era may be obtained from two books by María Salas, *Nosotras las solteras* (1955; We Old Maids [Barcelona: Juan Flores]) and *Solteras de hoy* (1966; Unmarried Women Today [Madrid: PPC]).

With the nation's first elections in forty years during the summer of 1978, after four decades with only one legal political organization, parties proliferated so that by the end of that year (the first in which other parties were legalized), more than two hundred had been established. Women's political groups were similarly splintered, and with the widespread indifference of middle-class Spanish women, it was not until the summer of 1983 that the Spanish Feminist Party held its first congress.[16] Other advances were achieved in the interim. Perhaps the most hotly debated and ultimately anticlimatic was the legalization of divorce at the end of August 1983. At least equally significant was the establishment in the same year of a national Instituto de la Mujer (Women's Institute) under the auspices of the Ministry of Culture, which has subsequently created many regional information centers on women's rights (a matter about which large sectors of the feminine population are still ignorant, given the newness of the changes and the fact that many lower-class women are functionally illiterate). A governmental agency comparable to Washington, D.C. bureaus, the Instituto de la Mujer has created a varied spectrum of support agencies in its scant four years of existence, including family planning centers, health care agencies, psychosocial assistance centers, hospitals, clinics, halfway houses for victims of abuse and domestic violence, and other emergency refuge centers and legal services for women. One of the problems in the cultural arena echoes a quandary in the feminist political sphere: the general lack of interest on the part of a large sector of the female population.[17] There has been some modest success—thanks in part to subsidies—with the magazine *Mujeres,* a bimonthly launched in 1984 with sections for Galician, Catalan, and Basque women as well as Castilian. This periodical has taken on such problems as women's disinterest in the daily news and the phenomenon of "lonely hearts" magazines and pulp novels (the publications most read by Spanish women today, according to sales figures).

Likewise in the cultural sphere, Spain's official dictionary, the *Diccionario de la Real Academia Española,* became a target late in 1985 when the Socialist government recommended to the Royal Academy a revision of language belittling women or otherwise deprecating them (e.g., the latest [1984] edition of the Dictionary of the Royal Academy included among its definitions of "mujer" [woman] such expressions as "pública," "ramera" [whore], "mundana" [worldly], "perdida" [fallen woman], and defined "maestra" [schoolmarm] as "mujer del maestro" [the schoolteacher's wife]). Thus, an effort is under way to eliminate sexism from the country's most prestigious dictionary, although many problems remain in areas of possibly more pressing concern, such as jobs. *Información Cultural* 37 (June 1986) reported that one of four women of working age is a maid (10) and referred to the Royal Decree of August 1985 ordering labor regulations to be drawn up covering domestic servants (these went into effect late in 1986, setting minimal employment standards).[18] Most women working in such jobs are not covered by social security or any form of retirement; 21 percent are totally illiterate, while 41 percent have only the rudiments of elementary education. "Live-in" maids suffer the worst working conditions of all and are most vulnerable.

Progress since the death of Franco has been significant, perhaps even impressive, but the distance still to be traveled is great. Not only was it necessary to start from a point well behind most of Europe, but also new complications have arisen with the rapidly increasing percentage of women in the work force and the bettering of women's economic status.[19] Spanish student demonstrations and riots early in 1987 drew attention to the problem of access to higher education: only the top 12 percent of Spanish students are admitted to universities, and there is little financial assistance. Given the tradition of de-emphasis upon education for women, the female population is disadvantaged in the competition both for university slots and intellectual distinction.

On a more positive note, Spanish women are writing in record numbers, and some of the most exciting literature in Spain today is being written by women. Abolition of the last vestiges of the Franco regime's censorship on 31 December 1978 did not produce the great literary outpouring expected by some (in fact, the level of literary quality dropped considerably). Censorship obliges authors to exercise their ingenuity to circumvent it, and to do so by strictly literary means: figurative language, allegory, symbolism, allusion, judicious placing of narrative silences, neobaroque convolutions, indirectness, and so on.[20] The aesthetic values of texts produced under these conditions often exceed those written without restraints, which may verge on the diatribe or sermon, or otherwise diminish artistically because of excessive directness. Such dangers may pose more of a threat for fiction written by men: censorship takes many forms, and controls inscribed within societal norms are far more pervasive and effective than any provided by the political mechanisms of a given regime. Women writers must still work within the constraints of unofficial but perfectly real "gender censorship."

As Spain ends its first decade as a democracy,[21] an unparalleled four generations of women writers share the literary scene with three-quarters of a century of varying experiences, values, perspectives, and ideologies. The best notion of the change in the interim can be gained by comparing the women writers of the several generations, their themes and techniques, and observing the evolution (as well as revolution) achieved. Women writers' new numbers, new visibility, and new freedoms, their heightened levels of consciousness, education, and self-awareness, improved channels of communication, and increased contacts with one another offer hope that the best is yet to come.

Heritage of the Nineteenth Century

From mid-century to the advent of the Revolution of 1868 and realism, Spain's most prestigious novelist was a woman, Cecilia Böhl von Faber (1796–1877), "Fernán Caballero."[22] Frequently translated in Europe and America, her work was much admired and praised by foreign critics. Considered the first great writer of popular best-sellers, she is credited with restoring the Spanish novel to public favor. While her conservative, moralizing posture has contributed considerably to the aging of her work, she was a major innovator in her day, anticipating key facets of realism, and even now is arguably the most significant transitional link between romanticism and the regional and realistic movements in the novel. The feminist elements that may be gleaned from her treatment of women, marriage, family life, and the problems of personal happiness versus duty to family, church, and society are attenuated by her uncritical acceptance and staunch defense of patriarchal values.

Although born in Cuba (then a Spanish colony), Gertrudis Gómez de Avellaneda (1814–73) lived most of her adult life on the mainland.[23] Avellaneda was more "liberated" in her life-style than in her literary ideology, but both her life and work were important precedents upon which future women writers could build. Avellaneda has some aesthetic significance also as a precursor of realism, helping to construct a bridge between romantic fiction and more solid ground where the great realistic novels could flourish. She should be remembered for her ideas, especially her antislavery stance, her attack on prisons and ills of the criminal justice system, her presentation of women as victims of society's laws, her depiction of the stifling conformity and limitation of provincial domestic life, her analysis of education for young ladies, and, perhaps most important, her advocacy of women's intellectual capacities and her portraits of enlightened, cultured, and moderately liberated feminine models, as well as treatments of the conflict between a career and traditionally inscribed feminine roles. Beth Miller's essay, "Gertrude the Great: Avellaneda, Nineteenth-Century Feminist,"[24] updates views of Avellaneda's contributions.

Carolina Coronado (1823–1911) lived through the height of romanticism, the rise and decline of realism and naturalism, and the heyday of the Generation of 1898. More moderate than Avellaneda, she nevertheless opposed religious intolerance and pointed out the dangers for women who attempted to compete with men in cultural and humanistic pursuits. She lucidly portrayed the deleterious effects for women of the double standard of morality, and she condemned wife-beating.

Another and more prolific woman writer, the reputed author of more than a hundred works, María del Pilar Sinués y Navarro (1835–93), made women her primary and almost exclusive subjects, treating gender roles, marriage, motherhood, domestic life, feminine role models, the education of women, and topics supposedly of special or exclusively feminine interest. Her aesthetics were minimal and not at all innovative, and her ideology extremely conservative as evinced by her ardent espousal of patriarchal attitudes. Aside from her feminine thematics, Sinués's major contribution may have come as a spin-off of her enormous popular success, which served to demonstrate the existence of women as literary consumers, a previously overlooked presence in the publishing marketplace.

Ana García de la Torre, approximately a contemporary of Sinués, with Galdós and other leading realists (no biographical data are known), was progressive for the epoch in her presentation of problems of class, gender, and the proletariat, as well as for objective examination of the institution of marriage from a variety of perspectives. Among the first to portray the "working girl," she is unusual among Spanish women writers in treating utopian socialism, workers' movements, and "decent" alternative life-styles for women beyond marriage and the convent. Dolors Monserdà de Macía (1845–1919) is most significant for her exposé of materialism and amorality in the upper class. The Catalan novelist's denunciation was as innovative as was her depiction of the self-made woman and examination of several fairly complex socioeconomic issues. Her experimentation produced something resembling the internal monologue, endowing her with aesthetic significance as a precursor of fictional techniques of European modernism. Monserdà should be remembered also for her interest in the working class and problems of the working woman. She contributed to eliminating overidealization, sentimentalism, and moralizing from women's fiction, and moved toward rehabilitating the stereotypes of the embittered and solitary spinster. Portraying a broad spectrum of society, Monserda provided a comprehensive, objective, and realistic vision, helping to steer fiction by women into the mainstream of realism.

Emilia Pardo Bazán (1851–1921), one of the giants of nineteenth-century realism and naturalism, ranks on a par with Galdós, Clarín, and Valera, and clearly above other male writers.[25] Spain's most significant feminist in the past century, she is also that country's greatest woman writer, rightly credited with introducing naturalism to Spain.[26] Influential both in her theory and practice of the novel, she defended higher education for women and advocated better treatment of illegitimate children. Her presentation of female sexuality as natural rather than reprehensible, criticism of the double standard, and impersonal presentations of many instances of abuse of women and children are but a fraction of the necessary and significant foundations she constructed for the benefit of future writers. More important than her ideas, perhaps, was her example, and the tenacity with which she defended women's rights to areas previously reserved for men. Pardo Bazán, Monserdà, and several lesser contemporaries lived until well into the present century, so that new feminine writers appearing on the scene after 1900 were not alone, bereft of tradition and preceptors, as had been essentially the case a hundred years before. Their establishment of an initial feminist canon helps to explain the surprising quantity, quality, and visibility of women writers in Spain today.

Chapter Two
The Turn-of-the-Century Generation

Women narrators of the turn of the century are approximate historical contemporaries of the Generation of 1898 (Unamuno, the eldest, was born in 1864, and Juan Ramón Jiménez, the youngest, in 1881). Most of the women in question were born in the 1870s, a few in the 1860s, so that reckoning by birth dates places them within the same time frame. However, there is little indication of association or literary affinities with the male writers of the period. Some occasional evidence of cultural, literary, artistic, and intellectual coincidence with the Generation of 1898 does appear in these women's work, but the eldest of the group, Caterina Albert, belongs most properly with the naturalists of the close of the nineteenth century, and may be compared with Blasco Ibáñez, a contemporary of the Generation who is usually excluded. Carmen de Burgos's interest in the occult, the diabolic, and spiritualism coincides with Valle-Inclán's, whose works are rich in relevant motifs (for example, "la señorita medium" in *Tirano Banderas* and diabolic possession in "Mi hermana Antonia"). Burgos's satire of Calderonian honor echoes a preoccupation of Pérez de Ayala (*Tigre Juan, El curandero de su honra*), and her presentation of lower-class life in Madrid recalls several novels of Baroja. Concha Espina's ingenious burlesque of a foppish and mediocre modernist poet in *Despertar para morir* suggests that she shared Unamuno's negative evaluation of that movement. The books devoured by young Regina in Espina's *Agua de nieve* (the philosophies of Nietzsche, Schopenhauer, and Renan) comprise the works of the most significant thinkers who influenced the Generation. Espina's *costumbrista* attention to picturesque regional detail (more characteristic of the nineteenth-century although with appreciable stylistic differences) finds an occasional contemporary counterpart in many descriptive inventories of Azorín's fiction and essays. Such coincidences, however, are little more than what might be expected among writers from the same place and time. Espina's treatment of the theme of national regeneration, although it appears somewhat later in her work, is a more substantial thematic similarity, and she shares other common points with Ganivet and Maeztu (a passing interest in humanitarian socialism, in the latter instance, followed by a common reverting to political and religious conservatism). These scattered details are insufficient, however, as the basis of an argument for including the women writers of the period within the Generation of 1898, despite the arbitrariness of its roster.

A Major Catalan Cultivator of Rural Naturalism

Caterina Albert (1869–1966) was born to a family of rural Catalan gentry and spent most of her life in the small Mediterranean fishing village of L'Escala, on the Costa Brava. The rugged landscape and simple, robust people exerted a permanent influence on her literary works. Shy and quiet, Albert was largely self-taught, but learned French and Italian via travels, acquiring a broad and varied cultural background. Her early works were mostly poetry and drama, and in 1901 she published *Quatre monolegs* (Four Monologues), intended for the stage and following the Renaixença style of the famous Catalan dramatist, Angel Guimerà. All four verse monologues have feminist themes or implications: A woman reminisces about her life in "La tieta," while in "Pere Martir" the speaker is a servant by that name. "La Vepa" portrays a working-class woman, and "Germana Pau" is a nun in a sanatorium, whose speech is addressed to a fellow nun at her cell door. It is not for her verse theater that Albert is remembered, however, but as one of the best Catalan prose writers of all times. Many consider her this century's best writer of fiction in Catalan. Comparable to Pardo Bazán in her combination of rural themes and naturalistic techniques, she had another master (in addition to Zola): the great nineteenth-century Catalan novelist, Narçis Oller. Albert's output is smaller, comprising a single-volume edition of *Obres completes,* of some 1,900 pages.[1]

Whether because of timidity or caution, Albert wrote under a male pseudonym, "Victor Català." Her view of the rural world is generally somber, grim, and pessimistic, often brutal. When her identity became known, she was furiously attacked by modernists and the *Noucentistes* (early twentieth-century neoclassicists) who considered it improper for a woman to write such "crude" and violent works. Her writings were daring in subject and themes, and the starkly realistic depiction of rural life disconcerted the public, the more so when it was revealed that the author was a woman. Perhaps Albert's best works are the *Drames rurales* (1902; Rural Dramas), a collection of twelve powerful and desolate stories of country people in which life is painted in darkest hues, characters are plagued by disease, and the social problems depicted include alcoholism, violence, and poverty.

Terry views Albert's ruralist fiction as a "partial reassessment of narrative form" with a "deliberately fragmented structure encouraged by *modernism* [which] leads in the direction of fantasy and Symbolism." Català undertook the task of transforming "the older type of realism through an awareness of *modernista* aesthetics."[2] The *Guia de literatura catalana contemporania* (which drew up a critics' list of three hundred works nominated to figure among this century's fifty best titles in Catalan literature) included Albert's *Drames rurales* and *Caires vius* among the original nominees, and *Solitud* among the fifty finalists.[3] Aware of the potential shock value of her material, Català wrote a preface warning delicate urban damsels among the readership to steer clear. *Ombrìvoles* (1904; Shady Places) collects four additional stories that reiterate and continue thematics and techniques of the rural dramas.

Solitud (1905; Solitude), Albert's best-known novel, usually considered her masterpiece, achieved immediate success and was promptly translated into Spanish, German, French, Portuguese, and English. Sometimes termed realistic, it blends such naturalistic traits as detailed description and a deterministic view of life with lyricism, idealism, symbolic characters and vision, mythical and legendary elements, and the contrapuntal interplay of the most sublime and perverse motivations. Pastor, an idealized shepherd figure in the tradition of Rousseau, acquires mythic proportions, but is not fully integrated into the plot. Mila, the female protagonist, accompanies her ineffectual husband to a remote hermitage where he has taken a keeper's job. In the mountain isolation Mila's hard life is complicated by the baleful and deleterious influence of a demonic being, Anima, upon her husband, who rapidly disintegrates. After an outbreak of violence, Mila is alone but liberated. Without transgressing the bounds of verisimilitude, the narrative achieves a powerful impact that made it the model for a whole group of lesser novelists who followed Albert in the creation of a ruralist novel characterized by primitive, alienated characters, rugged scenes imbued with grandeur, material verisimilitude, and the everyday discourse of the common people. Català's most distinguished follower was Prudenci Bertrana. Less-talented writers exaggerated the wild settings and rude characters, and for some years Catalan literature was inundated by ruralist novels whose "peasant speech" was sometimes achieved by extreme vulgarity.

Caires vius (1907; Living Aspects), a third collection of short narratives, is preceded by an extensive authorial foreword, a meditation upon the role of literature in the modern revival of Catalan culture. As in *Solitud*, many stories feature legendary or mythical content. Jaume Vidal Alcover prefers Català's short stories to her longer fiction, considering the brief pieces artistically superior.[4] With the vicious attacks following revelation of the identity of "Victor Català," the author ceased writing until 1918, when she tried her hand at an urban novel, the three-volume *Un film (3.000 metres)* (A Film [3,000 Meters]), which failed with critics and public alike. The novel's experimental form was analogous to the film medium and specifically the serial films then in vogue. Deliberately imitating the *folletín* (nineteenth-century serial pulps) upon which these early films were based, Català incorporated several clichés of the genre that she perceived as reincarnate in the nascent cinema medium. Her transgeneric intertextuality was not grasped by critics or readers of the day. Anticipating the objectivist movement in postwar Spain by several decades, Albert attempted a variant of narrative objectivity resembling the camera's. The work's poor reception may have resulted also from Albert's treatment of an unfamiliar environment and cast of neopicaresque-type characters. *Un film* is a stylized, sordid tale of an abandoned orphan, Nonat (whose name suggests an Unamuno-style play on words, meaning "not born"). Nonat's obsessive desire to solve the mystery of his parents' identity, plus a congenital ambition, lead to delinquency and eventually death. The relative absence of plot (typical of objectivist works later in the century) and the episodic structure found in both the picaresque and "dehumanized" writings of the 1920s may also have contributed to the lack of acceptance.

Conflicting dates for her birth (from 1869 to 1873) notwithstanding, Albert lived to well past ninety, writing to an advanced age. Later works include several collections of short fiction: *La mare balena* (1920; the Mother Whale, seven stories), *Marines* (1928; two chapters of an unfinished novel); *Contrallums* (1930; Against the Light, eleven tales); *Vida molta* (1950; A Lot of Life, thirteen stories); and *Jubileu* (1951; Jubilee, eleven stories). A slightly different late collection is *Mosaic* (1946), containing lyrical, intimate essays on personal topics reflecting the writer's everyday life: her home, garden, relatives and friends, even the weather and humble household objects. Also included in her *Com-*

plete Works are journalistic articles, academic speeches, prefaces to other writers' works, and correspondence.

Caterina Albert was sometimes perceived as a neo-naturalist because her writings included naturalistic sordidness but were not based upon scientific theory. However, her use of symbolic elements and scenes of primitive rusticity, which were nonetheless enormously pictorial and sumptuously colored in their splendid landscapes, led other critics to class her with *Modernisme* (understood in Catalonia as a transcending of romanticism).[5] Not a feminist in the usual sense, Albert was not associated with women's causes, and her writings displayed no greater interest in the lives of women than of men. She definitely did not write on "women's topics," yet both her work and personality are of particular interest because the subtext of her fiction is a determined declaration of equality for women writers. Català refused to accept societally imposed limitations based on gender. In addition, her aesthetic innovations, the high quality of her work, her literary leadership, and unprecedented number of disciples acquired among male writers are all factors rendering her exceptional and unique.

An Aristocratic Expatriate

Sonia Casanova de Lutoslawski (1862–1958) was born in the village of Almeiras in the province of Coruña (Galicia). In 1887 she married a Polish nobleman-philosopher, and from that time on lived largely outside Spain. However, she maintained contacts with her homeland, collaborating in the Spanish press. Casanova learned Polish well enough to publish in that language and was an active participant in the turn-of-the-century women's movement, working especially in the field of health care to improve hygiene and combat tuberculosis. A cultivator of many genres, she published travelogues, histories, short and long fiction, essays, plays, and poetry, and became best known for her lyrics, characterized by a romantic quest for meaning and anguished, impossible love. Casanova achieved a measure of official recognition, symbolized by awarding of the Cross of Alfonxo XII, and was admitted to the Real Academia Gallega.

Fascinated by Russia from an early date, Casanova treated Russia or Russian characters in many of her works. Her first novel, *El doctor Wolski. Páginas de Polonia y Rusia* (undated, ca. 1905; Dr. Wolski. Pages from Poland and Russia), traces the vicissitudes of the relationship between an idealistic Polish doctor educated in Russia, and a skeptical, hedonistic Russian friend. Reminiscent at times of Unamuno's *Amor y pedagogía* with its demonstration of the inapplicability of scientific theory to the realities of human life, love, and procreation, *El doctor Wolski* presents a scientist who has developed a formula for genetic improvement of the human race that leads him to break the commitment to his Russian fiancée, tubercular from excess studying, in order to marry a robust Polish woman (who fails to produce heirs). The topic was sufficiently current in the early years of this century that it appears in Baroja's *El árbol de la ciencia,* and similar theories are satirized by Pérez de Ayala in *Prometeo.*

Lo eterno (1907, The Eternal), a short novel, treats a favorite topic of Valera, a priest's conflict between his ecclesiastical duty and vow of chastity and temptations of the flesh, and like Valera, Casanova attempts a psychological study. Hers, however, is tainted by melodrama and more than the required dose of plot complications. Having entered the priesthood in spite of the influence of his free-thinker father, the hero faces temptation in the form of an attractive young woman, seduced and abandoned. The possible solution offered by Protestantism, which allows clerics to marry, complicates his struggle before the conflict is resolved via the stereotypical device of martyrdom.

Más que amor: cartas (1909; More than Love: Letters) is an epistolary novel with possible autobiographical ingredients. An exiled Spanish widow who lives in Poland with her children attempts the regeneration of a philandering Madrid politician, known only slightly on the basis of a pair of widely separated encounters. Her efforts to infuse idealism and morality into the life of her correspondent come to naught. A personal experience of solitude and pessimism concerning human relationships emerges from the reading. In two collections of brief fiction, *El pecado* (1911, Sin) and *Exóticas* (1912), Casanova expresses more explicitly feminist concerns. Set largely in Galicia, the eleven stories of *El pecado* treat incompatibility of the sexes in love and marriage, and study feminine guilt and responsibility from a psychological standpoint. The short pieces of *Exóticas* include family scenes and sociological commentary, and in addition to social and feminist questions, recount Casanova's problems with Russian literary authorities and censors.

Princesa rusa (1922: The Russian Princess) sketches the "dolce vita" of the Russian nobility and the diversions of the frivolous international set, an aspect in which the interests of this novelist overlap those of Baroja. Casanova treats the problem of divorce in marriages of mixed nationality and religion, focusing on a Russian femme fatale married to a Spanish marquis. Pursuing her study of the contrasting values of the wealthy international exiles from Eastern Europe and traditional Spanish norms, in *Como en la vida* (1930: As in Life) the novelist compares the existence of the turn-of-the-century equivalent of the jet set with life in a rural Galician *pazo* (which the hero abandons, as he does his childhood sweetheart, for a widowed Russian princess). Disillusioned by her erotic betrayals, he finally returns to Spain to volunteer his services in Morocco in a romantic gesture toward self-redemption and the defense of traditional values. A more somber and "real" world appears in *Las catacumbas de Rusia roja* (1933; Red Russian Catacombs), which depicts the conflict between revolutionaries and counterrevolutionaries after the Bolshevik revolution. It might be termed a continuation of the previous novel insofar as the widowed Russian princess, Alix, reappears as the lover of an idealistic revolutionary hero whose first love is his mission. Traditional marriage is contrasted with free love, and romantic love with transcendent ideological commitment, in a plot whose trappings are again frequently those of melodrama (disguise, imprisonment, mysterious deaths).

Some Lesser Vernacular Writers

Palmira Ventòs i Cullell (1862–1917) wrote consistently under the masculine pseudonym of Felip Palma. Born and reared in Barcelona, she nonetheless depicts rural Catalonia in her works of fiction, as well as in her works for the theater. Realism and naturalism, the vogue during her formative and apprenticeship years, provide a pervasive background, although Ventòs adds elements of lyricism and comic relief (sometimes folkloric in nature), as well as a certain controlled sentimentality. At the time of her relatively early death Ventòs left a number of unpublished works. *Asprors de la vida* (1904; Asperities of Life), a collection of five short stories, pictures the harshness of rural life, human selfishness, cruelty, and evil in Catalan villages. In this respect, Ventòs may be seen as a continuer of the ruralism of Caterina Albert. Utilizing a variant of the pathetic fallacy, Ventòs depicts her characters as victims who play out their solitude and despair on the stage of an indifferent nature. *La caiguda* (1907; The Fall) is a novelette portraying human solitude on the individual level and human selfishness on the collective level. The brutish nature of mankind, together with the harshness of village existence found in the earlier collection, reappear in *La caiguda,* but are softened by sentimental themes and an emphasis on the harmonizing power of love. Although weakened by dependence on coincidence, the narrative still expresses a powerful vision.

Carme Karr i Alfonsetti (1865–1943), another Barcelona writer, was active in the *Modernisme* (Catalan modernism) movement, collaborating in a number of literary magazines, as well as editing a monthly for women, *Feminal.* She moved from publishing songs in Catalan to short fiction, plays, and essays on social, literary, and feminist issues. Karr founded and directed La Llar, a residential college for women teachers and students, and was one of the leaders of early Catalan feminism.

Bolves, quadrets (1906), a collection of seven pieces of brief fiction, is divided into two sections, each geographically unified. The first, a group of country vignettes, relies heavily on descriptions of nature, in the vein of Pereda and Espina, and concentrates on forgotten children and—by implicit ironic contrast—a childless woman. The second group is urban, contrasting the lives of the upper and lower classes of Barcelona, and implicitly indicting the injustice of social stratification. Along with the dichotomy of wealth and misery, the author employs another contrast, reality and illusion, and reiterates her sympathetic interest in children. In *Clixíes, estudis en prosa* (1906; Snapshots: Studies in Prose), another collection of short narratives, the unifying metaphor of photography is frequently employed, and many of the stories are titled as landscapes, interiors, snapshots, and the like. Most of the "photos" portray women who are in some way immobilized—trapped in an unsatisfactory marriage, trapped by social class with its conventions and restrictions, trapped by socioeconomic limitations. Karr also published a short novel, *La vida d'en Joan Franch* (1912; The Life of John Franch), *Cuentos a mis nietos* (1932; Stories for my Grandchildren), a recasting of myths and folktales, usually of exemplary nature, and *El libro de Puli* (1958; Pauline's Book), more cautionary tales for children.

Francisca Herrera Garrido (1869–1950), a member of the wealthy Galician aristocracy, was born in La Coruña, but lived most of her life in Madrid. Like Rosalía de Castro, whom she knew, she wrote both in Galician and Castilian. Rosalía was her literary model. Herrera Garrido was conservative and antifeminist, but nonetheless one of the first women to publish narratives written in Galician. Perhaps in recognition of this contribution to the dignity of the vernacular, she was elected to the Galician Royal Academy. Her output included poetry, short stories, and novels, among which are the novels entitled *Néveda* (1920), *Pepiña* (1922), *Réproba* (1926), and *Familia de lobos* (1928), and her short fiction, *A ialma de Mingos* (1922) and *Martes de antroido* (1925).

A Feminist Journalist and Teacher

One of the most prolific of this older group and a notable feminist is Carmen de Burgos Seguí (circa 1870–1932; birth dates listed range from 1867 to 1879). She often wrote under the pseudonym "Colombine." The daughter of the consul of Portugal in the Mediterranean province of Almería south of Valencia, Burgos was a multifaceted figure with a strong social consciousness who bore two children, and later divorced her husband (creating a local scandal) to move to Madrid as an early instance of the single parent. She returned to her studies and eventually won a teaching position in the Normal School (1901). Widely recognized for her work as a journalist, lecturer, translator (of Leopardi, Ruskin, and others), essayist, biographer, and novelist, Burgos collaborated with the press both in Spain and abroad. She was the first Spanish woman newspaper editor to function as a reporter and interviewer, and undertook the first public survey of divorce in Spain. An active suffragist, she also opposed the death penalty, and founded *La Revista Crítica* in support of Jews. Her bibliography includes hundreds of newspaper articles, more than fifty short stories, some dozen long novels and numerous short ones, often published serially in the popular press and sometimes not collected in volume form. In addition, Burgos published essays, speeches, and many practical books for women, manuals such as *Arte de saber vivir* (1910; How to Live Well), *La cocina moderna* (Modern Cooking), *Manual de cartas* (Handbook for Letter Writing), and *El tocador práctico* (1911; The Practical Dressing-Table). More socially oriented treatises included *El divorcio en España* (1904; Divorce in Spain), *La protección e higiene de los niños* (The Protection and Health of Children), and *La mujer moderna y sus derechos* (1927; The Modern Woman and her Rights). In addition, she published poetry and literary criticism as well as travel books.[6]

Many influences are present in her fiction, from the postromantic adventure novel exemplified in *El último contrabandista* (1920; The Last Smuggler) to deterministic naturalism, seen in *Los inadaptados* (1909, The Misfits), which belongs to some extent to the past century's veins of *costumbrismo* and local color. Based upon the regional traditions and customs of the isolated Valley of Rodalquilar near her childhood home in Almería, this rural drama presents the conflict between local autonomy sentiment and government officialdom (a topic that has again become timely in the post-Franco era). Her social and feminist preoccupations appear in *La malcasada* (n.d., The Unhappily Married Woman), while an interest in the supernatural produces *El Retorno* (The Reappearance, influenced by spiritualism and allegedly based on "fact"). Occult themes are explored in *Los espirituados* (1923; The Possessed), as well as *Los endemoniados de Jaca* (1932; Possessed by the Devil in Jaca). *Quiero vivir mi vida* (1931; I Want to Live My Own Life) incorporates then-current theories on psychology and sexuality, drawn from the popular physician-essayist, Gregorio Marañón, who provided a prologue for the book. In this ambitious novel Burgos studies the psychological and physical deterioration of a woman from the middle-class who struggles against the restrictions of her conventional bourgeois marriage, and finally kills her husband in a quest that has been variously interpreted as a search for communication and the expression of latent homosexuality.

The author's interest in women also appears in clear relief in *La rampa* (1917; The Ramp), dedicated to the "destitute and disoriented" women who had sought out Burgos for advice. Providing detailed description of the dilemma of a lower middle-class woman who is victimized because of her lack of job education and a consequent inability to support herself, Burgos re-creates the plight of a legion of other women mistreated by Spanish society. Holding advanced, liberal notions on love and motherhood, Burgos indicted the double standard and its incorporation in the nation's Civil Code via a number of short stories. Spanish law has traditionally been very lenient with the "outraged husband" who kills a wife either guilty or suspected of adultery (a situation echoed in many Spanish American countries). In "El artículo 438," whose title refers to the section of the law dealing with adultery, Burgos portrays an unscrupulous husband who abuses and finally murders his wife, but is acquitted by his peers when he alleges that it was a matter of "honor." The situation, presented as not uncommon, is meant to expose the inequality before the law of the middle-class wife. *En la sima* (1915; On Top) portrays a wealthy young widow who encounters the love of her adolescence, an impoverished aristocrat who had rejected her for a more advantageous match. Her struggle with the temptation to accept self-sacrifice, returning to a situation of exploi-

tation in exchange for his company (which she finally rejects), allows
Burgos to criticize the upper class and especially the titled aristocracy
at the same time she again undercuts the double standard.

Liberal women writers of the nineteenth and early twentieth centuries show a marked preference for widows when depicting "liberated"
behavior (cf. Pardo Bazán's *Sunstroke*). Perhaps this merely echoes the
"merry widow" stereotype, but it also happens to reflect social reality:
the widow enjoyed more autonomy—especially if economically se-
cure—and could afford the luxury of pleasing herself rather than a
prospective husband. Furthermore, she was not subject to the patriarchal restraints affecting wives and unmarried daughters. An additional
advantage from the writer's point of view is that the widow's more
liberated conduct was less likely to be seen as an attack upon the institution of matrimony or a rejection of filial or conjugal duties.

Eugenio de Nora[7], in his panoramic view of the Spanish novel since
1898, has considered "Colombine" merely a popularizer, although it
must be remembered that she consciously strove to make of her journalism and fiction the vehicles for communicating current issues to the
broadest public possible. In her deliberate use of the popular press for
didactic purposes, she anticipates the similar practice of Ortega y Gasset. Her goals were more pedagogical than aesthetic, resulting in a
sometimes heavy-handed or too-explicit didacticism and a tendency to
overromanticize, but these are balanced when not offset by the depth
of emotion of her finest works and her talents in impressionistic presentation of environment and skillful characterization. Burgos seemingly anticipates certain aspects of existentialism, excelling in the
presentation of a woman's "limit situation" and need to decide her
future course while hampered by a lifetime of patriarchal repression
that limits her awareness and ability to act. Although many works by
this writer are of difficult access, two of her novels have been recently
reprinted with introductions, *El hombre negro* (1912; The Evil Man) and
Villa-María.[8]

A Major Popular Success

A contemporary of Burgos but a very different personality both literarily and on the human level is Concepción (Concha) Espina (1869–
1955). Espina is termed the first Spanish woman writer to earn her
living exclusively from her writings, a possible overgeneralization, but
one that reflects her popularity. Twice nominated for the Nobel Prize

(once lost by a single vote), she won several other prizes for her work, including the Royal Academy's important Fastenrath Prize for *La esfinge maragata* (1914; *Mariflor*, 1924), the National Prize for Literature for *Altar mayor* (1926; High Altar), and a major theatrical prize for *El jayón* (1918; The Foundling). Espina's prestige was such that several of her works were translated, and she was named a cultural representative of King Alfonso XIII to the Antilles (1928). She later served as a Visiting Professor at Middlebury College, Vermont. Although generally conservative and rarely revealed as a feminist, Espina was one of the most successful women writers in the first quarter of the present century, and her visibility and popularity unquestionably contributed to strengthening the image and position of the woman writer. A complete biography is available in Mary Lee Bretz's *Concha Espina* in the Twayne World Authors Series (Boston, 1980), with a book-length treatment in Spanish of her life and works written by the novelist's daughter, Josefina de la Maza.[9] A relatively recent biographical and critical survey in Spanish, including unpublished letters, is the 1974 study by Alicia Canales.[10]

The author of novels, plays, and poetry, Espina is most closely associated with the regional variant of realism, with her early novels usually set in rural Santander (also portrayed by Pereda, whom she resembles both in detailed descriptions of nature and generally conservative ideology). The author of some fifty books in all, she was influenced more or less equally by postromantic sentimentalism and realistic currents, but remained essentially independent and apart from the major literary movements, focusing mainly on female protagonists. As a sentimentalist, she wrote many tales of unrequited or impossible love, but also had sufficient vision to portray some women characters as victims of their own sentimentality, trapped in an intellectual vacuum by the conflict between romantic illusion and the harsher realities of daily life and typical male-female relationships. Nora correctly perceives in Espina a "cultural and aesthetic lag,"[11] noting in her work a combination of "vigor and affectation, human strengths and foaming sentimentalism." In later novels, Espina moves outward beyond her native region and also beyond one-to-one relationships to the impact of varied social realities on her characters, usually women. Her plays were few, but concentrate upon internal moral dilemmas of women in their varied roles as mother, daughter, fiancée, and wife. Two collections of Espina's brief fiction explore a number of critical issues in Spanish history during the first half of the twentieth century, including the need for national reform, the conflict between traditional values and progress, materialism versus idealism, and the hostilities of Spain's Civil War. More specifically feminine themes range from disillusionment in love to an attempt to break down sexual and class stereotyping and the need for social reform.

The popular *folletín* (serialized novel of the nineteenth century) with its melodrama, suspense, and overdependence on coincidence, provided one of the models for Espina's first foray into long fiction, *La niña de Luzmela* (1909; The Girl from Luzmela), which also numbers the sentimental novel and moralistic subgenre among its forebears. She had already published a serialized novelette, *La ronda de los galanes* (Round of Gallants) in the same year, which passed unnoticed. [12] The latter features a simplistic dualism of characters (a black-and-white division into virtuous and evil), perceptible in several of Espina's fictional works. Plot takes primacy over characterization, and from the *folletín* the author appropriates two overworked motifs (also favored by the melodrama): illegitimacy and mysterious parental background.

The writer's concept of suffering as a fundamental part of human existence and her depiction of virtue in conflict with evil make another appearance in *Despertar para morir* (1910; To Wake Up and Die), although more sophistication is evident in this second treatment. The moral decadence of the aristocracy at the turn of the century is analyzed in the persons of wealthy members of Madrid's upper class spending the summer at a Cantabrian villa. The aristocracy's overemphasis on material values at the expense of moral and spiritual ones is satirized, as the novelist develops the tragic consequences of marriage as an economic transaction. Espina discovers a new formula with her third novel, *Agua de nieve* (1911; The Woman and the Sea, 1934). Suffering continues to be a major avenue for plumbing life's deeper meanings, but the earlier simplistic conflicts between good and evil are replaced by analysis of the Spanish woman and the heroine's internal struggles in the course of her quest for happiness.

Among Espina's best and most successful novels is *La esfinge maragata* (1914; *Mariflor*, 1924), which develops and refines choice aspects of her regionalistic vision of northern Spain while incorporating some of the fervor of the Generation of 1898 for national regeneration. *Mariflor* is set in the isolated, backward, and impoverished semidesert Maragatería district of León, bordering on Galicia. Following now-classic realistic/naturalistic procedure, Espina spent months there observing details of village life, geography, and social environment, and documenting the local dialect and folklore. Nora agrees that the novel is provincial, localistic, and *costumbrista,* but also sees it as an "indignant and vigorous denunciation of the social and family situations of women in which only the common, generic condition of the Spanish wife is stressed."[13] The formula again contains elements of the *novela rosa* and *folletín.* The narrative is structured largely on the basis of contrasts, such as the one between the illustrious past of Maragata and its miserable present. Florinda, the heroine, raised in Galicia (humid and green) returns to live with her grandmother, Dolores, in a desolate, sterile land. The once-wealthy and powerful family is now impoverished and vulnerable. Florinda—modern, independent, frank, curious, cultured, and optimistic, with an urban mentality—contrasts with her grandmother who is reticent, traditional, even feudal in her outlook, relatively uneducated, coarse, lacking in independence, and a typical example of the rural mentality. Striking an implicitly feminist note, another contrast is established between the women—strong, silent, long-suffering—and the men—brutal, domineering, and dehumanized, or else weak. Life in Maragatería is an endless cycle of emigration and living at the subsistence level.

Harsh economic realities and the traditions of the land assert themselves over her modernity and optimism, and Mariflor ends by accepting exactly the same economic basis for matrimony as generations of Maragatan women before her. What may be a happy ending for her grandmother and aunt, whose financial security is thereby guaranteed, is considerably less euphoric for the heroine. Espina's usual emphasis on suffering and altruism has not entirely disappeared but has been subordinated to the portrayal of adaptation to an extreme environment and the placing of individual needs after those of the group. The strong point of Espina's fiction is her descriptive power, her capacity for recreating geography, landscape, setting, and mood; and in *Mariflor* she excels in painting the atemporal region, forgotten by progress, with its xenophobia and misery, barren harshness, and stark, impoverished culture.

Unlike its predecessors in Espina's work, *El metal de los muertos* (1920; The Metal of the Dead) is most emphatically social protest fiction. World War I had intervened, Communism had become a world power, and Spain was experiencing the unrest and social problems of the pre-Civil War era. Responding to these circumstances, Espina moved closer to the Left, although her position continues to be moderate. *El metal de los muertos,* a social epic and her most ambitious work, has been ranked by most critics among her best achievements. Nora considers all Espina's writing to be necessary preparation for this work of "plenitude."[14] Again, the diligent author conducted personal observations of the area and way of life described, this time of the Río Tinto copper mines in the province of Huelva (Andalusia). Exploited from pre-Roman times, the mining operation was taken over by the British in 1873. Espina depicts a miners' strike between 1910 and 1920, a working-class struggle supported by a small group of bourgeois intellectuals inspired by humanitarian socialism (a term avoided by the novelist, whose chief organizer speaks instead of a return to early Christian values). Concern with pollution, industrial wastes, and poisonous by-products lends a contemporary air to this novel, written nearly seven decades ago. As the characters proceed toward Dite (Espina's name for Río Tinto, not coincidentally one of the names of Pluto, Greek god of hell and the dead), the surroundings become increasingly infertile, the air filled with gas, the earth bare of vegetation, and the rivers discolored by mineral wastes. Miners live in company houses built on the mountainside without sewage disposal, without medical facilities and schools, working long hours for minimal pay, the victims of cave-ins, unsafe machinery, and the poisonous atmosphere. Although she utilizes certain characters as narrative perspectives, Espina introduces a large cast ranging from brutalized local prostitutes to old-time miners, administrators, and labor officials, achieving a collective focus and something approaching the collective protagonist. The main plot is complicated by rather involved amorous subplots, but the novel's primary conflict remains the struggle between the forces of capitalism and the workers' welfare.

Espina's most nearly feminist novel is *La virgen prudente* (1929; The Wise Virgin), in which she examines societal pressures and cultural prejudices that condition women's attitudes, producing internal contradictions (a response to conflicting tendencies in society itself). An idealistic young lawyer, Aurora de España (Dawn of Spain), struggles with family, friends, and suitors, intent on independence in spite of their resistance to her unorthodox course. The protagonist's symbolic name reflects Espina's optimistic faith in women's capabilities and sets the tone for one of her most upbeat novels (which has appeared at least once under a variant title, *Aurora de España*). The contrast between The Wise Virgin and Espina's novels from the mid-thirties onward is enormous, as wartime experiences rendered Espina extremely pro-Franco for several years. Most of her postwar novels are politicized works of

national exaltation tending again to the melodrama of her apprenticeship years, with their Manichean duality of good and evil, light
and darkness, contributing little to her aesthetic achievement or
reputation.

Altar mayor (1926; High Altar), awarded the highest recognition of
any of Espina's works, the National Prize for Literature (the most prestigious literary prize won thus far in Spain by any woman writer), is
aesthetically inferior to *Mariflor*, lacks the dramatic impact and social
significance of *El metal de las muertos* (The Metal of the Dead), and at
its worst, reverts to the melodrama and flat, oversimplified characters
of her first novel. Essentially conceived as an exaltation of traditional
Spanish values and national history, it is set in Covadonga (Asturias)
where the Reconquest began in 711. In several ways, it belongs in the
same group as Angel Ganivet's *Idearium español* (1897), written three
decades earlier.

Blind from 1937 on, Espina nevertheless continued to write. Two
novels of her last years qualify as more memorable for the feminist
scholar. *El más fuerte* (1947; The Strongest) presents a male protagonist,
Adrián Montaves, who after eighteen years of successful marriage faces
(with his wife) the test of parenting three children through adolescence. In the process, Adrián acquires self-knowledge and becomes better acquainted with the younger generation, but his wife founders in a
futile effort to recover the past. Although not among Espina's more
celebrated works, *El más fuerte* remains one of her best executed studies
of family relationships and is especially valid in its depiction of feminine conditioning and the dilemma of the Spanish woman who has
been too narrowly prepared for too exclusive a role in life. Likewise of
interest for the feminist critic, *Un valle en el mar* (1950; A Valley in
the Sea) returns to Espina's native Cantabria to focus upon the theme
of rape and its consequences in a stratified rural society. While the
descriptive passages do not rank among the novelist's most finely nu-
anced depictions of the region's human and physical characteristics, the
delineation of social values is informative and fairly objective, and the
two central characters, Antonio and Salvadora, transcend the unidi-
mensional flatness and melodramatic traits of the minor personages to
rank among Espina's more worthy and memorable creations.

An independent figure who resists facile categorization, Espina
changes repeatedly during her half-century career, so that neither her
ideology nor her thematics remain constant. Her aesthetics are not

especially innovative, but her frequent changes in setting and subject matter indicate a desire to progress in the novelistic art. She was extremely interested in feminine psychology, although her analyses were less of individuals than a type, the woman who was forbearing, long-suffering, self-abnegating, chaste, born "to love and suffer" (like Mariflor). Espina's poetics are eclectic and personal, and the results are uneven. From today's perspective many of her works seem outmoded, the more so because she drew often upon the past century's more dated literary manifestations (postromanticism, melodrama, sentimentalism). Her move to the right at the time of the Civil War (motivated by her traditional Catholicism) has also hurt her fame and created an "ideology gap" for many of today's readers. Her diary of the war, *Esclavitud y libertad: diario de una prisionera* (1938; Slavery and Liberty: Diary of a Prisoner), helps to explain her changed attitude. Nevertheless, her writing as a whole is representative of a broad social spectrum as well as being of sociological interest because of her middle-class origins and identification. The enhanced respect that she won for women writers in official circles through her own acceptability and popular success continues to benefit her successors.

Invisible Feminism: A Ghost Writer

María de la O Lejárraga (1874–1974), born in a small town in northern Spain called San Millán de la Cogolla, was the eldest child of a large family of scientists and intellectuals. From 1880 onward, she lived in Madrid, attending the Normal School where she studied to become a language teacher. In 1897 she began writing works in collaboration with her future husband, Gregorio Martínez Sierra, six and a half years her junior. In 1900, when he was nineteen and she twenty-five, they married, thereafter publishing numerous stories and novels (written between 1898 and 1910). From 1909 onward, they concentrated increasingly upon the theater, producing more than fifty plays, many of them notable successes and at least one, *Cradle Song,* a smash hit. Although most of the works were signed by Gregorio, and others signed jointly, Patricia O'Connor has demonstrated conclusively in her study *Gregorio and María Martínez Sierra* that most, if not all, of the work is María's, as documented by the letters of Gregorio.[15] When the Civil War broke out in 1936, María was a commercial attaché of the Republic and spent most of the war in exile in France, moving to New

York in 1950. After living in Arizona and Mexico, she finally settled in Buenos Aires, where she continued her literary production, turning out several books and numerous articles, including memoirs, stories, and feminist essays.

The heroines of the works by the Martínez Sierras are not activists aggressively involved in the struggle for women's rights, but they actively seek their own fulfillment through work, study, or active participation in extradomestic pursuits. Although maternity is exalted as the ultimate expression of femininity and most of the pair's heroines are nurturing women, they are also intelligent, educated, independent, assertive, and unfailingly Spanish. Indeed, there seems to be a certain amount of mild xenophobia in works by the Martínez Sierras, since it is almost always foreigners who are caricatured and who play the most villainous roles. Older women, conservative or reactionary, appear conceived to illustrate the adverse effects of prolonged domestic incarceration and to contrast with the modern, career-oriented, younger woman who incarnates the ideal. The heroine is sufficiently idealized to constitute an unbalanced picture, lacking negative appetites and vices, incapable of jealousy, vanity, infidelity, and vengeance: she is a compendium of womanly virtues. O'Connor points out that "The model liberated woman in the Martínez Sierra plays . . . is intelligent but not pedantic, independent but not domineering, virtuous but not prudish, ambitious but not pushy, strong but not overbearing. She is, in a word [that is] abhorred by 'gut' feminists, feminine."[16] By contrast the men are almost always weak, immature, vacillating, childlike or infantile, undisciplined, and less than brilliant.

Almas ausentes (1900; Absent Souls), the first novel by the Martínez Sierras, features a narrator who does research on the mentally ill by spending some time in an asylum, where he is largely an observer. The novel's residual Gothic characteristics are visible in the gloomy castle serving as the asylum building, the collection of tormented personalities, the murder committed by an inmate, and the candidly innocent heroine, perhaps even the altruistic, almost saintly commitment of the director's assistant. Fortunately, the most objectionable excesses of melodrama have been avoided. *Horas de sol* (1901; Sunny Hours) presents a wealthy city girl vacationing in the country where she becomes enamored of a simple, rustic villager. The role of natural surroundings and the sunshine recall to a lesser degree the protagonism of an overwhelming Nature in Pardo Bazán's *La Madre Naturaleza*: here Nature is sensuous, inebriating, seductive. The innocent dream of love and happiness in the summer sunlight is interrupted almost on the last page when a letter arrives from a Madrid friend, recalling the social life of the capital and joking about a possible rural idyll.

In *Pascua florida* (1903; Easter Sunday) Josefina, a young widow, returns to her native mountain village for a stay with her aged, ailing grandfather, the local schoolmaster, thereby meeting Lucita, an idealized, nurturing, altruistic, maternal neighbor who takes care of the old man, and Lucita's brother Lorenzo, the local doctor. The traditional, conventional symbolism of spring with its connotations of new life, new hope, works its miracle of regeneration as the old man recovers, and Lorenzo and Josefina find love, completing the Easter "resurrection." *Sol de la tarde* (1904; Afternoon Sunshine), a collection of short pieces, displays a sensitive perception of nature, delicate word paintings of landscape, and modernist coloration. In one story an old priest and his sister care for a gypsy boy until he runs away with a passing caravan, oblivious to the old man's fondness. Several other stories concern feminine renunciation, or the dedication of self to others. There are various portraits of nuns (a favorite subject), often in the role of teachers, whether of orphans or the blind.

The contrast between peaceful village and outside world, between villagers and those from far away, appears again in *Tú eres la paz* (1906; You are Peace), the couple's most popular work of fiction, and most successful work in any genre after *Cradle Song*. Like many of their works, *Tú eres la paz* is based upon a sort of love triangle, with two women sharing the affections of one man. Ana María, who represents village values, is modest, intelligent, disciplined—a model of womanly virtue—and enamored of her cousin Agustín, an artist who is weak, pleasant but immature and indecisive. Both have been raised by their grandmother, who fondly expects their marriage. When he studies abroad, Ana conceals his affair with the foreign model, Carmelina. The latter's infidelity eventually facilitates the unlikely hero's comparison of the two women, Spanish and foreign, and as usually happens in works of the Martínez Sierras, the "native" emerges as superior. Carmelina decides to travel with a foreigner, leaving Agustín free to marry Ana María. Opposition between two women of the type established in *Tú eres la paz* is characteristic of these writers' fiction: Ana María is altruistic, disciplined, long-suffering, patient, virtuous, serious, maternal, and generously self-abnegating; Carmelina is egotistical, undisciplined, amoral, irresponsible, lacking maternal feelings, frivolous and—foreign.

El agua dormida (1907; Sleepy Waters) employs the narrative perspective of a child, who perceives everything through the eyes of innocence. The little girl's view of her mother is perhaps unconsciously
ironic. Miserably unhappy with the feminine lot, the latter attempts
to drown herself and her daughter to spare the child life as a woman,
and as she goes to sleep the little girl recalls her mother having told
her that all female children should have their heads knocked against a
wall at birth. Quite a different atmosphere and theme appear in *La
torre de marfil* (1908; The Ivory Tower), although the characters are
familiar types in the Martínez Sierras' fiction. Again, the young working woman of impeccable character is counterbalanced by the negative
archetype of the traditional smothering mother, who sublimates her
frustrations and hostility in excessive religiosity. There is again the
weak-willed, immature, and childlike man who compensates for the
nurturing his mother did not provide by unconsciously seeking a lover
who will be a mother figure. Clearly, aspects of the real-life relationship and personalities of the Martínez Sierras are portrayed via the heroine and her lover in this and a number of other works by these writers
that feature essentially the same types.

Todo es uno y lo mismo (1910; It's all the Same) returns to the here and
now of rather pedestrian reality, to the world of academia in which a
vacillating, immature college instructor or graduate assistant, Teófilo,
is oedipally in love with Teresita, young wife of his mentor, protector,
superior, and father figure. He refuses to admit the reality of the conjugal relationship, taking a vacation to escape temptation when the
husband is doing research abroad. After an affair with nurturing Maud
(while pretending that she is Teresita), he cynically concludes that all
women are alike. This same story reappears as the fourth and final part
of a longer novel, *El amor catedrático* (1910; Love is the Teacher), which
provides additional perspectives upon the potential triangle.

Although some fiction would be written later (María never abandoned it completely, and returned to it in exile), it ceased after this
point to be the dominant genre. Besides other fictional narratives,
María also wrote *Cartas a las mujeres de España* (1916; Letters to the
Women of Spain) and *Nuevas cartas a las mujeres de España* (1932; New
Letters to the Women of Spain); feminist essays, as were *Feminismo,
feminidad, españolismo* (1916; Feminism, Femininity, and Being Spanish) and *La mujer española ante la República* (1931; Spanish Women and
the Republic). Two books of memoirs written in exile provide significant evidence of María's evolving feminism as well as autobiographical

data: *Una mujer por los caminos de España* (1952; A Woman on Spain's Roads) and *Gregorio y yo* (1954; Gregorio and I).

María Martínez Sierra and her works continue to be something of an anomaly in the developing history of Spanish feminism in the twentieth century. Without agressiveness or polemics, she managed to outline for women a number of alternatives beyond the domestic realm. She combats the stereotype of the frustrated, embittered old maid with a series of young heroines who are independent, intelligent, nurturing, and assertive, their active, decisive strength subtly underscored by the weakness and immaturity of their male counterparts. The prominence of the love intrigue and pervasive presence of sentimentality betray a trace of conservatism that, together with the espousal of traditional virtues, assist in making the imbedded feminist attitudes more acceptable.

Two Lesser Feminist Writers

Isabel de Palencia (1872 or 1878 or 1881–196?) was born to a prominent family in Málaga, her mother being a Scottish Protestant and her father of Basque origin. After a convent education in French and English and having spent time in England, she founded a women's journal, *La Dama,* of which she was the chief editor and contributor. In addition, she was a translator of contemporary English and American literature, and the correspondent for British newspapers as well as a columnist for the famous Madrid daily, *El Sol.* An expert on women, children, education, and slavery, she was named Republican Spain's envoy to the League of Nations, and in 1936 was appointed ambassador to Sweden, subsequently going into exile in Mexico at the end of the Civil War in 1939. Her publications include historical and social essays, children's literature, and memoirs as well as novels. Her fiction is modeled upon Galdós and other nineteenth century realists, but her themes are more strictly contemporary. Having translated Havelock Ellis into Spanish, she became interested in the then-controversial question of reproductive theory, which inspired her first novel, *El sembrador sembró su semilla* (1928; The Sower Planted His Seed).

Maria Domènech i Escate de Canellas (1877–1952), an advocate of better education for women, founded a union for Catalan working women. She occasionally used a masculine pseudonym, Josep Miralles. Primarily a novelist, she also wrote short fiction. In *Contrallum* (1917; Against the Light) she undertakes the psychological analysis of a young man of a well-to-do provincial family who is smothered by class conventions. Forced to remain in the village and work in the family business, married to a girl he dislikes, and frustrated in all his aspirations, he ends a suicide. A number of other novels in Catalan, including *Neus* (1914), *Els gripaus d'or* (1919), *Herències* (1925), and *Al rodar del temps* (1946) are unavailable. *Confidències* (1946) is a collection of nine short stories, in which nine women express their most intimate concerns, usually in the first person, through monologues or dialogues.

The turn-of-the-century writers received a substantial legacy from their predecessors, and in many cases improved upon it, although the major achievements of Pardo Bazán continued to stand. Less iconoclastic than their male counterparts of the Generation of 1898, they were for the most part more conservative in their aesthetics, following the lead of the great nineteenth-century realists and naturalists rather than experimenting with genre and novelistic structure. Thematically, however, they were more innovative than their predecessors, as evidenced by the introduction of international scenarios in the works of Casanova, spiritualism, the occult and psychosexual disturbances in the works of Burgos, philosophical problems, social protest and ecological concerns in the writings of Espina, and the idealized unwed mother as heroine in *La torre de marfil* of María Martínez Sierra, as well as bitter denunciation of the feminine lot in *El agua dormida* of the same writer. Martínez Sierra's romantic tropical allegory, *La selva muda,* evokes Baroja's idealized presentation of jungle life in *Paradox, rey,* and the two writers coincide in viewing civilization as a corruptive force. María Martínez Sierra also joins with Unamuno and Baroja in portraying the lives of academics as plagued by fully as many problems as the existences of those less educated. While most of these are not major issues, they do provide evidence of a common intellectual patrimony, suggesting a possible narrowing of the gap between the masculine and feminine writers as groups.

Chapter Three
Minor Contemporaries of the *Novecentistas* and of the Generation of 1927

The first identifiably new, distinct group in Spain after the Generation of 1898 is the so-called *Novecentistas* (also called the Generation of 1914, partly because of World War I, partly because the first mature publications of the group appeared in that year). Some fifteen years later the famous poets of the Generation of 1927 (García Lorca, Rafael Alberti, Vicente Aleixandre, Pedro Salinas, Jorge Guillén, Luis Cernuda, and others) celebrated their first joint activity, an observance of the fourth centenary of Góngora. There are insufficient female novelists of real stature to constitute a counterpart "generation" contemporary with the *Novecentistas*. Following the "turn-of-the-century generation" comes a nucleus of less prolific and less well-known women writers, most of whom were born in the late 1880s and early 1890s. Like the *Novecentistas* (a group in which there were important critics, essayists, and thinkers, but a dearth of "creative" writers), this small cluster of coeval women contains no great novelist, although there are estimable lesser narrators.

In the larger, slightly younger group, approximate contemporaries of the Generation of 1927—born during the first decade, roughly, of the twentieth century—the level of creativity is much higher, and women in this chronological grouping share certain formative influences: the intellectual leadership of Ortega, the liberties of the Second Republic, the climax of the suffragist movement in Spain. On the whole, they begin writing relatively late in life, usually in their mid-thirties, and frequently display a demythologizing tendency, rejecting or modifying traditional views of women and of motherhood. The idealism and conservatism typical of so many women writers of the past century give way to a restrained, yet determined nonconformity. They are no longer limited to a relatively noncommittal presentation of injustices inherent in the feminine condition and occasional pictures of nondomestic (and/or nonconventual) roles for women, but begin to express more audible dissent: not merely women who work or who seek options beyond matrimony, but women who reject patriarchally inscribed definitions of womanhood or transgress patriarchally defined boundaries of motherhood. The feminist movement per se makes its appearance in the fiction of this group, as does a more decisive and specific formulation of the conflict between household duties and self-realization, whether expressed in writing or otherwise. With this generation, there also appear works demythologizing family relationships (for example, analysis of abnormal brother-sister relationships). Social criticism, a subject broached and then dropped by Concha Espina, becomes a more general preoccupation, along with heightened interest in children and adolescents as fictional protagonists. War (especially but not exclusively the Civil War) and exile also emerge as significant generational themes, since many of these writers experienced the trauma of the national conflict and its aftermath. These themes become still more visible in the writings of the postwar generation. Problems of the divorced or separated woman also receive more frequent fictional treatment with the advent of the contemporaries of the Generation of 1927.

Minor Narrators in Catalan

Carme Montoriol i Puig (1893–1966), a Catalan playwright, novelist, translator, and poet, lived most of her life in Barcelona. Her first artistic activities were in the realm of music and translation, which led her into writing for the theater, for which she produced her most successful pieces, although her works frequently provoked scandals because of their controversial subject matter. For example, her first play, *L'abisme* (1933; The Abyss), deals with a mother and daughter's love-hate relationship, tending to undercut the mythologized vision of traditional motherhood, while *L'huracà* (1935; The Hurricane) portrays incest between a mother and son. In her novel *Teresa o la vida amorosa d'una dona* (1932: Teresa, or the Love Life of a Woman), Montoriol portrays a woman who separates from her husband and begins a new, liberated existence thanks to work that provides economic independence. An active feminist during the Second Republic, Montoriol did not write after the Civil War, in part because the Franco regime had prohibited the use of Catalan. A collection of ten stories written between 1921 and 1936 was published under the title of *Diumenge de Juliol* (1936; July Sunday).

Celia Suñol (b. 1899), another Catalan novelist, has spent most of her life in her native Barcelona. The first woman writer in Catalan who broke the silence imposed by the Franco regime, she published her first novel, *Primera part* (First Part) in 1948. This fictionalized autobiography describes Barcelona in the beginning of the present century, as well as significant moments in Suñol's life: illnesses (bouts with tuberculosis and psychological crises), the death of her first husband, and her first contacts with the feminist movement. Widowed a second time after a few years, she supported her children by a variety of jobs: working in a bar, as a seamstress, and as a translator. Part of this experience resulted in a novel, *Bar,* prohibited by the Franco censorship because it ended with the protagonist's suicide. A similarly autobiographical collection of stories, *L'home de les fires i altres contes* (1950; The Man of the Fairs and Other Stories), contains material of interest for the feminist critic: the title tale, for example, depicts the conflict between writing and domestic duties. Literary creativity is upstaged by the need to cook and clean, until the would-be writer is so overwhelmed that writing is postponed for another day. Several of Suñol's stories and her general tone are evocative of later works in Catalan by Núria Pompeia and Maria Antònia Oliver. Her stories were unintentionally prophetic, for despite awareness of her talent, Suñol abandoned writing to take care of her children.

Aurora Bertrana (1899–1974) was the daughter of Prudenci Bertrana, a well-known Catalan writer numbered among the disciples of "Victor Català." Born in Gerona, Aurora was able to become a world traveler, visiting not only Europe and North Africa, but South America and Oceania, an experience repeatedly reflected in her fiction. Two of her early novels are marked by the tragedy of war: *Tres presoners* (1957; Three Prisoners), a simple but intensely emotional narrative set during the Spanish Civil War and portraying a situation that arises between three prisoners, and *Entre dos silencis* (1958; Between Two Silences), based on a real-life experience of Bertrana during World War II when she worked as a volunteer in a village that was totally destroyed. *La nimfa d'argila* (1959; The Clay Nymph), a study of infantile psychology, portrays a girl whose childhood is truncated, while *Fracàs* (1966; Failure), an essay in the area of social criticism, is a denunciation of the upper classes who cloak egocentrism with religiosity and respectability. *Vent de grop* (1967; Tailwind) is a love story set against the background of a small tourist center and fishing village on the Costa Brava, a simple evocation of emotional disappointment and frustration that occur between two young lovers when one decides to break off the relationship. Most of Bertrana's short-story collections have some thematic unity: *El Marroc sensual i fanàtic* (1936; Sensual and Fanatic Morocco) re-creates the writer's travel impressions, as does *Peikea, princesa caníbal i altres contes oceànics* (1980; Peikea, the Cannibal Princess and Other Oceanic Stories), which depicts a utopian society, an idealized landscape filled with tenderness and vitality. *Oviri i sis narracions més* (1965; Oviri and Six Other Stories) begins with close observation of a cat named Oviri and proceeds through six more tales with animal protagonists to probe the closeness of relationships between humans and animals. Bertrana has a well-defined individuality, owing both to her thematics, which transcend the rather narrow limits of most writing by women of that period, and to her finely crafted style.

Another Catalan novelist, political activist, and journalist, Anna Murià i Romani (b. 1904 in Barcelona), became involved in the women's movement at an early age, studying at the Institut de Cultura i Biblioteca Popular de la Dona Catalana (Catalan Woman's Institute of Culture and Popular Library) in 1927. Her many collaborations in the press of the period date from the same year, and her political activism began three years later, identified especially with leftist groups and the Catalan independence movement. During the Civil War she was a member of the central committee of the Estat Català, going into exile in France in January 1939 with the fall of Barcelona to the Franco forces. The beginning of her exile coincides with her meeting with Agustí Bartra, a Catalan novelist and poet whom she married that October, beginning their odyssey of exile in the Dominican Republic, Cuba, and Mexico, where they settled until 1970, finally returning to Catalonia in that year after an absence of some three decades.

Distinguished as a writer of children's fiction and for her critical studies of her husband's poetry, Murià has published a number of significant novels generally overlooked by the critics. *Joana Mas* (1933) is an ambitious attempt to contrast two very different types of women, the protagonist or title character whose life ambitions are realized when she marries a wealthy, older man, and her opposite, a single woman who achieves economic independence through her work, but fails to find emotional stability. Murià clearly intended to present contrasting models or alternatives for women, but is not fully successful in analyzing their personalities. In *La Peixera* (1938; The Fishbowl) Murià has apparently attempted to symbolize the entrapment of the worker in an economic situation without potential for future advancement or self-improvement. Although her protagonist is a young man, the circumstances portrayed are equally applicable to the working woman. Working as a clerk in a dreary office whose resemblance to a cell is enhanced by the presence of iron bars, he is able to see the sky only through a tiny ceiling aperture (hence the title image with its allusion to the limiting form of the bowl with its open top). The extremes of boredom and unvarying similarity of successive days, like the existence of the imprisoned fish, are unrelieved tedium. *Res no és veritat, Alicia* (1984; Nothing is True, Alicia) narrates the potentially incestuous, but unconsummated love between a brother and sister. From the perspective of the sister, Murià presents a complex and tangled web of relationships. When another woman is sentimentally linked to her brother, the protagonist turns to another man, hoping to find in him the virtues she perceived in her brother. An autobiography of the author ends the book.

Aquest serà el principi (1985; This Will be the Beginning) is Murià's most ambitious narrative work, a lengthy and complex novel of some five hundred pages, spanning three historical epochs: the early 1930s (proclamation of the Second Republic, up to the Civil War), exile (from the late 1930s on to perhaps 1970), and the period of return to Catalonia. Although there is obviously a certain autobiographical input, the work is not presented as an autobiography, and there is no character corresponding to or representing the author, who instead divides her vital experiences among several different figures. Paralleling the absence of a novelistic alter ego is the lack of a narrator or central narrative consciousness: all of the characters speak for themselves, the result being perspectivistic and impressionistic.

Rosa Maria Arquimbau, another Catalan novelist, born in Barcelona in 1910, has also written under the name of Rosa de Sant Jordi. Her first stories were penned at the age of fourteen, an early beginning that resulted in her being classed with writers of the 1930s. As a journalist, she collaborated with several leftist periodicals during the years of the Republic, and also began writing short pieces for the theater. The Civil War, exile, and subsequent difficulties for literature written in Catalan all affected her work, and she too spent nearly two decades without publishing. Her novelistic protagonists are usually women, seen outside the family or domestic setting. *Historia d'una noia i vint braçalets*

(1934; Story of a Girl and Twenty Bracelets) is a novel whose protagonist is a girl sent by her family to study in Barcelona. The twenty bracelets of the title symbolize special events in her life, and are used as narrative ploys to introduce new facets of her character. *Home i dona* (1936; Man and Woman), a short epistolary narrative, retraces a woman's efforts to live her own life following separation from her husband. Although women during the period of the Republic enjoyed more liberties than in the years either before or afterward, Spanish society in general was still quite strictly moralistic, and in this decidedly Victorian context the letter writer is a rather liberated woman for her time. Arquimbau's more recent fiction is exemplified by *40 ans perduts* (1971; Forty Years Lost), in which a young Barcelona dressmaker of proletarian background is suddenly catapulted to fame and finds herself able to decide what aristocrats will wear, a position to which she adjusts with ease, if not complete verisimilitude.

Minor Narrators in Castilian

Margarita Nelken y Mausberger (1896–1968), an influential feminist, politician, sociologist, and critic during the epoch of the Second Republic, joined the Communist party during the Civil War and went into exile in Mexico following the end of the conflict, later leaving the party. Best known for her books on women, including *La condición de la mujer en España* (1922?; The Condition of Women in Spain), an early analysis of Spanish feminism, and *Las escritoras españolas* (1930; Spanish Women Writers), she also wrote two novels, *La aventura de Roma* (1923; Roman Adventure) and *La trampa del arenal* (1923; Sand Trap), long out of print and inaccessible. Her sociohistorical treatise, *Por qué hicimos la Revolución* (1936?; Why We Made a Revolution), provides a history of Spanish workers before the 1930s and an eyewitness account of historic events during the turbulent years of the Second Republic, concentrating upon the government's repression of an uprising by leftists and workers in 1934.

Carmen de Icaza, born in 1899 in Madrid, was the daughter of the well-known writer and Mexican diplomat Francisco A. de Icaza. Her father's diplomatic career allowed Icaza a very cosmopolitan upbringing, as she studied in Spain, France, and Germany, and traveled extensively in Europe and the Americas. Her literary career began early: she published her first novel, *La boda* (1916; The Wedding), at the age of seventeen. This narrative appears to have been reworked and reissued under the title of *La boda del Duque Kurt* (1935; Duke Kurt's Wedding). In 1936 came her first significant commercial success with *Cristina de Guzmán,* published serially in *Blanco y negro* and quickly translated into French where it was serialized in a Parisian daily. It appeared in book form with the modified title, *Cristina de Guzmán, profesora de idiomas* (1936; Cristina de Guzmán, Foreign Language Teacher), and has been translated into Italian, Czech, Norwegian, Dutch, and Portuguese, with student editions done in Holland and the United States (edited as a reader for language students at Loyola University, 1958). In the following decade Icaza published a good many more novels: *¿Quién Sabe?* (1940; Who Knows?); *Vestida de tul* (1942; Dressed in Tulle), set in Madrid in the 1910s; *Soñar la vida* (1944; To Dream Life); *El tiempo vuelve* (1945; Time Returns); and *La fuente enterrada* (1947; The Buried Fountain). These and the novels written subsequently belong essentially to the *novela rosa* genre of sentimental romances, whose dominant characteristic is identified by Eugenio G. de Nora as "a constant deformation of reality in the direction of what is 'pleasant' . . . commercially adapted for a tender and almost exclusively feminine market."[1] The genre typically idealizes love; employs steroteyped figures, simplistically good or bad, usually belonging to the nobility; and as a whole is guilty of class bias, placing an excessive emphasis on grandeur, wealth, and distinction.

Further novels by Icaza include *Las horas contadas* (1951; Counted Hours), *Yo, la reina* (1955; I, the Queen), *Irene* (1958), and *La casa de enfrente* (1960; The House Across the Street). Icaza's works paint detailed portraits of the Madrid aristocracy and those in diplomatic circles. Nearly all of this writer's works enjoyed long-lasting and widespread popularity and have been translated into several languages; some were also adapted for the stage. Her significance is not in the area of mainstream literature but as a popular narrator with a wide audience. Icaza received several awards for her commitment to those in need: in the postwar period she headed a newspaper campaign to focus attention upon the plight of destitute women and children, she helped establish a social aid society and she held positions in the Spanish Red Cross.

Paulina Crusat (b. 1900), like Elisabeth Mulder and Carmen Kurtz, was born in Barcelona, but she wrote only in Castilian. Also like these slightly younger women, Crusat belonged to an upper-middle-class family, and was raised in a cultured atmosphere that stimulated her literary inclinations. Although Crusat won her first poetry prize at the age of twelve, she has not been a constant or prolific writer. After her marriage, she moved to Sevilla, where she has written literary criticism and novels. Nora attributes to her an excellent anthology of contemporary Catalan poets, published in 1952.[2] It appears that most of her fiction was published during the 1950s and 1960s; none has appeared since 1965. Crusat's *Mundo pequeño y fingido* (1953; Small, Feigned World) is frankly subjective and nonmimetic, a minor revolt against the "documentary" or "testimonial" realism in vogue at the time of publication. The characters are mostly aristocrats of the first generation of romanticism, who meet in Switzerland around 1820. The novelist makes no attempt at historical reconstruction, but via an excellent psychological exposition and analysis expresses her belief in the essential sameness of basic human problems throughout the ages. Eugenio de Nora terms it an "exemplary" psychological novel.[3] Crusat's major work is a series of two novels with a probable autobiographical basis. The first of the linked novels, jointly titled *Historia de un viaje* (Story of a Voyage) is *Aprendiz de persona* (1956; Apprentice Person), which describes the childhood and youth of the female protagonist, Monsi, concentrating on her developmental process and the changes undergone. Her adolescence is strictly subjected to societally inscribed rules, with little or no freedom, and no real opportunity for developing her own individuality. A glimpse of the protagonist after her marriage—a brief appearance as an adult at the end of the novel—indicates that matrimony finally provides her the chance to discover her own identity. Nora suggests that the title of the two-part series may contain an allusion to Virginia Woolf's *The Voyage Out,* and notes some affinity of spirit between the two writers.[4] In the second novel, *Las ocas blancas* (1959; The White Geese), Crusat evokes the Barcelona of 1916, a world that is deliberately old-fashioned and slightly unreal, framing her poetic evocation of the passage from adolescence to young adulthood. Declaring it to be "un libro de mujer" (a woman's book), she concentrates upon a detailed introduction to each of six teenage girls and their activities, beginning with the traditional attendance at the opera, tertulias (fixed and regular, informal gatherings), evening strolls, Carnival, musicals, dances, a New Year's Eve party, their first serious boyfriends, and first long dresses. The final impression resembles a debutante ball with flashbacks. *Relaciones solitarias* (1965; Solitary Relations) is a full-length epistolary novel, divided into four parts whose names correspond to the four seasons. Like most of this writer's works, it is out of print and inaccessible.

María de los Reyes Lafitte y Pérez del Pulgar, Countess of Campo Alange, was born in 1902 in Sevilla where she resided until her marriage in 1922 to a grandee of Spain. From 1931 to 1934 she and her husband lived in Paris, where she studied art and art history. Her first book, published in 1944, was a critical biography of the painter María Blanchard. A member of several Academies of Art and Literature, Campo Alange is a distinguished historian and sociologist of Spanish women, and is equally well known as an art critic. Her second book-length essay, *La guerra secreta de los sexos* (1948; The Secret War between the Sexes) sold out rapidly, and was reprinted. In it, Campo Alange presents a philosophical study of women throughout history, emphasizing feminine psychology, woman's position in society, and woman's reactions to men. *La flecha y la esponja* (1959; The Arrow and the Sponge), a short-story collection, reflects in its title the author's awareness of Freudian symbolism, with clear allusions to masculine and feminine signs. The seven tales contain a fictional elaboration of themes first enunciated in *La guera secreta de los sexos*. Masculine-feminine conflicts are re-created with great imagination and sensitivity and include some unexpected problems verging upon the psychopathic.

Other important feminist essays by Campo Alange include *La mujer como mito y como ser humano* (1961; Woman as Myth and as Human Being) and *La mujer en España, cien años de su historia (1860–1960)* (1963; Woman in Spain: One Hundred Years of History, [1860–1960]), a study of Spanish womanhood with a historico-literary focus. Here Campo Alange uses articles, interviews, letters, published and unpublished memoirs, polls, statistics, and even oral tradition to reconstruct the social and cultural evolution. While concrete examples are not disdained, the countess is more interested in the collective phenomenon than in individuals. *Concepción Arenal 1820–1893* (1973), another treatise of significance for women's studies, provides a detailed study of the life and times of one of Spain's pioneering feminists, with particular attention to her public life, her work for reform of the penitentiary system, and her activities as novelist and educator. Although there are references in a number of sources to novels by Campo Alange, nothing more specific has been located.

María Teresa León, born in Logroño in 1904, was the daughter of a military officer of aristocratic background. She began as a journalist while still very young, writing under the pseudonym of Isabel Inghirami in the *Diario de Burgos,* and later came under the influence of the vanguardist writers of the 1920s, more directly so following her marriage to poet Rafael Alberti, himself an erstwhile member of the vanguard. Like Alberti, León took a strong Republican stance, speaking out in favor of the poor and the workers. During the war she and her husband participated in rescue efforts of the Junta for Protection of National Artistic Treasures, and she collaborated with Antonio Machado in the wartime People's Theater. León is a novelist, essayist, and translator, in addition to her journalistic work, and a feminist in the tradition of Pardo Bazán. At war's end she and Alberti went into exile, first in France, then in Argentina, where they remained until 1963 before resettling in Rome. They returned to Spain only after the post-Franco transition to democracy.

León has written stories for children, and among her first works of fiction are *Cuentos para soñar* (Stories for Dreaming), composed in the 1920s under the guise of tales told by a mother to her children. Some intertextuality can be seen: fairy tales in the collection incorporate recognizable figures from traditional juvenile literature, simultaneously reflecting the here-and-now, with references to technological innovations of the moment. Among León's works for younger readers are *Rodrigo Díaz de Vivar, el Cid Campeador* (1954; also published in Russian, 1958); *Doña Jimena Díaz de Vivar, gran señora de todos los deberes* (1960; Princess Jimena Díaz, Great Lady of All Duties; Russian text, 1971); and *Cervantes, el soldado que nos enseñó a hablar* (1978; Cervantes, the Soldier Who Taught Us to Speak), popularized biographies of great figures of Spain's political and literary history.

Although her later stories became markedly socialistic, León's first collection of tales with rural themes, *La bella del mal amor* (1930; The Beauty Wrongly Loved), is utterly lacking in political or social overtones but is clearly tinged by the popular lyricism of medieval ballads (an epoch whose continuing appeal for León is evinced by her adaptation of the figures of Spain's great medieval hero, el Cid, and his wife for juvenile readers). The six tales of this collection allude specifically to the medieval ballad tradition, through epigraphs (as with the title tale and "La amada del diablo"), through the names of characters (sometimes Visigothic, as with Manfredo and Malvina), or by drawing upon oral tradition and legend. Clearly, the attraction of this popular form to León's poetic sensibility cannot be discounted as an element in her commitment to proletarian causes.

Shortly afterward León published *Rosa-Fría, patinadora de la luna* (1934; Cold Rosa, Skater of the Moon) with illustrations done by her husband. Somewhere between children's fiction and poetic fantasy for a more mature audience, this collection constitutes a bridge between her early juvenile fiction and her work for adults. These short stories are written in the vein of the Generation of 1927, with emphasis on metaphor, mystery, and lyricism. The nine lyric tales feature a number of animal protagonists, together with a few marginal human figures, in a dreamlike atmosphere. The Civil War and much politicization intervened before León's next work, and both the civil strife and problems of loss, defeat, and exile become important in subsequent writings. *Cuentos de la España actual* (1937; Tales of Present-Day Spain) is the most ideologically tendentious of León's fiction, with many pieces apparently composed exclusively to treat social injustice, contribute to the formation of class consciousness, and expose social oppression. Violence and hatred between classes, hunger, exploitation, and similar themes reflecting Communist party ideology evince León's growing commitment. In a number of autobiographically based stories, the narrative consciousness is a thinly disguised persona of the author, recalling her privileged childhood, as in "Sistema pedagógico" (Pedagogical Methods) and "Infancia quemada" (Burned Childhood), in which she witnesses the burning of her former private academy by a revolutionary mob.

Contra viento y marea (1941; Against Wind and High Seas), León's first novel, is a combative exemplification of the view that life is a struggle against enormous odds, deriving its meaning from solidarity with other sufferers. León wishes to depict experiences of the Civil War, placing them in a historical context to contribute added meaning. The first part is set in Cuba, portraying sufferings of the poor in the years following the War of 1898; then the action shifts to contemporary unrest and political activism in the years immediately before the moment of writing. When news of the Spanish Civil War reaches Havana, a volunteer force sails to aid the Republic. The second part, set in Spain, portrays the siege and surrender of Madrid in which the participation of the Cuban volunteers is of little importance (historically accurate, but desultory and flawed as a narrative structure). Lacking a protagonist or major character, the work is essentially a series of portraits or linked vignettes.

One year later León published a short-story collection reflecting her experience of the Civil War and exile, largely in Mexico, with the resulting presence of some indigenous Mexican mythology. *Morirás lejos* (1942; You'll Die Far Away) includes stories of greater technical skill and elaboration than in *Cuentos de la España actual* (where little beyond the ideological dimension survived). *Morías lejos* exhibits increased attention to character development, with care given to psychological motivation, and more emphasis on language per se. Often contrasting the situations of different classes via representative generic characters, this collection continues to subject aesthetics to ideology, but is less propagandistic, occasionally evocative or introspective, and sometimes approaches baroque elaborateness of style.

Las pereqrinaciones de Teresa (1950; Teresa's Pilgrimages) contains nine short stories sharing the presence of the symbolic character Teresa (a homonymic persona of the writer). One of León's most interesting works for the feminist critic, it includes profound explorations of feminine psychology, passions, and resignation, as well as submission to fate. Women appear in their daily settings, often domestic, with domestic and familial burdens, generally in a lower-class environment, although the writer stresses factors universal to the feminine condition, not determined by class. Even greater distancing from socialist thematics and commitment appears in León's next novel, *Juego limpio* (1959; Playing Fair), purportedly the memoirs of Friar Camilo who abandons his convent because of disturbances during the Civil War. Some of his experiences coincide with the autobiography of the writer: for example, after being wounded at the front, Camilo joins the Guerrillas del Teatro, a group providing theatrical entertainment for soldiers in the trenches and combat-zone hospitals. There are literary portraits of León and Alberti, as well as León Felipe and Pablo Neruda. Other wartime experiences are re-created in portrayals of the evacuation of refugees from Madrid to Cuenca and then Valencia, following the shifting Republican government after the fall of the capital, and incorporating many descriptions of hunger and affliction. León also depicts the departure of the International Brigades, expresses her deep, abiding love for the people of Spain, and exhibits uncommon sensitivity to nature's changing moods.

Fábulas del tiempo amargo (1962; Fables of the Bitter Time), another short-story collection, has a content somewhat belying its name, as it refers not so much to the recent, bitter past, as to a more atemporal, universal reality. There is, however, an air of nostalgia and some allusion to experiences of exile. The style is poetic, the prose rich and even baroque at times, with more attention to language than at any time after León's prewar works. Concern for aesthetics, a reflection of early vanguardist exposure, results in a belated, attenuated surrealism, with more emphasis on dreams, the oneiric and subconscious. Again, León alludes to mythology of indigenous America, and seemingly attempts to recuperate the past through memory. Quotidian reality has not totally disappeared but is diffused and relegated to the background, being visible in glimpses of daily life in exile and occasional denunciations of social injustice.

A very different work, but not surprising from an intellectual (and a text that has parallels in the work of Rosa Chacel), is *Menesteos, marinero de abril* (1965; Menesteos, April Seaman). The "April" motif harks back to youthful works of Alberti (as does the mariner), while the classical protagonist resembles Chacel's Greek utopian idealist in her *Novelas antes de tiempo*. León's explanation is simpler and more personal: she treats the mythological origins of Cádiz (boyhood home of her husband), emphasizing the character of Menesteos, a sailor mentioned in the *Iliad,* later associated with the seaport of three-thousand-year-old Cádiz. León makes a romantic quest of Menesteos's voyage: he lands on the beach of Cádiz in search of a long-lost love, and builds a sanctuary house in memory of the passion of his youth.

León's nonnarrative works include *La historia tiene la palabra* (1944; History Will Have the Last Word), a report on the fate of Spain's artistic treasures during the Civil War; *El gran amor de Gustavo Adolfo Bécquer* (1946; Becquer's Great Love), a historico-fictional biography of Spain's great postromantic poet, together with some of his rhymes; *Sonríe China* (1958; China Smiles), travel impressions of a visit to Communist China; and *Memoria de la melancolía* (1970; Memoir of Melancholy), notes on personal and collective experiences of exile in the aftermath of the Civil War. *Una estrella roja* (1979; A Red Star), one of León's most accessible works—most of her earlier titles are out of print or unavailable, having been published by small presses in Latin America—is an anthology of short stories previously printed in *Cuentos de la España actual, Morirás lejos,* and *Fábulas del tiempo amargo.* The title tale recounts the death of a little girl, an anarchist's daughter sent daily by her father to carry bombs and incendiary materials, until one day she is killed by her cargo. As she had been a friend of some Communist organizers, the father requests a red star to bury with the child.

Eulalia Galvarriato was born in 1905 in Madrid, where she has resided most of her life. A highly cultured woman, she has long lived in contact with literati and scholars because of her marriage to poet-critic Dámaso Alonso (for many years, the President of the Royal Spanish

Academy). A delicate, lyrical novelist and short-story writer, she was a finalist for the 1946 Nadal Prize with *Cinco sombras* (1947; Five Shadows), much admired by critics of the day. Citing its quasi-musical movement, Eugenio de Nora considers it "exceptional in many aspects,"[5] and quotes José Luis Cano's review in *Insula* (July 1947) to the effect that *Cinco Sombras* is "an accomplished work of art." Nora praises the purity, precision, and economy of Galvarriato's language and concludes that the work approaches "irreproachable perfection."[6] Although this novel betrays not a hint of protest, it presents a situation that should interest feminist critics: the five "shadows" are daughters of a domineering, possessive patriarch who becomes reclusive and antisocial following the death of his wife. The action is re-created via retrospective evocation by a more contemporary narrator, but most of it transpires in the late nineteenth century. Only one male, the son of an old friend, is allowed to visit the home, and so becomes the girls' only link with the outside world (and the means by which their story is reconstructed many decades later). The father's dictatorial tyranny frustrates the loves and possible marriages of the older girls, and when at last four of them join forces to help the fifth elope, the father retaliates by incarcerating the remaining four for months, confining them to their rooms without permitting them even to speak to one another. The married daughter dies following complications after childbirth, without having been allowed to return home to visit. Whimsically, the patriarch suddenly decides to arrange a marriage for the second daughter (who is silently in love with the one official visitor but dares not confess it). She is rescued by the third sister who accepts the match in her place, but drowns when a boat capsizes on her honeymoon. As the sisters die one by one, only shadows remain in the darkened parlor, arround the sewing box which was the focus of their lives. In spite of the lyrical, low-key tone, Galvarriato's portrayal of these five women— initially beautiful, lively, vibrant girls, reduced to muted shadows by paternalistic tyranny—is something of a feminist protest in spite of itself.[7] Galvarriato has also written a number of highly regarded short stories, and recently she published a collection of brief fiction, lyric essays, and prose poems, *Raíces bajo el tiempo* (1986; Roots Beneath Time),[8] which are frequently autobiographical, tender evocations of childhood friendships or long-ago encounters, mystic moments half-forgotten or dimly understood, reflections of the intimate inner life of a sensitive, introverted dreamer.

Concha Suárez del Otero (b. 1908), a native of Asturias, began her education in Oviedo, later receiving her doctorate from the University of Madrid, where she taught Spanish literature. A somewhat precocious beginning saw publication of her first adolescent novel, *Mabel* (1928), when the author was barely twenty. Set in a remote Austrian mountain village, the novel constitutes a re-creation of the life of a young schoolteacher, the daughter of a once-prominent family, now economically ruined. The protagonist (somewhat in the vein of heroines of the past century such as Pardo Bazán's Feíta, but also resembling Dolores Medio's alter ego in her 1962 *Diario de una maestra*) adapts successfully to her straits and the necessity for work, learning to communicate with people of very different backgrounds from her own. Another adolescent novel, *Vulgaridades* (1930; Ordinary Things), also set in the author's native Asturias, traces the friendship of two girls, Marta and Carmen, dreamers whose aspirations are slowly transformed by reality. There follows a nineteen-year hiatus in the literary career of Suárez del Otero, who spent the period from 1930 to 1949 without publishing. Her output since that time is rather evenly distributed between the several genres: essays, poetry, the novel, and short stories. She has received numerous literary awards and is an active contributor of critical articles for newspapers and periodicals.

Among the mature novels of Suárez del Otero is *Satanás no duerme* (1958; Satan Doesn't Sleep), somewhat in the tradition of the high school reunion. One month before the outbreak of the Spanish Civil War in June 1936, six graduating high school friends in Madrid make a pact, swearing to meet again in ten years. Their lives and loves in the intervening decade—beginning with the traumas of the war and concluding with its aftermath—are traced by the narrative, which introduces a number of unexpected turns and curious incidents. When the long-awaited reunion takes place, the one-time friends realize how much has changed and how little they now have in common. A more recent work that features a female protagonist is *Me llamo Clara* (1968; My Name is Clara). Considered by some to be Suárez del Otero's best narrative achievement, this is something of an exercise in metafiction, a novel within a novel (the first part includes a lengthy fragment of the protagonist's manuscript of an autobiographical novel she is writing in return for a publisher's cash advance). Fiction is not her primary vocation, but instead an attempt at self-preservation subsequent to the loss of her teaching job. Before finishing the novel, however, Clara accepts a position as a tour guide with a Madrid travel agency and sets off in pursuit of adventure across half a dozen European countries. An ill-fated romance and frustrated marriage plans end with Clara's return to Spain. Although the outcome is sufficiently inconclusive to allow for a sequel, the author seems to have abandoned Clara without further adventures.

A Cosmopolitan Traditionalist

Elisabeth Mulder de Daumer was born in 1904 in Barcelona of a South American mother and Dutch-born father. Comparable to Bertrana in her travels and sophistication and the presence of the exotic in her novels, she enjoyed the benefits of a cosmopolitan and refined education. Her techniques are rather traditional, and for the most part, her focus is preferentially upon the upper class. Mulder's early works were collections of poetry, published before the Civil War, and she achieved a modest renown in this genre. Traces of lyricism persist in several of her novels. Mulder also worked as a translator, producing Spanish versions of works by Baudelaire, Duhamel, Shelley, Keats, Pearl Buck, and Pushkin, among others.

Usually subjective, nostalgic or melancholic, sentimental and introspective, this writer's works emphasize analysis of the emotions, a trait that—together with the upper-class focus—resulted in their being classed as escapist by postwar critics with a predilection for critical or "social" realism. *Una sombra entre los dos* (1934; A Shadow between the Two), her first novel, which suffers the usual limitations of the thesis novel, has been seen as an important feminist statement, perhaps the only work by Mulder that can be so described. *La historia de Java* (1935: The Story of Java) evokes a beautiful, green-eyed cat, impossible to domesticate.

Because she remained in Spain following the war, Mulder's postwar novels are subject to the limitations of the censorship of the period. *Crepúsculo de una ninfa* (1942; Twilight of a Nymph) is typical of most rather tentative fiction of the early postwar years in its avoidance of problematic subject matter. In *Crepúsculo* Mulder offers a sentimental, melancholy, and lyrical treatment of the pathetic rural idyll and self-destructive emotions of a woman who is in love with a man with a terminal illness. *El hombre que acabó en las islas* (1944; The Man Who Ended Up in the Islands) begins the incorporation of spatial exoticism, its second part being set in Stockholm. The first part, which has been compared to aspects of Carmen Laforet's *Nada* (published one year later), contains some elements of *tremendismo*, primarily of the psychological variety, although the novel as a whole would best be described as a pastiche, for subsequent parts reflect romantic and gothic influences. There is definite escapism in the latter portions as the skeptical, hedonistic hero, Juan Miguel, renounces his past and civilization for an "animalistic earthly paradise,"[9] in the perpetual inactivity of the remote Antilles.

Las hogueras de otoño (1945; Autumn Bonfires) is one of Mulder's more valuable studies from the sociological perspective, returning to a realistic Spanish context to portray a mid-life crisis in the relationship of a mature couple. Insights into upper-class life of the period constitute its principal sociological interest. *Preludio a la muerte* (1946; Prelude to Death) reconstructs the relationship of two women who meet while studying in Switzerland, and become both friends and rivals. The foreign setting is one of the more common devices by which postwar writers attempted to circumnavigate the censors, and may explain the author's success in presenting a potentially censurable ending, the suicide of the disillusioned protagonist. With its sensitive insights into friendship and love, refined perceptions and sensations, profound and dramatic psychological analysis, this novel has been considered Mulder's best.

Alba Grey (1947) is more deserving of the "escapist" label, beginning in the mansion of a dying marquis and proceeding to a tour of Egypt by way of Italy. Alba struggles between the violent, absorbing passion inspired by Gian Carlo, and the more serene, spiritual love offered by Lorenzo, always against the backdrop of a heavily aristocratic decor and cast of cosmopolitan Italian nobility. Although relatively well received by conservative Spanish critics, this novel suffers from obvious contrivance of plot and more stylized rhetoric than some of the author's other fiction. It ends with a marriage of convenience. In *El vendedor de vidas* (1953; The Seller of Lives), an astrologer who foresees his own death without realizing it is the center of a well-structured reconstruction of the somber atmosphere of postwar Spain, as viewed from the perspective of lower-class Barcelona. The novel spans the years between the clairvoyant's vision of the fatal future incident and his own actual demise, which happens as foreseen. Absence in Mulder of the engagement characterizing works of the younger writers of the 1950s makes her work interesting as a complement to their portrayals of the same period.

During the early postwar years, characterized by a self-exaltation on the part of Falangists (later termed *triunfalismo*), treatments of the Civil War ("our glorious crusade") were unabashedly partisan and anti-Republican. With time, the first efforts to present a less partisan view of the war (epitomized by José María Gironella and his enormously successful novel, *The Cypresses Believe in God*) brought other fictional treatments of the traumatic experience of national conflict. Presentation of a pro-Republican perspective was impossible, but it slowly became feasible to move from glorification of the Franco forces toward a "war is hell" emphasis, which is the context in which Mulder's *Eran cuatro* (1954; There Were Four of Them) should be situated. A mother whose four sons died in the war undertakes a symbolic quest for reconciliation, visiting important sites and persons in the lives of her sons, three of whom served the victorious Nationalists (as aviator, soldier, and spy, respectively), while the fourth was a Republican and an anarchist. Failing in her desperate emotional attempt to mediate a postmortem reduction of the conflict that had claimed her sons, the mother slips first into madness and eventually death. *Luna de las máscaras* (1958; Moon of the Masks), one of Mulder's best-executed novels, has been seen as a necessary complement to certain products of novelistic engagement (for example, the works of Juan Goytisolo or of García Hortelano and others who portrayed the "dolce vita" of the upper classes) in the 1950s and 1960s, often focusing on the habitués of Mediterranean tourist centers or artists' colonies. When novels from the opposing ideological camps are read together, the total picture with its contrasts and resulting balance is of more value as a historical chronicle. In *Luna de las máscaras* Mulder re-creates a love triangle, two of whose participants are a famous sculptor and a well-known actress. The characters' remembrances and introspective thoughts are precipitated by an automobile accident.

With the exception of mention in Nora's panoramic work on the contemporary Spanish novel, Mulder has not attracted the attention of the international fraternity of Hispanists, not even those specializing in the postwar novel. Nevertheless, during the 1950s and early 1960s she was highly regarded by many Spanish critics and writers. Nora reflects this esteem when he judges Mulder as the only woman of the period potentially comparable to Pardo Bazán.[10] Nora is not usually overgenerous, but in this instance his judgment is out of phase: in the intervening quarter-century, Mulder has been as completely forgotten as many women writers of the nineteenth century. Some part of her decline in popularity may be due to her view of society as vitiated: she sees her sociological context as characterized by depressing vital sterility, which endows her fiction with bitter melancholy. And some of her better literary qualities—exquisite sensibility, refinement of perceptions and sensations, ability to capture subtle shadings, and elegance of expression—recall the cult of "pure" prose by the "dehumanized" narrators of the Generation of 1927, also now out of favor.

Chapter Four
Major Writers Appearing during the Republic

The First Academician

Carmen Conde Abellán was born in 1907 in the coastal town of Cartagena where she spent her youth, an experience endowing her work with a Mediterranean air. A poet, novelist, and critic, as well as the author of historical and literary essays, Conde is the first woman to be admitted to the Royal Spanish Academy, founded in 1714 (she was elected in 1978, at age seventy-one). An only child whose mother opposed her writing because it was a "man's thing, like brandy,"[1] she wrote furtively and began to publish at the age of fifteen, her first poems appearing in the local press in 1925. *Brocal* (Opening), her first book of verse, was published in 1929. After completing her pedagogical study at the Normal School in Albacete, Conde married poet Antonio Oliver Belmás in 1931.

Conde and her husband cooperated in founding the significant vanguard review, *El gallo crisis,* together with Miguel Hernández and Ramón Sijé. Most of Conde's early writings reflect the tutelage of Gabriel Miró, Juan Ramón Jiménez, and Gabriela Mistral. Critical acclaim first came with *Júbilos* (1934; Jubilations), poems in a surrealistic and ultraistic vein, with a prologue by Mistral. During the war Conde followed her husband, who served in the Republican army, and afterward took refuge with friends in Madrid. In 1945 she resumed her poetic career with *Ansia de gracia* (1945; Desire for Grace), one of her most important verse collections. *Mujer sin edén* (1947; Woman Without Eden) and *Sea la luz* (1947; Let There Be Light) contain a more personal poetry, although surrealistic echoes remain. Love is envisioned as the prime mover of the universe. During the following decade Conde's poetic production continued to be prolific, including *Iluminada tierra* (1951; Illuminated Land), *Mientras los hombres mueren* (1953; While Men Die, expressing her reactions to the war), and *Vivientes de los siglos* (1954; Survivors of the Centuries), which won the Simón Bolívar Award.

Conde's first efforts in prose were in the area of children's literature, ranging from novelized biography to plays and both brief and long fiction, signed with the pseudonym Florentina del Mar (a result of her ambiguous situation vis-à-vis the Franco regime and its censorship—since both she and her husband were tried by military tribunals for having written in *El Sol* during the Republican era). According to the *Columbia Dictionary of Modern European Literature,* 2d ed. (New York, 1980), *Soplo que va y no vuelve* (1944; Breath Which Goes, Never to Return) is a novel published during the early postwar years under this pseudonym. It is of difficult access. The first novel for adults, *Vidas contra su espejo* (1944; Lives against Their Mirror) was written in 1935 but remained unpublished for almost a decade. Reminiscent of works of the Generation of 1927, it is a lyric, passive novel in which abstractions and meditations predominate. Set in a Valencian or Murcian ambience recalling works of Miró, this novel's aesthetically self-conscious, impressionistic prose also evokes Miró's style. The five principal characters—two men and three women—all Decadentist aesthetes—end by pairing off after the suicide of the "fifth wheel." The major interest is intellectual, and the "action" consists largely of thoughts, feelings, and conversation. A lyric style—logically reflecting Conde's poetic training—is employed to examine the theme of intellectual love as opposed to a more instinctual passion (recalling such works as Unamuno's *Amor y pedagogía*).

En manos del silencio (1950; In the Hands of Silence), one of Conde's most dramatic efforts in the novelistic genre, is compared by Nora[2] to fictions of Unamuno because of its schematic concentration. This work explores love, guilt, passion, communication, marriage, isolation, and incest, for which reason Nora places it among the "most audacious and equivocal literary explorations in European postwar literature."[3] A middle-aged man conducts affairs with both the wife and daughter of a friend, leaving both women pregnant. The barriers to communication between the four major characters are the principal area of analysis. Although the husband/father of the two women may seem an innocent bystander, the novelist does not exonerate him from a share of responsibility; all are equally guilty, and end tragically, in death or madness.

Las oscuras raíces (1953; Dark Roots), a lyric canto to human love and passion, involves a double triangle. Four couples, whose destinies have crossed or coincided since all of them have lived at some point in the same seaside house, serve the novelist as bases for her exploration of the implications of fate and consuming passion. The protagonist or antagonist is the house (symbol of destiny or fate), apparently accursed, since all who live in it have their marital happiness destroyed by the intrusion of third parties. Mystery and an air of Greek tragedy hang over the characters, who move as in a dream, incessantly in motion between the house and various countries of Europe while the devouring fires of passion grow progressively more destructive. A quasi-detective element is introduced with the fourth couple, who attempt to unravel various mysteries shrouding the house and the lives of its inhabitants and to overcome the powers of destiny.

Cobre (1953; Copper) contains two novelettes, each approximately 120 pages in length, *Destino hallado* (Found Destiny) and *Solamente un viaje* (Only a Journey). The first reiterates Conde's interest in the theme of destiny, retracing the social and psychological development of the protagonist, a young female painter. This work also explores the effects of the Civil War on several individuals. Because of its depiction of a woman as a professional artist (a role heretofore seldom seen in fiction written by Spanish women) *Destino hallado* will interest feminist critics. The action is set in an unnamed provincial town, but descriptions suggest Cartagena (which is definitely the setting for Conde's next fiction, *La rambla*). Still more pertinent for women's studies is the second novelette, *Solamente un viaje,* which focuses upon a young wife and her growing indifference toward, as well as incipient rejection of, the husband she initially loved. The villain is not another man, or not at the outset, but—significantly—the monotony of boring domestic routines and the ennui of household confinement. The journey to which the title refers is a trip to Italy, which becomes a voyage of self-discovery. Freedom from familiar surroundings and her repetitive schedule allows the protagonist finally to confront reality.

Later poetry collections, reflecting a transition to a more personal and lyrical vein, include *Los monólogos de la hija* (1959; The Daughter's Monologues), *Derribado arcángel* (1960; Fallen Archangel), *Poemas del Mar Menor* (1962; Poems of the Mar Menor), and *Jaguar, puro, inmarchito* (1963; Pure, Unspotted Jaguar), her reactions to a trip to America. One of the writer's highest honors came when an anthology of her poetry, *Obra poética (1929-1966)* (1967; Poetic Works) received the National Literary Award. Conde's poetry of vitalism and passion has been compared to that of Spanish Nobel laureate, Vicente Aleixandre. She has treated themes from social protest to nonconformist youth and the dead in the Civil War, selfishness, rebellion, and the most fundamental human values, time and its ruinous passage, eroding memories, love, ethics, and even metaphysical convictions. Pain, bitterness, death, God, nature, childhood, and loneliness are also frequent emphases of this subjective poetry, full of remembrances, nostalgia, and childhood sensations. The influence of Miró appears in Conde's chromatic aestheticism and in her linguistic richness. The cosmovision expressed by Conde's poetry is both universal and uniquely feminine.

La rambla (1977; The Boulevard), a framing novel with four interpolated tales is an original sort of collection of short fiction, actually written many years before publication, as Conde indicates.[4] Indirectly, *La rambla* reflects one of the war's effects on this writer's work, a moving toward more "human" (i.e., sociopolitical) thematics, and away from abstract intellectualism. Composition probably dates from the late 1940s or early 1950s. The protagonist or narrative consciousness experiences both love and pity for the miners and fishermen of Cartagena and the nearby area of La Unión in the arid, impoverished territory of Murcia. An expression of the author's enduring affection for her native region, it is written in a concise, direct, poetic style, impregnated with localisms and regional dialect. The major story line concerns a wife's discovery that her husband had killed a man two decades previously, with a resultant erosion of her trust and eventually of the very foundations of the marriage. Exploring communication and various emotions—disappointment, guilt, disillusionment, remorse, anguish—the collection also contains more objective elements such as the poverty of the miners, which is treated realistically, with a detachment approaching the documentary. A significant portion of the realistic sections of *La rambla* retraces the industrialization of Cartagena, while another (which reflects social concerns) paints the paternalistic and patriarchal attitudes of the region and epoch. These aspects make *La rambla* Conde's closest approach to the "social novel," although the autobiographical substrata and recollections and prevailing lyricism situate the work at considerable remove, stylistically, from the narratives of "critical Realism."

Creció espesa la yerba (1979; Thick Grew the Grass) takes its title and theme from Solzehnitsyn's *Gulag Archipelago:* "The grass grew thick on the tomb of my youth." This psychological novel is also of potential interest for feminist critics, as it presents an in-depth analysis of the female protagonist who returns to the home of her youth to rediscover her past self. The process of remembering is painful owing to a childhood trauma, suppressed by her conscious memory. In slow stages she confronts the anguish of a past incestuous experience. *Soy la madre*

(1980; I'm the Mother) is also of potential interest for the feminist critic owing to its exploration of the problems of rape and its consequences, and the competing roles of woman and mother. Laurencia, raped by the wealthy *cacique,* don Diego, while still an adolescent, later marries Juan, and bears a son, Francisco. When the child is five, Juan is brought home dead, allegedly of a heart attack. Laurencia (and others, including the village doctor and priest) suspect that don Diego is involved. During more than a decade, while her son and Diego's son Pedro become friends, both Laurencia and Diego prohibit the friendship. Pedro expounds his hatred of his father and fear of becoming like him, and deliberately administers himself a fatal overdose of heroin.

Following Pedro's death, don Diego is overwhelmed with grief and guilt, and before dying, he wills his fortune to Laurencia, whose initial rejection of the money is reconsidered in favor of educating her son. Acceptance introduces the struggle between her concept of herself as a mother, only and exclusively, and her needs and rights as a woman. Marcos loves and wishes to marry Laurencia, but she is unable to accept either his love or her own incipient sexuality; so traumatic had been the experience of rape that during her marrigae to Juan, she never enjoyed their sexual relationship. Although she loves and desires Marcos, not until her son's wedding does she finally surrender to her own desire. Conde succeeds in presenting the trauma Laurencia experiences in relating to another man, even many years after being raped, and also paints with clarity and detail the struggle, finally verging upon mild schizophrenia, between Laurencia's competing roles. The egotistical and occasionally exploitative aspects of filial devotion are well addressed, and Francisco will apparently have his life managed by a strong and efficient wife who steps into the place ceded her by his mother.

Conde's fiction is relatively traditional in form and occasionally impresses the reader as belonging to a bygone age, more because of the mentality and inhibitions of the narrative consciousness than because of thematics. Arduous problems of conscience, spiritual dilemmas, and social issues are the substance of Conde's better works. The writer's emphasis on love and her interest in children place her in the realm traditionally (and somewhat pejoratively) associated with women writers, while her exploration of such topics as incest and rape seem to situate her among more progressive feminist authors, as would her less dramatic but completely real concern with the jading effects of household routines for the conjugal relationship and limitations imposed by domestic confinement upon self-realization. Conde was considered daring for her time and, like Victor Català, accused of crudeness and "masculinity." Her election to the Royal Academy is one indicator of societal change in Spain in the interim.

A Candidate for the Cervantes Prize

Rosa Chacel was born in the provincial Castilian capital of Valladolid in 1898, where she spent her first ten years, and began to study art at the age of eight. Her family moved to Madrid in 1908, and she continued her studies of painting and sculpture at the Escuela de Artes y Oficios first and then at the Escuela Superior de Bellas Artes de San Fernando. In 1972 Chacel published a memoir or first portion of her autobiography, *Desde el amanecer: Autobiografía de mis primeros diez años* (Since Dawn: Autobiography of My First Ten Years). More than 350 pages in length, the memoir does not follow a linear chronology, but a more fragmented progression carefully analyzing seemingly insignificant details as to their possible implications for personality development.

After some ten years in Madrid, Chacel's delicate health forced her to discontinue study in the unheated building at San Fernando (site of the old university), and she became a member of the Madrid Ateneo (Atheneum or private library) in 1918, a significant moment for her contacts with literature. During the 1920s, like other future members of the Generation of 1927, she became a disciple of Ortega y Gasset, later contributing to Spain's most significant literary and intellectual periodical of the day, the *Revista de Occidente* (founded by Ortega). Chacel married a fellow painter, Timoteo Pérez Rubio, and from 1922 through 1929, the couple lived and studied in Rome. Indeed, from that point onward, she would reside more abroad than in Spain (living in England, Germany, Greece, France, the United States, Argentina, Mexico, and Brazil).

Chacel's interest in literature continued, however, and upon publication of the Spanish translation of James Joyce's *Portrait of the Artist as a Young Man (Retrato del artista adolescente),* she saw in it all that a novel could or should be. "This admirable little work of Joyce marked my narrative decision," she observed half a century later, noting that the embryo of all her future writing is to be found in her first novel, *Estación, ida y vuelta* (1930; Station/Season, Round Trip), completed toward the end of her stay in Italy. "It is like the key that governs all my prose."[5] The conceit or wordplay of the title, a neo-baroque trait characteristic of the beginnings of many of the writers of Chacel's generation, exploits the double meaning of *estación,* both station and season, which allows a simultaneous allusion to a round trip and to the round of seasons, thereby hinting at the novel's cyclic structure. Chacel's work traces the formation of a young novelist, and represents a degree of fusion of form and content: the writer's preoccupation with form is evident from the beginning, and her prose in this first novel is lively, with vivacious imagery and occasional Proustian touches in the mechanisms of involuntary memory and frequent self-analysis. Influenced more than others of her generation by Ortega's *Ideas on the Novel* (1925), Chacel set out to apply quite literally Ortega's notions on heightened psychological realism in keeping with his perspectivist vision and contemporary psychological theory.[6] Plot is minimal and action all but nonexistent in *Estación, ida y vuelta,* which is similarly devoid of dialogue, being devoted almost totally to the minute analysis of varied and changing perspectives on an unfortunate love affair (an approach that also appears in Chacel's next several novels). The novelist is particularly interested in "describing the action before the act," not the story of a man's actions but his thoughts. The influence of Marcel Proust upon the conception of this first novel is also pointed out by Chacel herself who mentions that she read *A la recherche du temps perdu* in French in Rome while writing *Estación, ida y vuelta.*[7] Chacel's artistic background is evident in her continual visualization of objects, the disciplined complexity of her prose, and distancing (which is yet not the "dehumanization" for which the generation was both praised and blamed).[8]

During the war she contributed poems to the Loyalist magazine, *Hora de España,* and her next literary effort proved to be a book of sonnets, *A la orilla de un pozo* (1936; By The Shore of a Well), whose title again indicates her tendency to wordplay, since *orilla* has several meanings—bank, shore, side, edge—but is not usually associated with wells. Given her association with liberals and Republican intellectuals, it is not surprising that Chacel chose to leave Spain in 1937, even though her exile was not exclusively or primarily political in its motivations, for Chacel is essentially apolitical—she looks upon politics as ephemeral, and is interested in more lasting issues. Her next novel, *Teresa* (1941), was published in Buenos Aires, where her third and fourth novels would also appear. *Teresa* is a novelized biography of Teresa Mancha, the mistress of romantic poet José de Espronceda. Chacel uses the feminine perspective predominantly, presenting the woman's view on the romance, the difficulties of giving up everything for love in a society that chastises only the female partner, the experience of exile and alienation, illness, and desperation, and finally death in solitude and oblivion.

Memorias de Leticia Valle (1945; The Memoirs of Leticia Valle) is a Spanish variant on the Lolita theme. Chacel has indicated that its gestation dates back to the period when she was writing *Estación* in Italy and read a Dostoyevski novel in which a middle-aged man hangs himself after seducing a young girl. Remembering a comparable case in Valladolid during her childhood—a schoolmaster who seduced a ten-year-old girl—Chacel recalled in an interview her suspicion that it had been the child who took the initiative because the man was so handsome, and she declared that she would one day write a novel in which a little girl seduces a respectable gentleman, and the gentleman has to hang himself.[9] The protagonist, eleven-year-old Leticia writes a diary in the effort to understand her life through reconstructing it. Leticia is a precocious adolescent, psychologically troubled and morally ambiguous, neither a child nor yet an adult, for whom the episode has aspects of the rite of passage. Other themes include jealousy, the education of the artist, and possible sexual abuse and child molestation (quite unheard-of problems for the Spanish novel of the early 1940s). The novelistic version is not as clear as the novelist's interview on the matter of who seduces whom.

One of Chacel's major works is *La sinrazón* (1960; Unreason), republished in Andorra in 1970 and in Spain in 1977, at which time it won the Premio de la Crítica (Critics' Prize), one of the country's most prestigious awards (Chacel has twice achieved this recognition, a feat accomplished by few other novelists). An extensive, almost motionless autobiographical narrative by a male protagonist, *La sinrazón* retraces the life of Argentinian Santiago Hernández from 1918 until his death in 1941. Raised in Europe from the age of a year, he is educated by an uncle, obtaining a degree in chemistry. Returning to Argentina in 1930, he marries, has children, takes over a pharmaceutical business, and then has an affair with a woman from his past. This provokes the loss of his wife and children, and perhaps his death, as his prolonged soul-searching culminates with his demise. As in her previous novel, Chacel uses the diary technique, ideally adapted for her literary aims of character analysis. Santiago's confessional effort at understanding his life, his loss of innocence and of his hold on life forms the entire text of the novel. His search for self-fulfillment and pleasure is a result of his lack of beliefs (religious, political, humanitarian), and he places too much faith in the identity-defining power of professional and financial success. Whether through coincidence, fortuitously or otherwise, the protagonist is able to accomplish apparently impossible feats through the exercise of will (which may be the intervention of luck, a point the novelist leaves deliberately obscure), and thus life is not a sufficient challenge to him. Prolonged analysis leads him to the realization of his need for God, for faith, for something transcendent, beyond himself (here echoing Unamuno, as well as Ortega, both of whom influence Chacel's thought).[10] He concentrates all his psychic power on seeing the wing of a dead butterfly move, as a sign of the existence of God (he previously accomplished astonishing results through the exercise of will). Santiago is found dead and the butterfly's wing is broken. *La sinrazón* is one of Unamuno's terms for faith (since acceptance of the tenets of faith goes against scientific reason), and it is in part through this irrationality that Santiago comes to have some comprehension of his own loss of innocence.

Barrio de Maravillas (1976; Maravillas Neighborhood) is the autonomous first part of a trilogy based in large part upon autobiographical materials. The trilogy as a whole is planned as a reconstruction of the lives of two female protagonists from the turn of the century up to the present, concentrating upon the Madrid neighborhood where Chacel resided from 1908 to 1910, the time of her initial acquaintance with the capital. Beginning when the protagonists are girls, the novelist's questioning, probing, analytical procedure seeks answers to fundamental enigmas of life such as the essence of being, the purpose of life, and the nature of human identity and consciousness. Chacel has described the novel as a history of her generation (the writers of the Generation of 1927), and thus she concentrates especially upon aesthetics, upon the girls' introduction to the arts, including not only literature, painting, and sculpture, in which she herself participated, but also music and cinema in the years before World War I. While undoubtedly the aesthetic significance of *Barrio de Maravillas* is primarily as a view of the arts in Spain before 1914, Chacel also presents a profound and important study of female adolescence.

Although she originally intended to entitle the second part of the trilogy *La escuela de Platón* (The Platonic School), according to indications in several interviews, Chacel changed her mind and instead published it with the title *Acrópolis* (1984). The formula of "internal dialogue" (or what Unamuno dubbed *monodiálogos*), one of Chacel's most constant devices, is utilized again in her attempt to illuminate the secret, personal route of thought. The transformation undergone by memories in the course of literary elaboration is probed, and the relationship between memory and history scrutinized. Two female protagonists, Isabel and Elena, appear in the years preceding the Republic (1914–31), and their lives serve as a pretext to retrace the lives of those about them—the history of Spain, its art, and social reality, which cross through the consciousness of the characters together with love, personal quirks, and debilities, illness, love of life, and a search for orientation. Chacel's prose—always dense, intellectual, and philosophically complex—becomes still more baroque, combining a variety of techniques which range from the internal monologue to the traditional omniscient narrator, to Platonic dialogue and discursive digressions. *Acrópolis* is a self-contained and independent narrative unit, as was its predecessor (i.e., the "plot" is not dependent upon acquaintance with the events of the first part, although as in all of Chacel's novels, plot is almost nonexistent). The third part, according to Chacel's declaration in the lecture series at the March Foundation, should be entitled "Ciencias Naturales" (Natural Sciences). Following the plan originally outlined, this third and final portion of the trilogy should comprise the postwar period.

In addition to these longer narratives, Chacel has published essays, and a recent book of poetry, *Versos prohibidos* (1978; Prohibited Verse), a collection of sonnets, odes, and other metrical forms, including "moral epistles." Essay volumes include *La confesión* (1971; Confession) and *Saturnal* (1972). In *La confesión* Chacel studies those confessions that she considers the greatest, most important, and dramatic of history, those motivated by a sense of guilt: those of St. Augustine, Rousseau, and Kierkegaard, as well as Galdós, Unamuno, and Cervantes, forming the trio of writers Chacel considers the most decisive for Spanish literature. *Don Quijote* is seen as a confession, a last will and testament born of the conviction that "to believe and to love, one must be crazy" (29). Clearly influenced by Ortega and Unamuno, Chacel sees in Cervantes the conclusion that, in the world in which he lived, one had to lose either faith or reason. Her study of the confession as genre simultaneously exhibits her familiarity with a wide range of critical texts. In the case of all three—Cervantes, Galdós, Unamuno—Chacel encounters evidence of concealment, rather than full confession, symbolized in a variety of novelistic characters.

Saturnal (The Feast of Saturn),[11] some three hundred pages of small print, was nearly four decades in gestation. Chacel's preface identifies it as the outgrowth of an article published in *Revista de Occidente* in 1931, "Esquema de los actuales problemas prácticos del amor" (Outline of Present Practical Problems of Love). An abiding concern of Chacel, the problems of love became the subject of a 1959–60 Guggenheim Foundation grant, under which some two-thirds of the final text was drafted in New York. A pondered, probing, meditative, and questioning text, *Saturnal* has sexual equality as its basic, implicit postulate. Ortega's tutelage is frequently apparent in the measured, logical manner of argument and development, as well as in the sustained, dispassionate and reasoned tone. After a survey of other authors who have treated the subject in modern times, together with indications of their similarities and differences, Chacel proceeds to attempt to isolate the essence of feminine psychology—not physiology—that is, what it is that makes the female psyche different, peculiar, and concludes that on a deep, ancestral level, it is the fear of rape. Many feminist studies are discussed, invariably to signal Chacel's discrepancies, ranging from Virginia Woolf to Beauvoir to Campo Alange. Briefly, Chacel touches upon related topics: homosexuality, maternity, and prostitution.[12] An unexpected major focus is the cinema, seen as especially significant in shaping the modern mentality. Among many digressions, one which Chacel identifies as a distinguishing "sign of the times" is the unisex phenomenon (women have moved into what once was exclusively masculine territory, while men have become more feminine).[13] The approach in the third section is more sociological, with a consideration of public morality and law, slavery and servitude, riches and power, difference and equality, among many other topics. Chacel's concern is with the problems of good and evil, tolerance and intolerance, war and the "right to kill." Her consideration of sexual relationships is paradigmatic, symbolic of all others.

Chacel's short-story collections, *Sobre el piélago* (1952; On the Open Sea) and *Ofrenda a una virgen loca* (1961; Offering to a Mad Virgin), were brought together with some previously uncollected and even unpublished stories in a single volume, *Icada, Nevda, Diada* (1971). The title is based on three variations of the word *nada* (nothing) and sounds one of the existential concerns of the writer, nothingness. Another major preoccupation of the collection is death, including suicide, also clearly linked to the title. Twelve stories are included in the first collection, and as is the case with Chacel's novels, plot is relatively insignificant, while the elaboration of subtle shades of meaning, visionary impressions, and an exquisitely worked prose take precedence over both action and characterization.

Novelas antes de tiempo (1981; Novels Ahead of Time), a collection of four unfinished novel projects, summarizes the works that Chacel planned to write, but feared she might never have time to finish (she was eighty-two when the summaries were published). Each fragment appeared previously in literary magazines and is followed by an essay in which Chacel discusses the process of creation of fictional works, explaining problems and outlining her plan for the remainder of the work in question. If there is a common denominator to the collection, aside from the creative process per se, it is the concept of life as a search, a quest: in *Suma,* a novel of Buenos Aires which begins in San Juan and contains characters from Chacel's neighborhood, an intellectual searches for perfection in nature, and similarly, *La fundación de Eudoxia* presents an intellectual's quest for a perfect society. Chacel's foreword explains that she had conceived of the persona for this work as a young Greek expatriate, indigent, with an intellectual beauty consisting in part in the incomprehensibility of his projected utopia, a being so at odds with the materialistic environment of the commercial neighborhood in which he is presented that his presence in the bar (subject of the completed fragment) can be compared to the luminous passage of a comet, observed but not understood, and touching no one.

The protagonist of *Margarita (zurcidora),* an aging woman, engages in internal dialogue, an extended free-association process that is derived in a general way from autobiographical materials, literarily transformed. To a great extent, it is a catalog of sensations and perceptions (alarm clock, bell, neighborhood sounds, the cry of a locust) interspersed with thoughts (the time, whether to get up or wait another ten minutes, memories, fantasies). *El pastor* (The Shepherd) is the oldest of the four novelistic embryos, as Chacel explains in her preface, the only one that is "completely Spanish" (the others having been conceptualized during her years as an expatriate). Sometime during the 1920s she read a translation of a novel by the Andalusian Arab, Abentofail, *El filósofo autodidacta* (The Self-Taught Philosopher), and decided to write someday another novel in which those things voluntarily silenced in Abentofail's narrative would be said. *El pastor* narrates the history of a boy born on a tropical desert island. Adopted by a gazelle whose baby has died, he is raised among the animals, speaks all their languages, and develops a speculative spirit. The death of his "mother" gazelle, his shock and rejection of the event lead him to attempt to explain the cause of death, and he comes to postulate a soul in her that has escaped, and to find the body despicable by comparison. He therefore devotes himself to meditation upon the soul, contemplating the world of forms and aspiring to reach the essence, perfection, immortality. The novel has been termed a "metaphysical *Robinson Crusoe.*" *Los títulos* (1981; Titles) is a collection of critical articles, and *Alcancía* (1982; Piggy-Bank) is Chacel's diary.

Chacel continues to be active, agile, and alert, and involved in her writing. After having twice won the Premio de la Crítica (in 1976 for *Barrio de Maravillas,* and in 1977 for the Spanish edition of *La sinrazón*), the aging writer came suddenly to the literary forefront in Spain. When in 1978 the Royal Spanish Academy decided to open its doors to women for the first time, Chacel was one of the nominees. One of Spain's most respected intellectuals and critics, Julián Marías, said of Chacel that she "has no equivalent" in the Spanish narrative: "she can't be exchanged for anyone else, which means that without her, our literature—that of the Spanish language—would be incomplete."[14] Chacel was also a contender for the Cervantes Prize in 1985, an award given not for a single work but for the totality of a writer's production. Spanish literature's most significant recognition, it functions not on a national basis but worldwide and is given only to those writers whose contributions are judged to have enriched the cultural heritage of all Spanish-speaking countries. Although Chacel was not ultimately selected, her inclusion among the finalists constituted one of the most important instances of recognition of the worth of a Spanish woman writer.

A Humorist with a Flair for Sorrow

Mercedes Ballesteros de Gaibrois was born in Madrid in 1913 (according to *España, hoy* [17 November 1971, p. 55], not 1891 as reported in *Women Writers of Spain*).[15] Her family belonged to the traditional Spanish nobility: her father was the historian, Antonio Ballesteros Beretta, Count of Beretta; her mother was Colombian. Both parents were scholars and academicians. A writer of newspaper and periodical articles from the 1940s onward, Ballesteros published her first works of fiction in 1939: *Paris-Niza* (From Paris to Nice), *La extraña boda de Glori Dunn* (The Strange Wedding of Glori Dunn), and *La aventura de una chica audaz* (The Adventure of an Audacious Girl), all out of print and inaccessible. In addition to some unnamed books of poetry attributed to her by Nora,[16] she has also written plays and critical essays (including a biography of Avellaneda, of interest for women's studies), novels, and short stories, and is well known as a lecturer.

Ballesteros is one of the very few women in Spain to have achieved success as a humorist: she has written innumerable brief, humorous, and subtly ironic essays on a wide variety of topics which range from vacations to cocktail parties, Christmas, fate, literary trends, shopping, common social rites and rituals, the shortcomings of modern education, varied people, situations, places, and more. Examples include the collections *Este mundo* (1950; This World, reprinted in 1959 in two parts entitled *Invierno* [Winter] and *Verano* [Summer]); *Así es la vida* (1953; That's Life), a collection of articles first published in the periodical press; and *El personal* (1975; Personnel). Nora groups her works of humor together with those of a nucleus of writers influenced by Ramón Gómez de la Serna. Ballesteros has written under a number of pseudonyms, including Silvia Visconti, Rocq Morris, and especially Baronesa Alberta.

As a narrator, Ballesteros has a natural facility for capturing subtle psychological shadings and nuances of meaning, an eye for miniscule detail, and a smiling, tolerant, but incisive humor. Her prose is succinct and terse, unpretentious yet elegant and direct. She is a gifted narrator who creates situations of enormous credibility, which have nevertheless a certain sense of timelessness. (A line repeated by characters in her first major novel, *La cometa y el eco* (1956; The Kite and the Echo), expresses the idea that time does not pass: "Time is always there, quiet and eternal. We are the ones who pass."[17] Time in an eternal sense—as the universal structure in which life and death are inserted—is a major preoccupation of Ballesteros' fiction.

In *La cometa y el eco,* which spans some twenty years in the life of the orphaned protagonist, Augusta, and of the family with which she lives, the author focuses primarily upon women. Nora, who devotes only one paragraph to Ballesteros' fiction, terms this her "first important work as a novelist of humor."[18] But humor is hard to find in *La cometa y el eco*; serious, without being somber or pessimistic, it has at most a pair of amusing exchanges between children. The work is set in a Valencian fishing village where the family has a summer home, and in the city, where they spend the winters in an old-fashioned but genteel mansion. Only a teenager, the orphan Augusta has a long acquaintance with

death and loneliness before she is taken in by remote relatives. Over
the years, without having consciously planned it, Augusta becomes the
caretaker of the grandmother in her extreme old age. Two intellectual
and platonic incipient relationships—one with a middle-aged history
teacher who tutored her, the other with a younger friend of one of the
brothers in the family—are both ended by the man's death, and at
novel's end Augusta in her mid-thirties seems destined to be a spinster.

The grandmother, a fragile yet strong character, both generous and
frank, is nonetheless a product of the past century. Very much a partisan of the patriarchal establishment, she has a definite antipathy to
the stereotypical wives with their litany of complaints about husbands'
shortcomings and infidelities; her sympathies are with the men. "For
her, to be born a man was a misfortune. The worst thing of all was
having to put up with women" (85). There are varying portraits of
women in the novel, representing a wide range of ages and social
classes. The most memorable of the women after the protagonist is
unquestionably the grandmother, who is upright and kind, although
a far cry from feminist. Jacinta, the provincial social-climber whom
Victor marries while both are students at the University of Madrid,
treats her husband coldly because of her mother's advice that if she is
too affectionate, he will soon grow tired of her (237). Augusta, by
contrast, behaves with considerable naturalness, and although she
never attends the university, devotes her life to reading and study.

The title figures, the kite and the echo, are symbols of time and
something approaching metaphysical communication (between the living and those who have gone before). These metaphors also serve to
underline the circular structure of the novel, an intrinsic expression of
its philosophical substrata: Augusta, Victor, and Pepet fly kites the
first day of her stay with the family, and again at the end of the novel.
Years before, lonely young Augusta had let hers fly heavenward, a silent outcry directed to her dead father. The echo, connected to a natural chamber in the rocks nearby, is a link with the past and the future,
by virtue of its repeating "Leo"—the name of a long-dead girl who
lived in the same house, and that of the orphan who arrives at the
novel's end—to continue the cycle that began with Augusta. Although
the action ends shortly after the Civil War, the reader is left with a
curious sensation of more recent times (by contrast with Carmen
Conde's *Yo soy la madre,* which supposedly portrays the moment of
writing—1980—and yet leaves an impression of turn-of-the-century
values and worldview).

Eclipse de tierra (1954; *Nothing is Impossible,* trans. Frances Partridge, 1956) is a novelette or long short story, a mixture of fantasy and reality with a child protagonist whose boarding-school escapades occasionally recall the ambience of the picaresque, and for those well versed in Spanish fiction of the period, may evoke Rafael Sánchez-Ferlosio's *Alfanhuí,* which similarly treats a child protagonist who is simultaneously innocent and worldly wise, with an instinctive wisdom bordering on the magical (another example of this sort of character, in a novel that lacks the fantastic dimension, is El Nini in Miguel Delibes's *Las ratas* [1962]). Because of the lyrical tone and the similar age of the child protagonists, *Eclipse de tierra* has been compared with Ballesteros's novel of some dozen years later, *El chico,* but such a comparison does not apply to the archetypal nature of the child in this work (whose title literally means Eclipse of the Earth). Like Alfanhuí, the boy protagonist is a descendant of the "sorcerer's apprentice," and perhaps of Till Eulenspiegel, as is El Nini in a more limited sense, but this same comparison is not applicable to the nameless boy in *El chico.*

Taller (1960; The Workshop) is not the first novel to deal with seamstresses or dressmaking—a well-represented occupation in Spanish women's fiction because it continued to employ a good many women up through the 1960s. A considerable popular success, *Taller* was adapted for the stage with the title *Las chicas del taller* (1963; The Girls in the Workshop). The setting is a very fashionable dress salon in Madrid. All main characters are women (seamstresses and the owner of the shop). Belonging partly to the same neorealist grouping as Dolores Medio's *El pez sigue flotando* (or other works of the present century that portray the separate lives of a group of characters who happen for some reason to occupy the same space and time), it is less closely identified with the socialist sentiment inspiring "social" realism in Spain. There is a pronounced psychological emphasis, and several problems of interest for feminist critics are broached: frustration, despair (springing from both socioeconomic and psychological causes), homosexuality, rejection, abortion, loneliness, and feelings of inadequacy or lack of self-worth.

Mi hermano y yo por esos mundos (1962; My Brother and I Around Those Parts of the World) is written in the first person from the perspective of a child-narrator, an anonymous little girl of perhaps ten years old (it is divided in two parts, the second of which was published separately: *El perro del extraño rabo,* 1953; The Dog with the Strange Tail). Although not written specifically for children, it has something of the air of juvenile fiction, including a number of absurdist elements in the situations into which the precocious child narrator and her brother stumble. Like much Spanish juvenile fiction, this work lacks any real character development, reaches no psychologically mandated conclusions, has no perceptible plot structure, no inherently meaningful or necessary beginning and end. Ballesteros compares it to life, in which "no knots are tied, and nothing is concluded." The first part, entitled "No Fuimos a Mesopotamia" (We Didn't Go to Mesopotamia), belongs in a vague way to literature governed by the journey topos, as does the second part, which details the escapades of the preteen siblings while visiting relatives in Italy.

La sed (1965; Thirst) is symbolically entitled; the thirst of Justa is a thirst for herself, a search for identity and meaning in her life. Justa, the protagonist, resembles the tragic heroine of García Lorca's *Yerma*, whose muted drama is her barrenness, the inability to bear children, but there the similarity ends. Justa suffers not from a frustration of maternal instinct alone—perhaps not even primarily—but from a lack of fulfillment of a more existential variety, a need to feel that her life amounts to something, that she is not merely a shadow passing through the world. Justa does not achieve a firm sense of selfhood, but exists in function of other persons in her life, primarily men: her grandfather (an old Portuguese professor, a somewhat idealized figure of the stereotypical intellectual), Carlos (her husband), Juan (a former sweetheart), and Lorenzo, her cousin. The men represent different forms of love, as well as potential alternative paths for self-development that Justa does not decisively commit herself to explore.

El chico (1967; The Boy [published with *Eclipse de tierra* in some editions]) is another novelette or short novel depicting events in the life of an anonymous boy. In this case the boy is twelve years old, and comes from a squalid proletarian background, having lived since he can remember with Nieves, supposedly an aunt who has raised him from birth through sacrifice and struggle, running a produce stand. The boy begins to work as a bellhop but, returning home to find a crowd around his apartment, he learns that his "aunt" has just died of a stroke, and that she was in fact his mother. His goatherd father comes from a rural hamlet to take him to live with a retarded younger daughter and his wife, Andrea. She sets the hut afire and elopes with her lover, leaving her retarded child inside. The boy is severely burned in rescuing her, and both drown when he rushes to a nearby pond to cool their burning flesh. In the end, the boy believes he sees God when his earthly father arrives too late to rescue the two children. Still innocent and pure in heart, the boy perceives the world as a better place, so that the religious symbolism of resurrection employed at the ending is fully within the atmosphere and tone of the story development. Constant or enduring aspects of Ballesteros's thematics which reappear in *El chico* include both her long-standing interest in the orphan (already present in *La cometa y el eco*) and the belief that life is wonderful, no matter how painful or hopeless individual experiences or moments may be.

Ballesteros possesses well-developed storytelling skills, and her fiction both holds the reader's interest and unobtrusively demands recognition that it is well told and elegantly written. Ideologically, the author must be classed as generally conservative, occasionally moderate; aesthetically, too, she is rather conservative, except for mild experimentation with absence of plot in a few pieces of fiction. One of Ballesteros's strong points is her psychological penetration, and she is usually at her best in the characterization of women and children; men, by comparison, are less fully developed and often somewhat shadowy. On the level of ideas, she tends to uphold traditional values of marriage and family, and to agree with the truism that money cannot buy happiness. She promotes spiritual values over material success, criticizes prejudice, hypocrisy, and egotism—all very much within the mainstream of traditional Christian morality, but with a minimum of emphasis upon religion per se. None of her techniques or ideas are startling in any sense, but the consistently high quality of her writing has undoubtedly enhanced the general perception of women writers in Spain.

Chapter Five
The Most Significant Writer in Catalan

Mercè Rodoreda was born in Barcelona in 1909, the only daughter of a rather typical upper-middle-class Catalan family. Her childhood was lonely, as she was withdrawn from school at age nine, and at an early age she became an avid reader (the major source of her preparation as a writer). Her explorations of the neighborhood in these years provide the basic settings for her future stories. From her grandfather she learned a love of and familiarity with flowers, which play an important role in many of her narratives. Somewhat typically, she served her literary apprenticeship writing for several magazines and newspapers in the city, especially the *Revista de Catalunya, Clarisme, Mirador, Companya, Meridià,* and others. Apparently she also wrote poetry, for mention is made in the *Guia de literatura catalana contemporania*[1] of her having won the title of "Mestre en Gai Saber" (mastery of the troubador's art), probably awarded in a competition such as the Jocs Florals.

During the years preceding the Civil War she began producing fiction, both novels and short stories, most of which she would subsequently repudiate, including a short novel with the intriguing title, *¿Sóc una dona honrada?* (1932; Am I an Honest Woman?). *Un dia en la vida d'un home* (1934; A Day in a Man's Life), *Del que hom no put fugir* (1934; What No One Can Flee From), and *Crim* (1936; Crime) were all excluded from editions of her complete works and are now inaccessible. These early works reflect Rodoreda's contact with the literary environment of Barcelona and her introduction to the Club dels Novellistes, where she came under the influence of the Sabadell group of vanguardists, including Françesc Trabal, Joan Oliver, and Armand Obiols, as well as other writers of the day, specifically Père Quart and C. A. Jordana. Carme Arnau[2] considers two of these early novels, *Un dia en la vida d'un home* and *Crim,* to be atypical, while the remaining two are seen as characteristic of the writer's production as a whole.

¿Soc una dona honrada? utilizes a dual diary format, one being the memoir of Teresa, the heroine (a dreamer, like most of the author's female protagonists), whose vice, like that of Don Quixote, is reading novels and imagining herself in the leading role. The other diary entries are authored by a man, presumably the would-be lover—the plot revolves around a temptation to adultery, which does not go beyond the stage of temptation. Essentially a psychological novel, *¿Sóc una dona honrada?* (Am I an Honest Woman?) has portions that clearly anticipate the writer's later use of the internal monologue, especially in the presentation of Teresa's doubts. Morality, in the form of bourgeois condemnation of adulterous relationships, obliges Teresa to relinquish the opportunity to live a novelistic heroine's existence. In a similar vein, *Del que hom no put fugir* examines the solitary life of a woman, but with a less individualized and more generic or collective, typical nature, an aspect that is patent in the use of the seasons of the year and the way in which events (and the state of mind of the protagonist) are correlated with the advancing year. Beginning in the spring-time, with optimism and the traditional hopefulness of new beginnings, the plot concerns the flight from Barcelona of a solitary girl—an orphan and only child, alienated and given to reading like so many of Rodoreda's protagonists—who takes refuge in a remote mountain village with the hope of escaping her past and forgetting her lover who is now married. Her spirits are initially buoyed by the warmth of the sun and the hope of achieving a reconciliation of her existence with societal mores and morality, but as the year advances and cold weather approaches, that hope dies and she is forced to face the impossibility of escaping from herself (hence the significance of the title). However, by means of several intercalated tales or subplots, the author also suggests that tragedy is inherent in the feminine condition: the rape and subsequent madness and suicide of Cinta, the miller's daughter (a sort of alter ego of the protagonist), another tragic tale related by the woman innkeeper concerning the death of her son, as well as the tragedy of a neighbor who gives birth to a deformed infant, whom she later kills—all contribute to reinforcing the subliminal message that the feminine condition is inescapably tragic. Nevertheless, the final psychosis and attempted suicide of the protagonist (apparently intended to be interpreted as inevitable because of its integration into the chronology of the dying year) seems insufficiently motivated, since little attention is devoted to the heroine during the presentation of the series of other women's tragedies. Because of its setting in the remote moun-

tain village, as well as the somber and violent details, *Del que hom no put fugir* (What No One Can Flee From) has been compared to the "rural dramas" of Victor Català.

Carme Arnau cites Rodoreda's mention of *Un dia en la vida d'un home* as having been inspired by a work of Françesc Trabal (a member of the vanguardist Sabadell group), *Hi ha homes que ploren perque el sol es pon* (There are People Who Cry Because the Sun Goes Down).[3] In both works the plot revolves around the failed attempt by the principal characters to escape an imprisoning society, symbolized by one of that society's basic institutions, matrimony. The classic love triangle also appears. Given the influence of Trabal, however, Rodoreda's protagonist is a man—a totally atypical instance among her novels. Even more atypical is the fact that a woman—or specific type of woman, the married bourgeoise—is the "villainess," who causes her husband's unhappiness and frustrates his desire for escape. As an emblem of the bourgeois establishment, the legitimate wife symbolizes reason, while the third member of the triangle, a much younger woman, symbolizes passion and liberty. The shortcomings of the wife in Rodoreda's work are in effect her having internalized too effectively the double standard, and so become too much a model of the "official" wife, of whom it is observed that a quarter-century of marriage has not taught her to laugh nor to kiss her husband with tenderness. A subversive aspect of this text is the clear espousal of more natural, freer relationships between the sexes, especially in the matter of love, instead of the repression imposed by bourgeois morality. Although it is atypical for Rodoreda to utilize a male protagonist, this novel nonetheless contains other elements found throughout her fiction, such as the denunciation of the frustrating nature of love relationships because of societal conditioning, and the role of literary models (novels, movies) in leading her characters to behave in a fashion resembling the lives of fictional heroes.

Crim is similarly atypical, since it employs all the clichés of the mystery novel, and is set in an environment that is completely British, right down to the names of the characters. As Rodoreda indicates in the prologue, *Crim* is a "parody of the detective novel, a sort of centipede, without head or tail."[4] Unlike Rodoreda's other works, then, this is a novel whose referent is not reality but literature, an exercise in intertextuality, and the characters are similarly "literary," stylized, worldly and elegant, properly made up, with no preoccupations more serious than the next change of lovers. A metaliterary aspect involves references to Catalan literary life, both to the previous generation and that of the writer. Whether because of Rodoreda's lack of satisfaction with the experiment, or because it was not a route that offered promise for future development, this novel represents a parenthesis in her development, a vein that is not further explored.

Rodoreda's first important narrative is *Aloma,* a poetic and symbolic novel set in prewar Barcelona, which was awarded the Crexells Prize of 1937 and published by the Institució de les Lletres Catalanes in 1938 (although *Women Writers of Spain* states that it remained unpublished until 1969, at which time it was substantially revised and rewritten). As is true of the remainder of Rodoreda's mature production, this novel focuses upon the character of a woman, almost an adolescent, emphasizing problems posed by the protagonist's gender and her sexual relationships. *Aloma* already contains the lyricism and many constant themes of the writer's definitive style. The protagonist, Aloma, who exhibits various weaknesses (she is solitary, introverted, passive, and romantic) is also quietly strong and enduring. Her peaceful nature is essentially at odds with the aggressive world in which she lives, an opposition that allows Rodoreda to develop a profound meditation upon the human condition in the modern world. The Catalan critic, Carme Arnau, has seen *Aloma* as a narrative of the loss of innocence, since the action revolves about an adolescent girl and her romantic dreams concerning a cousin's impending return from America. However, Robert (the cousin) is no fairy-tale prince: he is a mature man who seduces and abandons Aloma, leaving her pregnant, with her broken dreams. In her narrow, closed home environment, Aloma lives in an atmosphere of tension that pushes her to the brink of suicide, but love for the child she is carrying helps her to overcome the temptation. Both Aloma and her sister-in-law Anna are innocent, trusting victims of male egotism. Fittingly, the males who destroy them are in turn preyed upon by equally selfish and insensitive females, Violeta and Coral. On the psychological level, *Aloma* has definite tragic overtones, but Rodoreda avoids melodrama through a controlled, evocative style and recurrent imagery (including flowers—her favorite device—and cats), rhetorical oppositions, and contrasting pairs. While this first surviving novel does not yet display the brilliance found in Rodoreda's postwar fiction (in part because it lacks the experienced perspective of the mature author), it does contain the germs of her later handling of female characters.

The writer's exile, beginning in 1939, included a long period of difficulties and demoralization (a situation aggravated by her finding herself in France during World War II). For some fifteen years she struggled to make a living, residing first in Bordeaux, then Paris, and finally Geneva, where she settled until the time of her return to Catalonia after some twenty-three years in exile. The economic straits of Rodoreda's early years in exile apparently left little time for writing, although she collaborated sporadically with widely scattered Catalan magazines of the diaspora, such as the *Revista de Catalunya* in which she published "Tarda al cinema" (Afternoon at the Movies), "El gelat rosa" (Pink Ice), and "Nocturn" in 1947 (3d epoch, No. 103, July-September 1947). In Geneva, around 1954, Rodoreda began to write more frequently, her first important collection of these years, *Vint-i-dos contes* (1957; Twenty-Two Tales) receiving the Victor Català Prize. From this point onward Rodoreda's narratives are of outstanding quality, although of limited quantity. Most of the tales of *Vint-i-dos contes* center upon female protagonists and are uniformly rather somber, if not tragic in tone.

The collection displays a variety of techniques, but an essential unity of theme, portraying women somehow at odds with the world, their circumstances, or more uniquely personal aspects of their existence. In "La sang" (Blood) jealousy comes between a married couple, distancing the wife from her husband, and in "Fil a l'agulla' (The Needle's Edge), a variation upon themes enunciated in *Aloma,* a girl whose future has been frustrated by circumstance, daydreams fantasies of revenge in which she essays various means of killing the sickly cousin she once hoped to marry. "Estiu" (Summer) portrays domestic entrapment (of both partners, in this case): the wife, bored, sickly, confined to home and household duties, impatient and abrasive; the husband, distanced and daydreaming of girls he follows in the street, as he blames the heat for his lack of attentiveness. "El mirall" (The Mirror) addresses the problem of aging—which women writers have treated more extensively than their male counterparts—utilizing an image that is both polysemous and frequently repeated in women's fiction, the looking glass, before which an aged beauty recalls her youthful loves.

An especially pathetic tale is "Divendres 8 de juny" (Friday, June 8th) in which an impoverished young mother, whose child was the result of rape, drowns the infant and then herself. Similarly tragic and self-destructive is "Abans de morir" (Before Dying) in which a wife plans to commit suicide after learning of her husband's infidelity. It could well serve as a sequel to "Commençament" (Beginning), which portrays a couple with a sickly young son and a relationship that has lost its magic. The husband's bad day at the office included spilling ink on his pants and insulting the attractive new typist because of his bad humor, and he is further annoyed by his wife's immediate intuitive realization that he is upset. Recounting the incident at her behest brings him to confront his unchivalrous conduct, and walking to work the following day, he stops to buy roses for the typist. The failure of marriage is a basic theme of half a dozen stories in the collection, including (in addition to this one) "La sang," "Estiu," "Nocturn," "Fil a l'agulla," and "Mort de Lisa Sperling."

Eight pieces treat the beginning of male-female relationships in terms that indicate the ultimate impossibility of happiness, including "Tarda al cinema" (Afternoon at the Movies) and "Promessos" (Promises), both of which describe couples who are sad without knowing why. "Felicitat" (Happiness) and "Darrers moments" (Final Moments) present the sudden and unexplained extinguishing of love. "La blusa vermella" (The Yellow Blouse) portrays a boy's suffering because of having fallen in love with a girl he sees daily—accompanied by another man. In "El gelat rosa" (Pink Ice Cream) a girl becomes engaged, but continues to think of the first love who abandoned her. "Carnaval," whose underlying deceptiveness is symbolized via allusion to the masks of Mardi Gras, relates the chance encounter of a young man and woman, each of whom invents a fictional past as a means of escape from the boredom of their present lives. Robbery in the street provides a means of access to their true backgrounds. While she tends to concentrate upon female characters, Rodoreda also portrays men who are atypical, as in "Un home sol" (A Lonely Man), which analyzes the anguish of a solitary man waiting in an uninhabited house for someone or something that never arrives. At last he flees, without the reader ever knowing whether his fear is simply the result of his imagination or has a real basis. "Cop de lluna" (Moon Blow) is one of her most concrete references to the political situation after the Civil War: a half-mad old Frenchman requests a Spanish refugee to help him with the work in the fields, but the treatment that the political exile receives is so inhuman that he is tempted to kill his "benefactor"—although he ends by retreating into a kind of feminine passivity. Rodoreda is at her best in the subtle analysis of shadings and nuances of psychological complexities, and her probing of problematic relationships in the post-war world belongs fully to the mature period of her literary creativity.

La plaça del Diamant (1962; *The Pigeon Girl,* 1967; *The Time of the Doves,* 1983; translation and introduction by David Rosenthal) has been rendered into at least seven languages, including two translations into English. This deceptively simple novel is an absolute masterpiece of European literature, a work of a level of significance and perfection that must have surprised even Rodoreda's most fervent admirers. Once again, she focuses upon daily life, choosing a lower-class woman as narrative point of view and protagonist. Natalia, the somewhat un-likely heroine, suffers in marriage almost as much as in the Civil War because of the blind egotism of men in the patriarchal society that has formed her and the men around her, specifically her husband, Quimet (who is not totally to blame for his indifference to, and unawareness of, her emotional needs and problems). Never having had a propitious environment for developing a sense of selfhood, Natalia has a serious identity problem, compounded by solitude, beginning when she was orphaned at an early age and thus deprived of her prime role model. She finds herself totally alone, a victim of the radical absence of com-munication (a probable reflection of the writer's sensations during her years in exile). The world thus seems absurd or incomprehensible to her. Her feeble self-image is further weakened by Quimet, the first husband, whom she meets at a dance, who relegates her to the same status as a pigeon (while these birds are considerably more important to Quimet than to the average man, his equating of Natalia with them is seen in his changing her name to Colometa). Unable to communicate her frustration to Quimet (a vital isolation reinforced by the use of the internal discourse that predominates in the novel), Natalia passively expresses her aggression by neglecting the pigeons.

When Quimet is reported killed while fighting for the Republic, Natalia's financial and psychological situations are so desperate that she contemplates killing her two children and then committing suicide because no one cares about them. A second marriage to the shopkeeper Antonio brings a measure of economic stability, but her emotional cri-sis intensifies. Natalia lives increasingly in a world of daydreams, nightmares, and recollections, separated more and more from her ex-ternal reality.[5] The possibility that Quimet may be alive after all, a prisoner of war who may return, aggravates her psychic malaise, to-gether with a guilt complex motivated by her remarriage. A humble woman whose anguish finds no outlet, Natalia falls ever deeper into a profound melancholy, retreating from the world. Her situation may be seen as a symbolic expression of the impotence of the individual faced with a crisis of historical reality, as was the Spanish Civil War, in which the only feasible reaction is an instinctive search for refuge (a notion reinforced by the several motifs of small animals, with their helpless-ness, and of dolls or stuffed animals, symbolizing the refuge in subjectivism). *The Time of the Doves* is thus a variant of the bildungsroman, which follows the life or process of maturation of its protagonist, one of the prototypical novelistic plots in which a youthful character attempts to discover both his or her own nature and that of the world, a symbolic voyage through a variety of experiences, sacrifices, and adventures leading to the eventual encounter with self. This is likewise the underlying structure of Rodoreda's next novel, *El carrer de les Camèlies*.

Although *El carrer de les Camèlies* (1966; The Street of Camellias) has not been translated into English, there is a Spanish version, *La calle de las Camelias* (1970), which may be more accessible for those who do not read Catalan. The psychological study of solitude is continued via the personal narrative of Cecilia, abandoned as an infant on Camellia Street. Her psychosocial crisis begins as an identity problem, but is slowly compounded by a series of life experiences, inseparable from the history of the country and its frustrated attempt at autonomy (the defeat of the Republic). In the same way that the woman in a paternalistic and authoritarian society is merely an extension of the male, her functions defined by her relationship to him, the oppressed country's role has been defined by totalitarian forces. Lacking any possibility of a normal relationship with her parents, Cecilia is necessarily isolated, and she learns to intensify this condition of distance as part of her ego-defense.

She becomes increasingly narcissistic and self-oriented, halted at a crucial stage in her personality development, a situation aggravated when poverty forces her from sewing blouses into prostitution (and thus she comes to look upon herself as a love object). But narcissism is also a refuge, a compensation for the love others have denied her. Not only is Cecilia obsessed with herself, but also with motherhood, a reflection of internalized social values (in a society where the primordial purpose of sexuality is procreation). Her frustrated maternal instinct results in repetitive dreams of having children, and a tendency to interpret the world around her in terms of pregnancy motifs. In addition, her life is a series of humiliations and rejections, as well as sadistic abuse from one of her lovers (Marcos), that exacerbates her incipient paranoia. Cecilia's case is decidedly more sordid and pathological than that of any of Rodoreda's prior protagonists. Linked to her biography is a series of men who typify varying levels of social decadence in postwar Spain, with each lover signaling a corresponding step up the social ladder by Cecilia, although such material improvement does not protect her from degradation and rejection at the hands of the series of lovers. Close to madness, like Natalia before her, and tempted by the thought of suicide, Cecilia is finally saved through her encounter with a different sort of man, basically good and affectionate, with more of the father than of the lover, an unexpected benefactor through whose kindness Cecilia is able to live a portion of the childhood denied her when she was small, thereby satisfying obliquely her Oedipus complex. Interestingly, her "salvation" is owing in large measure to finding a man similar to Natalia's "savior," a coincidence that subliminally underlines the lower-class woman's impotence in Spanish society: no amount of anguish or struggle on her own suffices.

Arnau[6] discusses Natalia and Cecilia as aspects of a single character, pointing out the motifs of labyrinth in their lives, with all that this figure traditionally signifies of initiation. In the latter novel, however, the vision of life is more exasperated, and love relationships appear even more doomed to frustration (since there is a multiplicity of men), and the relationships decline in quality with the introduction of sadism. The orphan and the mirror, recurring motifs in Rodoreda's fiction, are joined in this work by the leitmotiv of the flame, conventionally linked to eroticism (with all its destructive potential), symbolizing the exploitation of Cecilia just as the pigeons expressed Natalia's degradation. *El carrer de les camelies* is a still more extreme instance of feminine devaluation, and both events and symbols are correspondingly more harsh and dramatic as befits this culmination of Rodoreda's study of the margination of women in Spanish society.

In 1967 another major story collection appeared: *La meva Cristina i altres contes* (1984; *My Christina and Other Stories,* translated and with an introduction by David Rosenthal). The translator's foreword, with a certain hyperbole possibly inspired by Rodoreda's recent death (1983), terms her the most important Mediterranean woman writer since Sappho; nevertheless, Catalan critics are generally in accord in viewing her as that language's most significant writer of all time. The seventeen stories in the English version include one added from another collection, *Semblava de seda* (It Seemed Like Silk). Style varies tremendously from the bleakly realistic to surreal and hallucinatory, with lyric interludes and frequent changes of moods and tones. Some stories capture the irrational dream states or nightmarish delusions of the mentally or emotionally disturbed, while others are tied to the dreary, sordid ambience of the shanty-town child or the pedestrian surroundings and limited horizons of the nursemaid. Two or three of the stories

involve metamorphoses (one index of the increasing importance of the
fantastic in Rodoreda's writing of her mature years). In one case, the
narrator-protagonist becomes a salamander; in another, the narrator-
fisherman one day becomes a fish; and in the title tale, "My Christina,"
the shipwrecked sailor/narrative consciousness spends years inside a
whale, in a symbiotic-conflictive relationship that shows him adjusting
when his attempts to kill his hostess fail, and ultimately emerging
covered with incrustations, a pearl.

Metamorphosis may be seen as a metaphor for alienation, and at least
three other stories portray that loneliness and solitude that result from
extreme timidity ("That Wall, That Mimosa," "Rain," and "Memory
of Caux"). Failed emotional relationships are at the core of the last
three, with "Rain" portraying vividly the confused ambivalence of a
woman who has arranged a rendezvous with a new would-be lover, but
suffers from cold feet at the moment of truth and goes for a walk in
the rain instead of waiting to receive him. "Memory of Caux" presents
a man whose timidity prevented his making any sort of overture to the
woman (apparently favorably inclined) that he thinks of for years afterward as the one love of his life. All social levels appear, beginning with
the poorest, as seen in "The Nursemaid," where an adolescent servant
baby talks to her young charge; in "The Hen," a painting of misery in
a slum hut; and "Therafina," in which a mentally retarded maidservant
innocently recounts her history of abuse and exploitation. Misery is not
a monopoly of the lower classes, however, as is clear in the moral and
emotional improverishment of the titled aristocracy in "The Dolls'
Room"—the psychotic family heir relates only to his doll collection,
and eventually jumps to his death when his privacy with the dolls is
threatened. "A Flock of Lambs in All Colors" is a symbolic recreation
of the role played in a developing life by illusion and embodiments of
youth and happiness (identified with the lambs), always maintained at
a distance by parental authority.

"The Gentleman and the Moon" is almost totally fantastic, as an
elderly, lonely, senior citizen finds a way to climb to the moon on the
silvery beams, transcending his solitude. If there is a common denominator to the collection, it is the writer's selection of marginal mental-
ities as narrative perspectives: a majority of these tales employ the first-
person autobiographical mode, or one of its two variants: the epistle
("A Letter"; "The Dolls' Room") or one-sided dialogue ("The Nursemaid"; "Love"; "Therafina"; and "Memory of Caux"). Only two tales
employ third-person narrators ("Rain" and "The Sea"), and only the

latter makes use of conventional (two-way) dialogue. One of the most extreme commentaries on the feminine condition is found in "The Salamander," in which a girl is pursued in the forest by a married man and assaulted (it is a rape to which she finally submits). Surprised in their lovemaking by the jealous wife, the two are separated. The anonymous narrator is accused of witchcraft by the wife, and suffers several attacks from the superstitious villagers before finally being burned at the stake—when she observes the lover in attendance, arm around his wife. At the height of torment in the flames, she is metamorphosed into a salamander, and eludes pursuers, hiding beneath the lover's bed, where she stays an indefinite time. Routed by the wife again, she finally slips into a pond, where a wounded paw is chewed off by eels before she escapes into the mud and mire of the bottom. The phallic character of the eels, who prey upon her at her most desperate moment, is not likely to be gratuitous.

"My Christina" is a totally different account of the exploitation of the feminine—whether a maternal, nurturing wife, or a mother whose body is occupied by an ungrateful and uncaring offspring. Clearly symbolic, set beyond real or historical time, this long narrative presents the feminine principle (Christina) as sacrificial or expiatory, incapable of self-defense, much less retaliation, ultimately the victim of the being she has carried in her body.

Jardí vora el mar (1967; Garden By the Sea) has been seen as atypical of Rodoreda's narratives, since the ostensible main character is not a female (as is the case with all but one of the earlier novels). However, the old man who serves as a narrative perspective (or narrator within the novel) is not the protagonist or even a central character so much as an observer, a gardener who is in a privileged position from which to recount an outsider's version of the tragic course of events in a love triangle. Although Rodoreda begins to move away from the realistic style and techniques employed in *The Time of the Doves* and *El carrer de les Camèlies, Jardí vora el mar* is a logical and necessary transitional stage between her early objectivity and the much more subjective symbolist and surrealist techniques that appear in later novels and stories. Significantly, the garden motif (which is important in *Mirall trencat* and some of the stories collected in *La meva Christina i altres contes*) acquires primary visibility here for the first time as a symbol of innocence and the happiness of childhood (connotations that are also present in their association with Maria in the next novel), but in both cases the introduction/intrusion of adults and adult love brings unhappiness and trag-edy, and leads to death. Under guise of relating his observations of the house's history to a would-be buyer, the old gardener reconstructs the story of the love triangle, re-creating the atmosphere of nostalgia, ten-derness, and solitude that is typical of the author.

Mirall trencat (1974; Broken Mirror) is one of Rodoreda's most com-plex and difficult works; Arnau considers it the "most tragic" of the writer's production.[7] While not the usual family chronicle, *Mirall tren-cat* treats three generations of persons related by marriage or by blood, beginning at the turn of the century and spanning at least four decades, until after the end of the Spanish Civil War. There are in a sense two heroines, one from the first generation and one from the third. Teresa, who is secretly the mother of an illegitimate son, Jesús, marries Sal-vador (who is still in love with the memory of Barbara). The themes of secret passions, unshared emotions, solitude of sentiment, and lack of communication are pervasive, and their effects mark all three gen-erations. Teresa and Salvador's daughter, Sofia, marries Eladi but does not care for him; her secret thoughts are for her father and Lluiset, a youthful friend. Eladi (an indecisive dandy, and minor, mediocre don Juan figure) has an affair with Pilar, and has a mysterious illegitimate daughter, María, while he and Sofia have a son, Ramon. The two chil-dren are unaware of having the same father until a strong attraction has developed between them; Eladi's revelation results in Maria's re-nunciation of life; she prefers to die rather than renounce her childhood and her companion.

Death in the world of childhood is one of the major themes of *Mirall trencat* (not only Maria dies, but Jaume, another child of the group). Maria is the archetype of the "pure" child, and surrounded with many of the symbolists' favorite images: water, garden, mirror, the moon. She is usually dressed in white, and surrounded by white; the only other color associated with Maria is bright red, with its connotations of blood and death. After Maria drowns, her body is accidentally dis-covered by Armanda, the family cook and an important domestic stabilizing force. The girl's burial is followed by Eladi's death, a possible suicide, and later by the death of Teresa. Maria becomes a disquieting phantom who vaguely disturbs all who visit the house, while Armanda converts the house into a sanctuary or museum to pre-serve the memories of Maria and Teresa, whose rooms seem strangely alive.

The novel is divided into three parts, the first treating the youth and vitality of the family, marriages and births being the main events. The second part presents the family's decadence and a series of deaths, while the third and last is almost metaphysical, consisting in large part of monologues by the two dead heroines and their shadowy presence. The novel's tripartite structure is echoed by tripartite sentences, and arrangement of the chapters in groups of three forming units of meaning (or dealing with a given character, etc). Three aspects of time—past, present, and eternity—are interwoven and contrasted. Rodoreda's style is more "literary," more baroque than in the preceding works, more sentimental and decadent, with much attention given to adjectivization and to the use of colors (consistently associated with certain characters). Once again Rodoreda's major emphasis is psychological. She stresses the imperfections of the family members, their disagreements and conflicts, with preferential emphasis upon the world of childhood, especially its intimate, internal aspects, which form the thematic center of the narrative, appearing repeatedly as the past of adult characters is interwoven with the present of the youthful ones. The infantile world is filled with ambiguity, illusion, cruelty, radical solitude, and alienation—impressing the reader in much the same fashion as that created in the postwar period by Ana María Matute.

Semblava de seda i altres contes (1978; It Seemed Like Silk and Other Stories; Spanish translation by Clara Janés, *Parecía de seda y otras narraciones,* 1981) contains a collection of ten short stories and a one-act play. "Ada Liz" tells of a prostitute in an indefinite land who saves money so that she can sometimes sleep alone, and who dreams of traveling on a ship. When at last she does, the captain "steals her dreams" (she wakes up with him without knowing how she came to be there). "En una nit obscura" (On a Dark Night) is a hallucinatory, surrealistic dream or delirious vision, experienced by a young soldier wounded and apparently suffering from gangrene, who fantasizes that he meets and loves a mysterious, yielding girl, Loki—who represents life, or his desire to live—but he is unable to return to her and realizes he is dead. "Nit i boira" (Night and Fog) is a grim, sordid memoir of a concentration camp inmate who recalls having to share his bed with the incontinent Meier, whose death the narrator concealed for days in order to have an extra cup of soup.

"Orleans, 3 quilometres" (Three Kilometers to Orleans) is probably based on Rodoreda's own experience of fleeing on foot when the Nazis invaded Paris. Also a war story, it is told from the perspective of refugees trying to reach Orleans, which is under bombardment by the Germans. "Viure al dia" (Living Day By Day), written in dialogue form, is an ironic commentary on the self-satisfied, intranscendent, bourgeois world suddenly shaken, truncated, by the outbreak of the Spanish Civil War (it is dated 18 July 1936, hours or perhaps only minutes before the war begins). "Pluja" (Rain), included in the English version of *My Christina* tells of the woman who leaves for a walk in the rain instead of waiting for the friend she expects to become a lover. "El bitllet de mil" (The Thousand Franc Note) recounts the humiliation and frustration of a housewife who tires of genteel poverty and decides to earn some money through prostitution. Her first customer replies to her demand for 500 francs that she is worth 1,000. Upon trying to cash the bill, she is told that it is counterfeit.

"Rom Negrita" (Rum) is very much in the vein of postwar socialist realism, a "slice-of-life" portrayal of several laborers in a neighborhood bar, whose major concern is the need to resell a slightly used pair of shoes belonging to one worker's son, while most of them enjoy looking at the barkeep's French wife. "Paralisi" (Paralisis) is written in the first-person, and has the air of a memoir; situated in Geneva, and evoking the time of the writer's residence there in exile, it tells of a visit to a doctor because of a psychosomatic lameness diagnosed as due to nervousness. "Semblava de seda" (It Seemed Like Silk) refers to a huge black feather—fallen from the wing of a black angel in a cemetery on the Day of the Dead (All Souls), as the narrator seeks a tomb that she has symbolically adopted, since "her" deceased is too far away to visit. Much of the narrative is hallucinatory, and the ending is quite surrealistic, the reader being left unsure whether the narrator is psychotic, dying, or simply delirious.

Viatges i flors (1980; Travels and Flowers) is actually two "collections" or groups of very short stories, almost prose poems, each group having a certain thematic unity. The "flowers" section was written in Geneva, over an extended period of time, and describes strangely beautiful but hardly natural flowers: "Ballerina Flower," "Desperate Flower," "Magical Flower," "Dead Flower," "Felicity Flower," "Water Flower," "Nameless Flower," "Ceremonious Flower," "Flower of Life," "Phantom Flower," and many more. The "journey" section, written somewhat hastily, in Romania, recounts largely imaginary or fantastic journeys, flights from reality or perhaps dreams, such as the "Journey to the Land of the Warriors," a satire on military parades; "Journey to the Land of Lost Children," which recaptures the sensation of being a lost child; "Journey to the Country of Abandoned Women," where the inhabitants eat leaves from a certain tree; "Journey to the Land of All Sorrow," "The Land of Cheeses," "Journey to the Land of Witchcraft," "To the Land of the Rainbow"; many more are lyric, largely static, descriptive fantasies. Stylistically they are very much in the vein of Rodoreda's other mature writing, perhaps with more than the usual amount of humor and emphasis on phonetic devices (such as frequent use of onomatopeia), but thematically these pieces are slight.

Quanta, quanta guerra (1980; So Much War; Spanish version, *Cuánta, cuánta guerra,* 1982) is a complex fusion of genres, a narrative whose structure follows that of the bildungsroman (and in fact does present an apprenticeship to life), but which also harks back to the picaresque, as well as owing something to the literary topos of life as journey or quest. Like the pícaro, Adrià is a poor boy, a widow's son whose travels are marked by progressive loss of innocence. Adrià, however, retains his candor, in spite of exposure to war, pillage, carnage, and suffering. Rodoreda's prologue explains the genesis of Adrià and of certain episodes, noting that she "barely believes in heroes," considering acts of heroism generally instinctive reactions, and that "man today is not heroic; he is satisfied with feeling powerful."[8] Adrià is not heroic, and his reasons for running off to war are never clearly formulated; the novelist comments that his impulse in leaving home is the "aspiration to liberty," but the boy is not consciously aware of anything more than being tired of working for his mother while his friend is leaving for adventure.

Too young initially to fight, Adrià works in the kitchen, lives close to bombings, death, and filth, deserts without being fully aware of the implications, is found and returned and leaves again, wandering always near the war zone, but never fighting. He suffers hunger, lice, fatigue, aggression, cold, wounds, and fever, meeting a wide variety of people, many of them good and kind, others egotistical, cruel, and treacherous. Uninterested in property, Adrià works for various people who feed or befriend him, taking little except food or bed, the war always near at hand, visible or audible in the distance when not close by. Adrià meets many classes, ages, and types of men—representative of humanity and its possibilities—and finally, weary of death and sorrow, decides to return home, without knowing if his home will still be there.

An indefinite time has passed, an indefinite distance has been traversed, and the boy is no longer a child: the war has also served as a rite of passage. Most of the novel is filled with lyric and surrealistic passages, juxtaposed to sometimes grotesquely direct encounters with the violence of war or the sordid aspects of reality. A filtering of events and perceptions through partial incomprehension or incomplete awareness of the narrative consciousness adds to the symbolist vagueness and mystery of ambience.

Chapter Six
The First Postwar Generation: Lesser-Known Writers

With the unconditional surrender of the remnants of the Republican forces on 1 April 1939, the victorious rebels under General Franco began a systematic purge of the opposition. The borders of the country were sealed, and "escuadras negras" (death squads) went from village to village, executing those who had served the Republic, often including schoolmasters, postal clerks, and other municipal employees who had held the same posts since the days of the monarchy. Untold thousands were imprisoned, some for twenty years or more, and executions of political prisoners were carried out on a daily basis during the first several years, according to testimonies of surviving prisoners. Although the regime apparently kept no statistics on political executions, informed estimates by insiders put the figure between one and two million during the first ten years. Other Republicans went into hiding within the country, often confined in tiny spaces beneath the floor or in attics, where, with the help of relatives, they remained concealed for many years. After approximately two decades, the regime proclaimed an amnesty and many emerged; others waited, emerging with successive amnesties, but some continued their concealment until after the death of Franco—a total of forty years. Many refugees who had escaped across the border into France were interned in concentration camps in the south of France, and later transferred by the Nazis to camps in central Europe. Of approximately 800,000 such Spanish Republican refugees, only 90,000 lived through World War II. Those who managed to reach Russia may have been more fortunate, but were not allowed to leave that country. Republican sympathizers who escaped from Spain before the war's end and reached the Americas found freedom, but still faced the rigors of life in exile, new beginnings, and an uncertain future.

Within Spain, the cultural purges were comparable in their severity to the political ones. All bookstores in the country were closed during some two to three weeks, and all "subversive" or potentially "dangerous" works were confiscated and destroyed, including nearly all the writings of the Generation of 1898, the realists and naturalists of the nineteenth century (tainted by liberalism), and the vanguardists of the Generation of 1927, whose experimentalism was anathema to the regime. The only foreign books escaping destruction were the works of Portuguese, Italian, and German Fascists. Everything printed within the country (including even matchbooks, maps, and playing cards) was censored, although officially censorship was said not to exist. Its semi-secret nature made it more formidable, for writers never knew exactly what might be censurable; simply turning a manuscript over to the euphemistically named Servicio de Libros (Book Service) required courage, for the author of a work deemed subversive might be summarily imprisoned. Three censors—moral, religious, and political—ruled on each work, and it could be prohibited on any of these grounds. Small wonder that literature during the early postwar years in Spain suffered as a result. The times were not propitious financially, either, with half the country's housing destroyed, the industry in ruins, and the economy at a standstill (agriculture had been interrupted for the better part of four years, for example). With the rest of the Western world involved in World War II, neither machinery nor material assistance was available from the outside, so that recovery for Spain was slow and painful. Only a fortunate few had the money for books or time to read them, and almost never could writers live by their writing (the exception being newspaper journalists). The women who began to write in those years faced the same difficulties as their male counterparts, plus additional constraints inherent in the official hostility of the regime to any form of "liberation" for women.

A Multilingual Writer for Children and Adults

Carmen de Rafael Marés was born in Barcelona in 1911, in a well-to-do family of unusually cosmopolitan background. Both paternal and maternal grandparents had lived in the New World, the writer's father being born in Cuba, her mother in Baltimore. Paternal and maternal forebears alike returned to Spain toward the end of the nineteenth century, and the writer's parents were married in Barcelona. The familial environment was out of the ordinary for Spain: three languages were spoken in the home, Spanish (Castilian), French, and English—but not

Catalan, even though the grandparents were originally of Catalan extraction. Customs and attitudes in the home likewise differed from those prevalent in Spain.[1]

Carmen studied in private Catholic schools in Barcelona until the age of sixteen, when she was sent to England to a private school there, receiving a first-class certificate from the National Union of Teachers. At twenty-three, she married Pedro Kurz, a French national of German ancestry, and in 1935 they moved to France (she added the *t* to her husband's name after beginning to write). The traumatic experience of the Spanish Civil War, which marked nearly all the postwar writers with profound scars, was barely a distant echo. However, Kurtz experienced World War II much more directly than did most Spaniards: her husband was sent to the front and taken prisoner at the Maginot Line in the summer of 1940. Kurtz began to work in the Spanish consulate in Marseilles, seeking his release which she secured late in 1941.

Returning to Spain in 1943, Kurtz commenced in 1944 writing juvenile fiction (up to one hundred stories were published under an unidentified pseudonym). Her successful children's stories garnered several literary prizes. At least six movies have been based on her juvenile novels (she has produced some thirty books for young readers under her own name). Most popular of her children's books are fifteen novels concerning the adventures of a twelve-year-old boy named Oscar and his pet goose Kina. Several of these have been translated to German and Polish.[2] Because she uses her husband's name when the custom for married women in Spain is to retain the father's family name, "Carmen Kurtz" is considered a pseudonym (some bibliographies list her works under the heading of Carmen de Rafael Marés). Kurtz's juvenile fiction is unexceptionally didactic, but also entertains.

After a decade of success in writing for younger readers, Kurtz tried her hand at the novel for adults, publishing *Duermen bajo las aguas* (1954; They Sleep Beneath the Waters [City of Barcelona Prize, 1955]). The autobiographical bias of many first novels appears in this thinly fictionalized account of the writer's childhood, marriage, and life in France. Two novels were published in 1956, the first completed being *La vieja ley* (1956; The Old Law), a work of considerable potential interest for feminist critics. Concentrating upon the stifling provincial world of a young Spanish bourgeois woman living from the 1920s through the 1940s, the novel is a protest against those limitations. The title alludes to an "old law" that requires us to love and be loved, and the search for love is predictably one of the novel's major themes. Reciprocity of love is stressed, not merely the quest for happiness. Technique can be considered mildly experimental, as Kurtz utilizes a modified perspectivism. The novel consists of ten chapters, narrated from the viewpoint of five different characters: the first four correspond, respectively, to four men who have varying forms of emotional involvements with Victoria, the protagonist, and the remaining chapters and epilogue are narrated by her in the first person.

El desconocido (1956; The Stranger) may well be inspired in part by the writer's experience of separation from her husband during the war and subsequent reunion after some four years of living apart. This novel, which won the 1956 Planeta Prize, retraces the fortunes of a couple who are reunited after a twelve-year separation (and it could in theory apply to many families in Spain whose men were political prisoners for prolonged periods, or families that had some members living as refugees or in exile). In *El desconocido* the husband was a member of Spain's "División Azul," Spanish volunteers who fought on the German side against the Russians in World War II. Taken prisoner in 1942, the husband returns in 1954. Again, a modified form of perspectivism is used, in this case a dual perspective, as the trauma of separation and equally traumatic reunion are presented alternately from the standpoint of wife and husband, the version of one sometimes complementing, sometimes contradicting the other. Each of the novel's three "books" is subdivided into two parts, "He" and "She." The first book, parallelistically retrospective, presents recollections and flashbacks of their whirlwind romance, brief marriage, and long separation, recapitulated from each partner's perspective as the moment of reencounter approaches.

In the second book, focused upon the couple's first few days after being reunited, the crucial difficulties of adjustment are portrayed, with emphasis upon the wife's hostility and resistance: Dominica loves the man she remembers, not the stranger who has returned, and she resents Antonio's belief that he continues to have marital rights. The third book presents a crisis, as Dominica's despondency leads to a suicide attempt. Aroused from sleep by her faint cry, Antonio is able to save her, and realizes that a fresh start must be made. He therefore courts her once again, and subsequently the two are able to move in the direction of real communication and togetherness. Kurtz displays profound understanding of the emotional problems for both husband and wife in this tense and painful situation, emphasizing especially the

inevitable misunderstandings and the barriers to communication, often
by the technique of contrasting one character's words with the other's
thoughts.[3]

Detrás de la piedra (1958; Behind the Rock) is allegedly based upon
a true-life story. Set in the gray, monotonous, fictional village of Nebia
in northern Spain, the narrative begins when the sleepy region's som-
nolence is interrupted by a robbery. Within hours one of the local
inhabitants is arrested as a suspect. *Detrás de la piedra* presents the
stifling atmosphere of boredom characterizing Spanish provincial life,
and much of the action transpires behind bars. The novel is narrated
in the first person by Julio, a middle-class family man and industrial
engineer, who has been imprisoned in a small provincial jail for a crime
he did not commit, although the reader is left in the dark as to Julio's
guilt or innocence until very near the novel's end. The experience of
imprisonment and the psychological crisis it provokes are elements that
link this novel with the situation of Antonio in *El desconocido*. The
"rock" or stone of the title alludes obliquely to prison walls, and thus
serves to focus the attention upon confinement, barriers, and the resulting existential crisis. Action is set late in the decade of the 1940s,
and it would appear that the probable political implications were considered by the censors, who retained the novel a year, and by Editorial
Planeta, which did not dare to publish the work, although Planeta is
the publisher of most of Kurtz's adult novels.[4]

Al lado del hombre (1961; Beside the Man) concerns both the search
for self or identity and the role of sexual awakening in that encounter.
Like *El desconocido,* this novel has only two major characters and treats
male-female relations, depending largely upon emotional probing or
psychological analysis. Most of the narrative is retrospective, beginning at the climactic point in the characters' relationship and retracing
the steps taken to reach that point, a process that includes (via flashbacks) those aspects of their earlier lives necessary to complete the characterization. A simple narrative with a circular structure, *Al lado del
hombre* recounts the meeting between a young woman (Carla) and a
middle-aged man who occupy adjoining seats on the train from Bilbao
to Barcelona, and their brief affair upon arrival there undertaken without either making any future commitment. Both are intellectualized,
and the man leans markedly in the direction of pedantry. The amorous
encounter might be considered in some sense a rite of passage or initiation for Carla into adult sexuality, and the journey motif enhances
the concept of passage. Because of its presentation of an extramarital

relationship that is not followed by rapid and exemplary punishment of the participants, this novel had considerable difficulty with the censorship. Melchor Fernández Almagro, one of the deans of Spanish critics in the 1960s, gave Kurtz's fifth novel a favorable review in *La vanguardia española*,[5] expressing his view that Kurtz had earned a place in the front rank of Spanish novelists of that day, without distinction as to gender.

In 1962 Kurtz's husband died, and her only grandchild was born. She completed a short novel, *En la oscuridad* (1963; In the Darkness), a finalist for the Premio Café Gijón, apparently never published.[6] Written soon afterward, *El becerro de oro* (1964; The Golden Calf) has a title that all readers familiar with the Old Testament will recognize as alluding to the worship of a false god, and, in fact, this is the theme explored: the worship of money, which is not only the root of evil, but idolatrous. Obsession with money appears as a generic bourgeois illness, and only those who do not succumb to the cult of the false deity emerge as happy, while others suffer a series of problems culminating with one man's suicide. Paradoxically, the death of Bernardino, whom others had considered mediocre, a nonentity, acts as a catalyst, vitalizing the survivors, giving meaning and purpose to their existence, and aiding in self-discoveries. After his death, Bernardino becomes the real protagonist of the novel.

Las algas (1966; Seaweed) is related in a tangential way to *El becerro de oro* insofar as both novels delve into the question of values; money—the driving force behind tourism—is again a source of evil, since exploitation of the Costa Brava town of Sescalas as a tourist center signals the beginning of both moral and ecological ruin. With a simplistic idealization reminiscent of the *beatus ille* topos, Kurtz here identifies the country area and residents with authenticity, the city and its dwellers with superficiality and falseness. Two women (both loved by the narrator) function to a limited extent as allegories of these qualities. The woman from the small town of Sescalas is identified with true love, while the woman tourist from the city is a false and destructive siren whose attractions mask deadly peril. Insofar as the novel can be considered a warning against the negative potential for the environment and for individual Spaniards represented by the booming tourist industry, Kurtz is somewhat ahead of her time, for it is not until the following decade that Spain's rapid development as a tourist center began to create more widespread concern among ecologists in the Peninsula.

En la punta de los dedos (1968; At Your Fingertips) returns to a theme enunciated in several earlier novels, the limitations and frustration of provincial life in Spain. However, it is only one of several themes introduced here, with old age, loneliness, unhappiness in marriage, and the search for happiness also figuring among the major preoccupations. Unlike any of Kurtz's earlier works, *En la punta de los dedos* features a collective protagonist, the whole town as perceived by an omniscient narrator. For the most part, the narrative viewpoint is situated in the street, following one character until he or she meets or contacts another, a structure that recalls aspects of the technique employed in Camilo José Cela's *Tobogán de hambrientos* (1962).

Entre dos oscuridades (1969; Between Two Darknesses) is the most somber of Kurtz's novels, death appearing in sharper relief than in any of her other works. Given the fact that the executioner is an uncommon narrative focus, and an equally uncommon object for psychological analysis, it is interesting to compare this novel with Pardo Bazán's *La piedra angular* that also has as its main character an executioner. The emphasis is somewhat different, as Kurtz presents a reconstruction of the lives and crimes of five different people (who were among the victims of the narrative consciousness, who recalls some of those he executed). *Cándidas palomas* (1975; Innocent Doves) is comparably light-hearted, something of a mid-point between Kurtz's children's fiction and the typical tenor of her novels for adults. Although there are five schoolgirls ranging in age from five to twelve, the novel emphasizes the friendship of a twelve-year-old, pre-adolescent girl and the middle-aged female swimming teacher at her private school. The work appears intended at least in part as a tribute to the youngsters of the girl's generation with their innocence and vitality. Kurtz may be portraying her own relationship with her granddaughter. In any event, the novel contains a sensitive exploration of the problematic circumstances of the spinster, of the pros and cons of being single as one approaches the mid-century mark, and a critical scrutiny of loneliness versus independence precipitated by the necessity of deciding how to respond to a somewhat unexpected proposal of marriage.

Kurtz's major novelistic undertaking is her trilogy, *Sic transit* (Thus Goes Glory), the reconstruction of the history of three generations of Catalan emigrants (quite obviously based in some part on the chronicle of her own family). The three parts of the trilogy are *Al otro lado del mar* (1973; Beyond the Sea), *El viaje* (1975; The Voyage) and *El regreso* (1976; The Return). The title of *Al otro lado del mar* alludes simultaneously to the sojourn of the ancestors of the doctor-narrator's family in America, and to the desire of the representative of latest generation to leave Spain. The several generations of the strong but tormented Roura family become focal points for exploration of the entrepreneur and of individualism, the formation and development of a class that played an important role in the industrialization of Catalonia and the emergence of the industrial bourgeoisie. After introducing characters from three generations, the novel narrows its focus to character analysis and a restrained exploration of various personal dramas, including a study of problems of aging.

In part two, *El viaje,* a second family of emigrants and pioneers is introduced—the Roberts—whose psychological and social history is integrated with that of the Rouras. The focus is now upon the great-great-grandfather's generation and emigration to America (specifically, the United States and Cuba) where the second generation is born, founding the dynasty whose third, fourth, and fifth generations appeared in the first novel of the trilogy. The chronological framework spans approximately sixty years of the nineteenth century, beginning when the seventeen-year-old orphan emigrant arrives in New York in 1834, and tracing his rise, marriage, and finally his death, after the outbreak of war in Cuba at the end of the century. These events constitute the beginning of the action chronicled, and thus *El viaje* would have been the first volume of the trilogy if linear succession were followed. Among the significant historical events portrayed are the war with Mexico, the Civil War in the United States (1861–65), and the Spanish-American War in 1898. These conflicts are viewed from perspectives that readers in the United States are unlikely to have encountered (i.e., that of the Spaniard). In a brief review of *El viaje,*[7] Alfonso Martínez Mena observes that Kurtz's tapestry of the archetypal family of Catalan emigrants, embracing a century and a half of dynastic, social, and political history, is a saga that compares favorably with Ignacio Agustí's trilogy, "La ceniza fue árbol," portraying the development of Catalonia's industrial bourgeoisie of the early twentieth century. *El regreso* takes up the history of the two families again at the point when their descendants return to Spain, and is narrated by Ricardo, grandson of the narrator of *El Viaje,* who continues the chronicle up to the present-tense moment of writing (i.e., the mid-seventies). Ricardo encounters his own identity through this discovery of his roots, and comes also to understand the importance of family ties.

In addition to the novelette *En la oscuridad,* Kurtz has two collections of short stories, *El último camino* (1961; The Last Road), and *Siete tiempos* (1964; Seven Times). For both collections, death is an important and even obsessive theme, as are poverty, the suffering caused by war, and the stultification of life by the conformity and limitations of provincialism. The twenty-seven tales of *Siete tiempos* are divided into seven parts, each with a certain thematic unity or community of sentiment: death, life, solitude, love, war, Christmas, and hope. Reviewing *Siete tiempos* in *El español* (17 February 1964), Luis López Anglada classified Kurtz's stories "among the best of the genre," and observed that the collection as a whole exuded "poetry, grace, originality and tenderness, without the concessions to bad taste habitual among our novelists today." Loneliness, desolation, and alienation are also repetitive themes in Kurtz's stories, and the figure of the spinster appears with some frequency, while problems of old age receive special attention and sensitive treatment. Kurtz is in the vanguard in her gerontological concerns, for this theme is little treated by writers of either sex, with the exception of Miguel Delibes's *La hoja roja* (1959). Feminism, per se, and specifically feminist themes, are present rather infrequently and usually only by implication in Kurtz's adult fiction, but in her works for children, a more explicit formulation is given to feminist messages, such as the need for females to lead fulfilling lives, reject stereotyping, and overcome tradition (good examples occur in the children's story collection *Piedras y trompetas* [1981; Stones and Trumpets]). An independent writer who is much less known and esteemed than proportional merits of her work would dictate, Kurtz belongs to no identifiable school or ideological grouping.

An Intellectual Writer of Psychological Novels

Elena Soriano Jara was born in the village of Fuentidueña de Tajo, province of Madrid, in 1917. She obtained her *Licenciatura* in Philosophy and Letters, and is unusually well versed in French and English literature. An insightful critic, she founded (1970) and directed *El Urogallo,* perhaps the most important literary periodical of the seventies in Spain. Soriano published four novels during the 1950s, only the first with full censorial authorization. Her trilogy was not allowed to "circulate," i.e., she was permitted to print it at her own expense but not to have it distributed, since her treatment of female eroticism and passion and portrayal of marriage as something less than "happily ever after" was considered dangerous. Whether as the result of frustration or responsibilities to her children (born in these years), Soriano abandoned the novel after completing the trilogy. A writer of a very different sort, personal, subjective, and impassioned with little in common with objectivism, Soriano in purpose is closer to Ortega's theories on the novel (in fact, her novelistic practice is similar to Chacel's). She followed Ortega's principle that characters not be defined by the author but allowed to define themselves. Theoretically, Soriano is distant from the literature of *engagement* which came to the fore with the Mid-Century Generation in Spain.

Caza menor (1951; Small Game Hunting) with its baroque richness of vocabulary was adopted as a text in France and at some schools in the United States. Set in rural Castile, very similar to the area of Soriano's childhood and a spot well known to the author from many summers of residence, the novel spans the decade preceding the Civil War. Its atmosphere recalls Pardo Bazán's chronicle of the decadence of landed gentry in *Los pazos de Ulloa,* as well as that of Elena Quiroga's *Viento del norte,* published in the same year. Technique is essentially that of traditional Spanish realism, with touches of *costumbrismo* seen in the detailed descriptions of local customs. A pair of rural landowners has three sons, Andrés (a womanizer), Emilio, and Pascual (something of an intellectual, who joins the Falange). Emilio marries Ana, daughter of a wealthy neighboring farmer, and she becomes a pawn in the brothers' rivalries. Fleeing the advances of Andrés, Ana is thrown by her horse from a cliff and killed; not long afterward, the war begins, and Pascual disguises himself as a peasant, attempting to reach the area held by the rebels, while Emilio is killed when he aims a gun at a squad of Loyalists who come seeking Pascual. Warned by one of the maids he has seduced, Andrés takes refuge in the mountains, from where he later sees the house and lands destroyed in bombardments. The novel ends inconclusively, inasmuch as the reader is left to imagine the fate of Pascual and Andrés, but the family and its holdings have been destroyed.

The trilogy, entitled "Mujer y hombre" (Man and Woman), consists of three independent novels with no common characters or connections of plot. Thematic unity exists, since each examines a different love relationship, neither happy nor normal, as the novelist inquires into the complex, elusive, and sometimes surprising relationships between the sexes. There is also a certain unity of emotion, of anguish on the part of characters who have sought to make of love a substitute for faith, reality, and even decency, seeking in it a basis for their lives. In

varying existential limit situations, they must confront the deceptiveness of this central "fact" of their existence. Of the trilogy's five most
important charcters, four experience crises as a result of the approach
of middle age: physical aging, inescapable evidence of the finitude of
existence, produces existential anguish. Other existential motifs include the problem of freedom, the issue of personal authenticity, and
relationships between the self and the other. In each case the action of
the novelistic present is precipitated by an individual emotional crisis
and covers a relatively short time span.[8]

La playa de los locos (Beach of Madmen) consists of a single long
letter, a variation on the extended internal monologue, written by the
protagonist to her lover of some twenty years before. An unusually
liberated woman, a professional who has just won the competition for
a teaching chair, she takes her first vacation alone at a small, solitary
Galician beach, where she meets a young man. Although he identifies
himself as a doctor, she suspects he is only a student, and does not
allow a physical consummation of their strongly erotic relationship. In
a few weeks, with the outbreak of war, he is taken away by mysterious
strangers (undoubtedly to be executed), and she is incredulous upon
hearing of his political involvement. Too stubborn to admit that she
may have misjudged her man, unable to face the possibility that he
may not return, she lives the next twenty years centering her whole
life on the obsession of this frustrated romance, never marrying, and
continuing to behave as though time is not passing. Menopause pre-
cipitates her decisive emotional crisis, as she rebels at the extinction of
her personality and the cessation of her fertility, desirability, and illusions. Forced to recognize that she has aged, anguished by the loss of
physical beauty, she returns to the beach in the hope of somehow re-
cuperating the past via a step-by-step reconstruction that eventually
forces her to accept reality, her radical solitude, and inauthenticity.

Espejismos (Mirages) is the term chosen by Soriano to designate states
of mind produced by crisis, self-doubt, and the anguish born of existential limit situations. A delicate and penetrating analysis of a marital
relationship grown stale, this second novel explores conjugal love and
its shortcomings, as well as other emotions affecting the marriage, and
like the other parts of the trilogy, possesses an intense unity. Again,
many years are summarized and intensely relived via internal flashbacks, while the action proper takes place in a matter of hours. The
narrative perspective shifts between Pedro and Adela, the only significant characters, beginning as they leave for the private hospital where

Adela is to undergo major surgery and exploring the thoughts of both as she waits to enter the operating room and as he waits while his wife is in surgery. Pedro—in a desperate attempt to hold onto his youth—has become involved with a girl young enough to be his daughter, even becoming engaged to her although divorce did not exist in Spain at this time (a large part of Soriano's subtext is the demonstration of the "immorality" of a system that perpetuates intimacy where there is no love). Suffering from guilt at his having insisted on the operation and his inability to feel appropriate concern for his wife, Pedro consciously attempts to play the role of afflicted husband but only succeeds in thinking that perhaps Adela will die, leaving him free to marry his young fiancée. As Adela is wheeled from the operating room, his first glance convinces him she is dead, and he falls to his knees crying that he has caused her death. So painful is his guilt that when the doctor tells him Adela will recover, he throws himself, sobbing, upon her unconscious form. Hardly a happy ending for either, it simply means that life will continue with the same problems, deceit, and alienation as before. Pedro incarnates the existential concept of escape from freedom: it is his inability to cope with even the illusion of freedom that explains his manifestly unhappy situation at novel's end. The novel's veiled but clearly implicit indictment of the legal and moral situation preventing divorce and perpetuating such relationships is sufficient explanation of this work's censorship.

Medea 55 (a title from which the novelist dropped the 55 in subsequent editions) is a modernization of the Greek myth, set in Latin America—probably out of fear that to use a Spanish setting could bring serious political complications (one of the two protagonists is a totally unscrupulous politician). Restrictions imposed upon action and characterization by the mythic framework make this work the least realistic of Soriano's novels. Daniela (Medea) and Miguel (Jason) meet during the Civil War. A mysterious foreigner, clearly leftist, Miguel accepts Daniela's passionate love because she can be useful to him, and makes her his mistress when her wealthy, conservative family opposes the marriage. Eloping with much of the family wealth, they begin a life of wandering and intrigue, across much of Europe and South America, including many times when Daniela's beauty and acting talents are cynically exploited by Miguel to influence those in power and advance his career. One almost idyllic moment in their life together occurs when an adored daughter was born, but her death as an infant results in Daniela's resolve to have no more. Rather than share Miguel's love or contaminate it with paternal sentiments, she secretly aborts herself time after time, letting him believe that she has become sterile. Finally, motivated by frustrated paternal urges as well as a desire for social status, Miguel decides to marry an innocent aristocrat. Not even Daniela's revelation that she is once more pregnant suffices to prevent the wedding. Filled with hatred, Daniela moves to destroy any potential for happiness in the union, sending the bride a complete documentary of her life with Miguel, illustrated by photographs, clippings, old love letters—all the intimate and sordid details. The convent-bred wife is stunned, repelled by her husband, catatonic.

The illusions on which love is based, the self-deception and deceits it occasions, the myriad forms love takes, its emotional and psychological perversions, are illustrated throughout the trilogy via a combination of the most diverse technical elements, from modified Aristotelian unities to the modern flashback and stream of consciousness for a highly personal result. Narrative intensity is achieved due to the singular unity of time, place, and action in the framework of personal crisis, while perspective is introduced by the use of introspection and retrospective recall. Soriano clearly draws upon observation, intuition, projection, and theoretical readings, and the influences of contemporary philosophy and psychology as well as specific literary theories are clear, as is a conscious experimentation with literary techniques. Soriano is a well-informed theorist who is embarked upon a simultaneous quest for artistic expression and answers to personal questions. It is unfortunate that she has not continued her novelistic output. For nearly three decades, her writing was limited to critical essays; a personal tragedy motivated her return to a more subjective form. The drug-related death of her son led to a long, anguished autobiographical exploration of the tragedy, *Confesión de una madre* (A Mother's Confession) in 1986.

Lawyer, Journalist, Feminist, Novelist

Mercedes Fórmica, born in Cádiz in 1918 of an elitist bourgeois family, was raised in several Andalusian cities, especially Sevilla. She had just begun her university studies in Madrid when the Civil War erupted, closing the schools. Her membership in the Falange undoubtedly facilitated her postwar career: she completed her law degree in 1945, and became a practicing lawyer. Her difficulties with the male-oriented system resulted in her becoming an advocate of women's

rights, devoted to demonstrating feminine competence in the exercise
of her profession while carrying out a journalistic campaign in favor of
legal and professional equality for women. Her first novels were published under the pseudonym "Elena Puerto," *Monte de Sancha* (1951)
being the first to appear under her own name. Although given little
attention by the critics, this novel is the first to appear in postwar
Spain that considers the Civil War in the light of the motives of both
sides and is not merely another instance of self-glorifying *triunfalismo*.
The novel focuses on the executions by working-class factions of the
upper-class families of foreign ancestry at the outbreak of the war,
studying the apparently political crimes committed during a state of
anarchy as the culmination of personal conflicts, including love in-
trigues, jealousy, and rejection. Thus those executed are not merely the
innocent victims of an abstract "red terror," but of more personal passions that they have provoked.

A year later Fórmica published *La ciudad perdida* (1951; The Lost
City), considered technically superior by Nora who detects a probable
influence of Graham Greene.[9] Set in Madrid at the moment of writing,
a decade after the close of the war, *La ciudad perdida* is a novel whose
"relevance" has increased with time. A fugitive member of the *maquis*
(clandestine pro-Republican guerrillas or resistance forces) who had
made an ill-fated sally into Madrid kidnaps a wealthy young widow
and holds her hostage. With considerable psychological penetration,
the novelist studies the strange couple formed by the alleged saboteur
and the socialite forced to serve as his shield and half-willing lover,
who evolves from fear to curiosity and sympathy, to compassion and
tenderness before her captor's violent death. Contemporary experience
with terrorism and hostage situations lends a context in which the
novel acquires acute verisimilitude.

A instancia de parte (1955; On Behalf of the Third Party) is Fórmica's
most feminist novel, and can be seen as an indictment of a *machista*
society that exploits and abuses women but also victimizes men. Pro-
regime critics found it excessively polemical and a mistaken attempt
at the thesis novel, while Nora finds the psychology to have been subjected to moralizing intent.[10] The author's legal background is evident
in the presentation of two intertwined case histories, the more artistic
and interesting of the two that of a woman trapped by the legal system
in Spain and its criminalization of adultery. After twelve years of marriage, a man who has tired of his wife manages legally to rid himself
of her by arranging with an unscrupulous third party to "prove" her

guilty of adultery (on the word of the mercenary he has hired). Jailed, deprived of her son, held incommunicado and finally deported to her native Philippines, the woman is a symbol of the defenselessness of married women in Spain, described by Nora as "an animated illustration of the idea that 'the law is a trap, set so that only women are caught in it.' "[11]

One of Fórmica's more interesting works, with a bearing on feminist issues, her next is not a novel but a historical investigation of a legendary topic. *La hija de don Juan de Austria. Ana de Jesús en el proceso al pastelero de Madrigal* (1973; Don Juan de Austria's Daughter, Ana de Jesús at the Trial of the Pastry-Cook of Madrigal) received the Fastenrath Prize awarded by the Royal Spanish Academy. An exploration of the legal uses of sixteenth-century Spain which reveals the pressures to which women were subjected, the book includes transcriptions of documents discovered by Fórmica and is an important contribution to any history to be written from a feminist perspective.

Fórmica has initiated publication of a series of memoirs, the first two volumes of which are *Visto y vivido, 1931–1937. Pequeña historia de ayer* (1982; Seen and Lived, 1931–1937; Short History of Yesterday) and *Escucho el silencio. Pequeña historia de ayer II* (1984: I Listen to the Silence). The first volume consists of the writer's childhood in Andalusia, her initial university days in Madrid, including joining the Falange, the outbreak of the Civil War, and its early months in Málaga (covered in her first novel). In her second volume Fórmica focuses on the war years and immediate postwar era, especially from the viewpoint of cultural survival, her experiences of forceful intellectuals either dead or exiled after the war: Republican poets Alberti, Guillén, Lorca, Machado, Hernández, and political figures from both sides, including Azaña, la Pasionaria, and Falangist founder José-Antonio. Living influences for Fórmica, for younger generations they were only names. Fórmica's intellectual integrity and her lucid efforts to achieve the difficult synthesis of many conflicting cultural tendencies make her a challenging and significant figure though her fictional production is small (she is presently completing a fourth novel, an interpretation of modern Sevilla in the light of its heterodox past, as discovered in her historical investigations).

Radio Journalist, Cultural Essayist, and Novelist

Born in Barcelona in 1916 of a well-to-do family, Mercedes Salisachs studied business administration and received a degree in merchandising shortly before the outbreak of the Civil War. Married in 1935, she had five children (one son, Miguel, was killed in an accident in 1958, profoundly affecting the writer).[12] In the postwar period her humanistic bent asserted itself, and Salisachs became a lecturer on art as well as writing and directing programs on topics of artistic interest for Radio Nacional and covering cultural affairs for National Spanish Television in its infancy. In addition to her writing (close to twenty novels), Salisachs and a partner operated an interior decorating business. A world traveler, she has had a number of significant critical and commercial successes, including some best-sellers (some have had more than twenty editions). Her works have been translated into English, Finnish, French, German, Italian, Portuguese, and Swedish.

Primera mañana, última mañana (1955; First Morning, Last Morning), her first novel, was signed with the pseudonym María Ecín (she also used the pseudonym "A. Dan" according to Nora, who gives her only half a dozen lines[13]). Salisachs was five years (1948–53) in writing this novel, which covers "fifty years of Spanish life in all of its aspects: social, artistic, human,"[14] and she considers it her best work. Some 430 pages of small print, the novel is narrated from the viewpoint of a male artist, and constitutes (according to the cover blurb) "an implacable portrait of the Madrid aristocracy and Catalan upper class." Rómulo, the protagonist, from Madrid, marries Clara, of a wealthy family from Barcelona, which facilitates his devoting himself to artistic experimentation, a variety of affairs, and a sort of perpetual alienation without commitment or struggle. Rómulo serves as a detached perspective on the first half of this century, fathering two daughters with whom he never communicates, and avoiding his wife, whose aging and obesity he describes as though viewing the work of an unknown and unskilled artist.

Carretera intermedia (1956; Second-Class Highway) is set on the Riviera, and features a female protagonist, unusual for the period in that she is a scientist, a chemist. Her profession is not significant in the action of the narrative, although in the past it was the cause of friction in her marriage (her husband accused her of neglecting their child for her laboratory). Bibiana, fortyish and plain, is recovering from a nervous breakdown following the death of her child and abandonment by her husband, ending a loveless marriage. Reluctant to initiate an affair earlier in life, Bibiana awakens to sexuality at a mature age, but is rejected by the man she loves, who declines to consummate the relationship because of his religious principles. Without revealing a feminist viewpoint, this novel may be termed feminist in its subject matter and its concern with the protagonist's dilemma, a loss of vital context together with the loss of her child and wife/mother roles. *Una mujer llega al pueblo* (1956; A Woman Arrives in the Village), one of Salisach's more successful works, translated into eight languages, has a rural setting, radically different from the ambience described in her previous novels. She focuses upon the psychological repercussions provoked by the appearance of a strange woman in the isolated hamlet, the reactions of mixed sentiments, and the influence of a certain xenophobia. During this very productive period in the writer's life six novels appeared in the space of two years; a number of them are now out of print or inaccessible. *Más allá de los raíles* (Beyond the Rails), *Adán helicóptero* (Adam Helicopter), and *Pasos conocidos* (Well-known Footsteps) all appeared in 1957, the last being identified as a collection of two novels and nine stories.

Vendimia interrumpida (1960; Interrupted Wine Harvest) is a personal favorite of the novelist, who considers it her most authentic work. *La estación de las hojas amarillas* (1963; The Season of Yellow Leaves) is a love story, set during the Civil War, but the war is of little importance: what matters is the intimate psychology of the characters, the description of a world of selfish passions in conflict with more generous impulses that do not manage to prevail. In a sense, the relegation of the war to the background may be seen as symbolic. *El declive y la cuesta* (1966; The Slope and the Hillside) takes as its point of departure the "good thief," Dimas (converted to Christianity upon the cross), but concentrates upon his mother, who questions the meaning of her life, devoted to service to someone who dies as he did. *La última aventura* (1967; The Last Adventure) is another psychological study, linked to social problems, the story of a man in quest of an impossible happiness. An egotistical and shortsighted dreamer, he abandons his wife for the sake of a hoped-for new love, foredoomed to failure. Also during this period Salisachs produced a sort of do-it-yourself manual, *El gran libro de la decoración* (1969; The Great Book of Decorating). It would be six years, however, between *La última aventura* and her next novel.

Adagio confidencial (1973; Concert of Confidences), a neoromantic work, and one of her most successful best-sellers, reissued in paperback, examines the casual encounter between a man and woman who have not seen each other for twenty years. The dialogue between the couple, mature adults who evoke a past they can never quite forget, takes place in a few hours in an airport lounge, and constitutes an analysis of their frustrated relationship, as well as a clarification of many vague or misunderstood points concerning their mutual circle of friends in former years.

La gangrena (1975; Gangrene), the most famous and successful of Salisachs's novels, presents the thoughts of narrator-protagonist Carlos Hondero, jailed as a suspect in the murder of his second wife, Serena. During some three days he remembers essentially his entire life, beginning with a childhood spent with his beautiful mother (of the ruined Madrid aristocracy) and her lover, "Uncle" Rodolfo (who pays for Carlos's studies). The novel's historical framework includes the abdication of Alfonso XIII (introducing the Second Republic), the beginning and end of the Civil War, and events of the 1960s and early 1970s, such as the election of Pope Paul VI and the diplomacy of Henry Kissinger. This historical background is interwoven with a social fabric formed by more than one hundred characters, intended to permit situating Carlos within his sociohistorical context. A combination of internal monologue and dialogue, the novel shifts continually between past (Carlos's remembering) and present (his reflections while in jail). Present-tense thoughts appear at the beginning of each chapter, and then Carlos returns to his past, providing a chronological reconstruction as he attempts to discern the forces governing his course. His recollections are at the same time a reflection of the customs of the Catalan upper class with its parties, orgies, and prejudices, a re-creation of the process of economic development and social change, a covertly moralizing vision of nouveau riche aspirations and bourgeois hypocrisy, a panorama of life in Barcelona and its environs during some four decades. Although Carlos is a "self-made man," he owes a great deal to his first marriage to Alicia, daughter of a Catalan financier, whose death he indirectly causes with his cruelty and neglect. His sense of guilt for Alicia's death leads him not to defend himself against the accusation of responsibility for the second death (of which he is innocent, at least legally). The sickness of the title is ambition, which drives Carlos and which is inherited by his daughter, Carlota, with whom he has his most intimate and sincere communication. [15]

Viaje a Sodoma (1977; Trip to Sodom) has as its protagonist a boy, Jacobo, the hapless victim of his parents' divorce, who goes to spend a time with his uncle, a bohemian painter who lives a dissolute existence in a picturesque village on the Costa Brava. The luminous Mediterranean days and nights by the sea are magical to Jacobo, who is overwhelmed by the opportunity to associate with adults. A new, and for him, marvelous relationship with his uncle is established. The psycho-

logical analysis of the boy's sensibility and Salisachs's use of his perceptions to present the corrupt and decadent world surrounding the
painter are among her best novelistic achievements. The frustrated and
malevolent beings who make up the uncle's circle, puppets who live
from orgy to orgy, inevitably conflict with the childlike narrative consciousness, with the result that Jacobo's innocence and world of fantasy
are overwhelmed.

In 1978 Salisachs published a short-story collection, *El proyecto* (The
Project), and a year later, another novel, *La presencia* (1979; Presence).
Following very much the plan of *Adagio confidencial,* this novel portrays
a man and woman who meet in a village of the Costa Brava, and during
the course of a few hours, evoke crucial moments of their lives. United
by a common tragedy but separated by insuperable incompatibility,
they mentally reconstruct the circumstances that produced their definitive separation. Cristina, one of the protagonists, was born a Siamese
twin, joined at the shoulder to Herminia. They were separated and it
was said that the other twin died during the wartime operation, but
the body was never seen; Cristina is convinced that Herminia is alive
somewhere, and responsible for seizures that she suffers from time to
time. Her mother became incurably insane after the birth; her paternal
grandmother was also demented. The other protagonist, Claudio, is a
married man her father's age, with whom Christina's father is discussing a partnership for developing a resort area on their coastal property.
After she has an affair with Claudio, his wife Matilde is drowned when
Christina was supposedly teaching her to swim; she is accused of murder and confined to an insane asylum for twenty years (not admitting
her insanity, she agrees that it is the best defense). After the death of
Franco, with legal reforms affecting her case, she is released and returns
to the scene of the affair, at which time she and Claudio, separately,
reminisce. Christina lies down to die because "somewhere, Herminia
is communicating the contagion of her own death."[16] The author was
intrigued by the theory of the strange communication and similar histories of twins, and leaves unsolved the question of the mysterious
connections between Cristina and Herminia.

Derribos (1981; Demolition), a volume of memoirs, is subtitled "Intimate Chronicle of a Time Paid Out," while the cover terms it "the
secret life of a little girl who was a writer." From the evocation of the
figures of her grandparents, her terror upon discovering her grandmother's epileptic seizures, reflections on her childhood and family,
her personal contacts with famous people (Dalí in his youth, Andrés

Segovia), social occasions, and tender domestic episodes, Salisachs sketches her early development as a writer against the background of the dictatorship of Primo de Rivera and the advent of the Republic. Rather than a formal autobiography, she explains that she reproduces only those moments that somehow marked her, influenced her development.

La sinfonía de las moscas (1982; Symphony of the Flies) is set in Barcelona in the 1950s, the time when it was actually written; the author withheld it, fearing it would be censored. Essentially, the novel deals with the hopes and expectations of change introduced in the life of the protagonist, Julio (almost sixty and employed in a publishing house), when he receives the news that he has won approximately two million pesetas in the lottery. Julio's family life is a sordid triangle with his sister-in-law, Finita (they drug his wife to sleep together), and his daughter Julita attempts suicide upon learning of the arrangement. Juana, his "successful" sister, is the mistress of a financier, his son Paco wants to be a priest, while Pilar, the seventy-year-old grandmother, imbibes and imagines herself an opera star (she was a singer in her youth). Despite his age, Julio still talks of becoming a novelist, and like his mother and sisters, has delusions of grandeur. The unrealistic illusions and hopes aroused in Julio by the lottery prize unleash a chain of disasters, as he wastes most of the money with a prostitute. In a scene reminiscent of the *esperpentos* of Valle-Inclán, the grandmother attempts to renew her opera career but loses her false teeth; returning home in humiliation, she insults her grandson, who disappears and is finally found in the morgue, victim of an automobile accident that may have been suicide. Genoveva, the protagonist's niece, is jailed and Julita is jilted, while Julio remains seriously ill and the family without food in the house at novel's end. Although on one level the novel deals with the importance of dreams, hopes, and illusions, each character is to an extent also the victim of those same illusions.

El volumen de la ausencia (1983; The Volume of Absence) was a best-seller during 1983 and 1984. In a doctor's waiting room, a middle-aged woman evokes her past while she prepares herself for the diagnosis that may be an announcement of impending death. Upon hearing the prognosis, the patient begins to walk through the streets of Barcelona while she reconstructs her past and projects her future. The outcome of her cogitations, the decisions she makes, can affect many lives besides her own. Salisachs creates a fascinating world of ethical tensions, echoes of bygone times, unsolvable conflicts, and memories that sur-round the protagonist for four-and-a-half hours of increasing suspense. Having learned that she has a brain tumor and four to five months to live, she is tempted to return to a past love, to see if he continues to care for her, but at the last moment she returns home and says nothing to her family. Without having a feminist thesis, this again is a profoundly feminist text, and Ida's decision is personally and solitarily her own.

A Consistently Feminist Social Conscience

Concha Alós was born in Valencia in 1922 of a working-class family. They moved to Castellón, where she studied her *bachillerato*. During the Civil War her family fled to Murcia, underwent hunger, privation, and the imprisoning of her father. Her mother died, and the future writer had to keep house for her father and work to help support the family. After a few years she went to Palma in Majorca to study to become a school teacher, afterward spending some ten years teaching in Majorcan villages (an environment reflected in some of her fiction). She moved to Barcelona in 1960 and began to write, supporting herself by giving private classes until she won the well-endowed Planeta Prize with her third novel in 1964, after which she has devoted herself entirely to writing. Alós began as a social realist, preoccupied with injustice and inequality in society, and is concerned in her fiction with exposing and denouncing inequities, most particularly as they affect women. In addition to novels, she writes short stories and occasional television scripts.

Los enanos (1963; The Dwarfs) describes life in a pensión in a large Spanish city, a run-down boardinghouse whose inhabitants exist on the fringes of poverty. With neonaturalist touches in the style of Baroja, it combines somber and sober, direct observation of life with an anguished existentialist view of the human condition. Following Darwin (and Baroja), life is a jungle in which the strongest survive,[17] and in this vein, most human beings are dwarfs (while society is a giant). The concept of humanity as helpless before powerful forces is allegorically represented by the motif of drowned rats. Using a contrapuntal technique, Alós portrays a variety of generic and despairing characters, victims of isolation, frustration, incommunication, and the effects of war and its aftermath. Women, especially, are victimized, as Elizabeth Ordóñez has pointed out, by "a society infected by socially sanctioned rape, murder and other forms of violence directed specifically against women."[18]

In her second novel, *Los cien pájaros* (1963; A Hundred Birds), Alós depicts the sexual and social awakening of Christina, a working-class girl in a provincial city (perhaps Valencia). The narration is largely in first person, from the viewpoint of Christina, incorporating dialogue exchanges with her family, teachers, and others. There are flashbacks to important moments of her past, such as her first communion. Christina's job as private tutor of a little rich girl facilitates the contrast between upper-class ease and luxury and her own home, with her embittered, prematurely aged, and frustrated mother. Insecure and romantic, Christina has a short-lived affair with the married brother of her pupil, a playboy who gives her expensive presents, rents a villa for their meetings, and tires of her even before she learns she is pregnant. Barely eighteen, she decides to have her child, leaving home to spare her parents, and resisting the temptation of marriage to the working-class boy who loves her. The conclusion is no solution; the novel ends as she boards the train for Barcelona to face uncertainty and seek independence as well as existential acceptance of responsibility for her own actions. This is laudable, from a feminist viewpoint, but realistically very risky and impractical, unlikely even to be feasible in the Spanish society of that day.

Las hogueras (1964; Bonfires), which won the Planeta Prize, pictures the atmosphere of a Majorcan village where a wealthy foreign couple's somewhat parasitic existence is contrasted with the background of poverty and frustration characterizing the lives of the peasants. The foreign couple consists of a self-centered ex-model, Sibila, and the older husband she has married for security, a middle-aged businessman. Sexually frustrated, Sibila enters upon a passionate but meaningless erotic adventure with Daniel el Monegro, a brutal day laborer and truck driver, in which sex is nothing but violence. A contrast is established with the spinsterhood of the schoolteacher, Asunción, and all of the characters seem suffocated by passion or frustration, a notion reinforced by the leitmotiv of the fish out of water, gasping for breath. Existentially, however, they are inauthentic, and their barren souls are symbolized by the bonfires of the title, a reference to accidental summer fires and the barrenness they produce.

El caballo rojo (1966; The Red Horse Inn) is based upon the refugee experience of Alós and her parents as they fled Castellón and the approaching Franco forces. In spite of this point of departure, Alós employs a seemingly objectivist technique in a narration that aspires to impartiality. The characters are a heterogeneous group of Republican sympathizers temporarily brought together when one of their number manages to obtain a job as waiter in "El caballo rojo," which becomes a meeting place for refugees. A dominant note is *costumbrismo*, a depiction of local color and customs, and as is typical of the genre in Spain, character development is minimal and somewhat stereotypical. Much in the fashion of Dolores Medio's *El pez sigue flotando*, the narrative moves from one character to another, in a plotless portrayal of collective sufferings, discomforts, hunger, sorrows, and longings experienced by a group of refugees. Lacking a protagonist, the narrative reveals the gap between optimism, dreams or hope, and harsh realities.

Alós's second novel, which deals more or less directly with the Spanish Civil War, is *La madama* (1970; The Madam), whose time frame is slightly before that of *El caballo rojo*, covering the early months of the conflict. Also utilizing a third-person narrative perspective, this novel possesses greater unity—implicit in the title, which appropriately calls attention to the ascendancy or predominance acquired by an individual, much as the title of *El caballo rojo* signifies the collective or generic nature through its focus upon a group meeting place. Instead of the many families that appear in the earlier novel, *La madama* portrays only one, the Esprius, a formerly wealthy, bourgeois unit whose members falter under stress. One son is jailed as a political prisoner, while the widowed father, Aquiles—no hero—and remaining children struggle to reestablish the family's failing fortunes, but barely manage to survive. The extended chronicle of family decadence is interrupted by the arrival of "the Madam," who succeeds in her own struggle to survive by installing herself in the family, making herself indispensable, becoming pregnant, and finally marrying the widower (Aquiles does not marry her without the simulacrum of a struggle, insinuating the advisability of an abortion, but she counters with fear). Although at first "the Madam" with her energy and strength seems to embody hope for the future, she is revealed ultimately as destructive, almost one of the avenging Furies. Alternating with this story line is the subjective, introspective meditation of Clemente Espriù, the political prisoner, who reflects upon the experience of imprisonment, the death of his friend Román, fears and longings for his wife Cecilia, turning ever more inward, and becoming more neurotic and obsessed until he is almost catatonic. The two narrative planes—prison and beleaguered city—are fused by the repetition of similar motifs signifying degeneracy, suffering, degradation, anguish, and despair.

El rey de gatos (Narraciones antropófagas) (1972; King of Cats, Cannibalistic Tales) contains nine short stories with a wide variety of themes. "La otra bestia" (The Other Beast) relates how a woman murders her unfaithful husband, although it may also involve her suicide. In the title tale, a strange man who becomes progressively more anti-social retires to an isolated cabin with untold numbers of cats, and one day nothing is left but the cats. All of the stories suggest the world of fantasy or madness which is just beyond the touch, the mirror, the door or wall that limit everyday reality. Frequently narrated in first person, the stories explore themes such as the war between the sexes, identity crises, alienation, fear, jealousy, and the loss of the mysterious something that separates human from animal.

In *Os habla Electra* (1975; Electra Speaking), a Freudian study of mother-daughter relationships, Alós moves further from the surface plane of socialist realism toward psychological analysis and the re-creation of myth. Characters and the atmosphere around them are studied in detail, and the narrative fuses past and present, real and fantastic, memories and that which never was. *Os habla Electra* signifies a change in style and technique for Alós, who concentrates upon the dichotomy between fertility and the threat of destruction. References to the Electra myth occur primarily in the tragedy of the characters, rather than in specifics of the plot, as Alós sketches the struggle between patriarchal and matriarchal modes with the female (Electra, singular and plural) striving to regain identity or androgynous wholeness. Combining oneiric imagery and fragmented structure, Alós transcends the limits of social realism that defined her prior novels.

Something of the mythic atmosphere remains in *Argeo ha muerto, supongo* (1983; Argeo's Dead, I Suppose) in which the novelist explores the invisible bounds between the fantasy world of childhood and the secrets of adulthood. Autobiographical in format (a first-person, linear narrative), the story develops the themes of childhood as Paradise Lost, the loss of illusion, and the loss of first love. The narrator-protagonist Jano struggles with reconciling reality and the dream world as she attempts to cope with fragmentation of personality and frustrated passion for her foundling brother, Argeo. Infantile mythology includes the capability of transcending barriers and convention, and while the enchantment lasts, the youthful heroes achieve their greatest adventures. But time passes, and as happens with other animal species, human beings are subject to a life cycle: the magic of childhood disappears and communication with it, and then the only solution is introspection.

Alós's most recent novel is *El asesino de los sueños* (1986; The Assassin of Dreams). Written in alternating sequences of second-person, familiar (tú), and third-person, objective narration, *El asesino de los sueños* presents the aspirations of the mother (coinciding with the norms of conventional society) and contrasts them with her reality ("fallen woman"). A novel of complex intertextuality—mythological allusions, the principals of *Othello,* Melibea and Polyphemus, Ortega, Tennessee Williams, Sophocles, Camus, *Ulysses,* Dumas, and others—the narrative is set in the Balearic Islands and Barcelona. Melibea has always lived with her mother, Dionisia, an attractive and intelligent woman who has suffered in life and thus desires something better for her daughter, whom she persuades to marry the Duke of Altaba y Poison. Unfortunately, the girl becomes amorously involved with Marcelo, the Duke's secretary, in a relationship in which dreams play a major part, and where the line between dream, symbol, and reality becomes unclear, and prose and poetry are fused. One of Alós's least autobiographical and most imaginative novels, The Assassin of Dreams is both experimental and literarily mature.

Minor Narrators

Concha Castroviejo, born in Santiago de Compostela in 1915, lived in exile in Mexico from 1939 to 1950, and since then has resided in Madrid. Active in journalism, she has written short stories, children's books, and two novels of exile, as well as detective novels. *Los que se fueron* (1957; Those Who Left) traces the route of Spanish exiles to Paris after the Civil War and then to Mexico, where most of them sit around in cafes lamenting the fate of their homeland (also described in some detail by another exiled Spanish novelist, Max Aub). Castroviejo then focuses on Tiche, a widow with a young son, and her development of a successful career, as she makes an affirmative adjustment to the new life. *Víspera del odio* (1959; Eve of Hate) is a psychological novel that explores the genesis of a woman's hatred for her miserly older husband. Set against the background of the Civil War, which provides the impetus for the action, the novel portrays her wartime affair and escape with her Loyalist lover through war-ravaged zones, and the husband's revenge as he has the lover arrested as an atheistic Communist.

Isabel Calvo de Aguilar (b. 1916) is important more for her founding of the Asociación de Escritoras Españolas in the 1950s and for her biographical anthology of women writers than for her novels that are strictly for entertainment, including exotic Oriental mysteries and romantic tales of unrequited love. Among her titles are *El misterio del palacio chino* (1951; The Mystery of the Chinese Palace), *La isla de los siete pecados* (1952; The Island of Seven Sins), *La danzarina inmóvil* (1954; The Immobile Dancer), and *Doce sarcófagos de oro* (1955; Twelve Gold Sarcophagi).

Rosa María Cajal, born in Zaragoza in 1920, was moderately successful in the 1950s and 1960s but seems to have quit writing at that time. She treated feminist and existentialist themes in at least three of her novels. *Juan Risco* (1948) portrays a rather unlikely protagonist, a famous journalist who faked his own death by suicide in order to "free" his wife, Cristina, to marry an editor. Bitterly withdrawing from human society, he is almost completely alienated; only the neighbor's daughter is able to communicate with him. Susana falls in love with him, but he arranges for her to meet a publisher, who is to be her next lover. When the editor's wife, Cristina, dies, Juan's secret is revealed. The novel is not a document favoring divorce, for with Cristina dead, Risco as a widower is free, but his lack of identity and lack of commitment continue. *Primera derecha* (1955; Apartment 1-R) portrays Mama Petra, a matriarch whose entire life is her seven children (her husband is just another child), and who never leaves her house. Clearly Cajal meant the novel as an indictment of such a restricted existence, for she followed it immediately with *Un paso más* (1956; Just One Step More) in which a resolute village girl builds a business career in the city, achieving independence as a successful bookstore owner. She is contrasted with her female friends and relatives who are weak, conventional, shallow, and dependent, and to some extent with males who are less strong and determined than she.

Luisa Alberca Lorente, born in 1920 in the province of Ciudad Real, is the author of numerous novels, radio scripts, short stories, plays, and children's books. Well known and successful in her field, the *novela rosa* or sentimental romance, she has had many of her novels translated into Portuguese.

Susana March, a Barcelona poet and novelist born in 1918, began publishing poetry at the age of twenty, and has produced at least five collections of lyrics. Her collected short stories appeared as *Narraciones* (1945; Narrations), and she has published five novels, and with her husband, Ricardo Fernández de la Reguera, has coauthored a series of historical novels modeled on those of Galdós, *Episodios nacionales contemporáneos*. Although she is not a militant feminist, much of her work deals with women and their lives, and feminine speakers are central in

her poetry and fiction, treating such themes as a woman's love for a
man, her children, or her mother. *Nina* (1949) portrays the protagonist's passion for a man that survives her lover's weakness and eventual
death, depicting a woman's love for an unworthy object which borders
upon the absurd. *Algo muere cada día* (1955; Something Dies Within
Us Every Day; *Les ruines et les jours*, 1960) is probably her most important novel, illuminating the lives of ordinary people in Barcelona during the Civil War, and tracing the development of María from
childhood to maturity. Narrated in the first person, the novel consistently utilizes the perspective of the protagonist as she marries, has
three children, later becomes a successful writer and the mainstay of
the family, independent and economically self-sufficient. Her relationships with men are unsatisfying and she feels that her deepest yearnings
are ignored or unfulfilled. María's most significant relationship is with
her mother. By contrast with *Nina,* this novel portrays the disintegration of a male-female relationship and indirectly criticizes the social
conventions that restrict and constrain individuals' lives. Other novels
of March include *Canto rodado* (1944; Rolling Stone) and *Nido de vencejos*
(1945; Nest of Swallows).

Mercedes Sáenz-Alonso, born in 1917 to a noble family of San Sebastián, is a professor at the University of Navarra, an internationally
known lecturer on art, history, and literature, and a literary critic
known for her book on Don Juan, as well as a newspaper correspondent, essayist, short-story writer, and author of travel books and postwar
realist novels. Two of her novels are set outside Spain. The first, *Bajos
fondos* (1949; The Depths), portrays a poverty-stricken area of London
before World War II and concentrates on four different family groups
living in the same tenement, with some characters verging on the mon-
strous. The second, *Altas esferas* (High Spheres), is a sort of sequel in
which one of the minor characters from the earlier novel becomes a
double agent, traveling across much of Europe, mixing with the elite,
and eventually betraying England. *El tiempo que se fue* (1951; The Time
That's Gone) portrays the ambience of the novelist's childhood, a noble
family in San Sebastián, with emphasis upon the war's effects—not
only its physical devastation, but the erosion of spirituality and threat
to the institution of the family. *La pequeña ciudad* (1952; The Small
City) portrays an ambitious small-town pharmacist who is almost destroyed by his inability to accept failure, while an upper-class friend
accepts similar frustration resignedly. As in all of this novelist's works,
the family is central to the narrative.

Eugenia Serrano (b. 1918), a journalist, short-story writer, essayist, and biographer is also the author of four novels, *Retorno a la tierra* (1945; Return to the Earth), *Chamberí-Club*; *Perdimos la primavera* (1953; We Lost Springtime); and more recently, *Pista de baile* (1963; Dance Floor). In the last-named, Constanza, the protagonist, is an artist who lives in the pseudo-bohemian ambience of homosexuals, alcohol and drug addicts, Communists, and heterodox intellectuals. Unable either to establish lasting relationships or tolerate solitude, she is fearful of aging at thirty, and concerned with losing her young lover. The dance floor is a symbol of sexual awakening and youth, and Constanza senses that she is slipping off its polished surface.

Angeles Villarta was born in Belmonte (Asturias) in 1921 and educated in Switzerland. The author of novels, essays, poems, and short stories, she is a prominent journalist and edited the comic periodical *Don Venerando*. Her novels, known only through secondary sources, include *Un pleno de amor* (1942; A Full Love), *Por encima de las nieblas* (1943; Above the Mists), *Muchachas que trabajan* (1944; Working Girls), *Ahora que soy estraperlista* (1949; Now That I'm a Black Marketeer), and *Con derecho a cocina* (1950; Cooking Privileges). *Una mujer fea* (1954; An Ugly Woman) won the 1953 Fémina Prize and portrays a marriage between Josefa, a shopkeeper's daughter, and Julián, illegitimate son of the last nobleman in the region, in an atmosphere of foreboding and superstition, with the townspeople functioning as a collective voice.

The writers in this group all experienced the Civil War as children, adolescents, or young adults—old enough to be aware that the world they had known was ending but, for the most part, too young to intervene actively. Many of them knew the trauma of exile in addition to the shock of war, and frequently their work is marked by these experiences as they portray the conflict and its aftermath. Generally, they are realists, interested in the psychological reverberations of violence and privation. Although the pro-Franco viewpoint is not totally absent, it is very much in the minority, even though most of these women wrote when the censorship made expression of views diverging from the official version of the war both hazardous and unrewarding. Although the writers are seldom fully objective, most strive for a balanced presentation—more noticeably so than in a majority of the works written during the same time span by male counterparts. Women writers tend to downplay ideologies in favor of other emphases, usually a focus upon human or spiritual problems and the suffering that war brings. While not overtly pacifistic, they usually echo to some degree the notion that war is hell. Typically, women writers present a behind-the-scenes view of war, away from the combat areas with few exceptions, and concentrating upon noncombatants. Obviously, for most women writers this is the realm of their own experience, and regardless of how many eyewitness accounts of battle they may have heard or read, they are less interested in attempting to reconstruct military ambience and operations than they are in presenting war's effects upon women and families, minds and hearts, beliefs and ways of life. Their sphere is thus what might be called the "intrahistory of war," to adapt Unamuno's terminology, and an important part of their contribution is the preservation of this human history which seldom finds its way into the historians' texts.

Chapter Seven
The First Postwar Generation: Writers of Relative Fame

The writers surveyed in this chapter are the most visible of postwar women narrators, having achieved the most prominence with commercial and critical successes. Usually enough criticism is available in English on their work to give an adequate idea of its nature. Where it is possible to refer to extant books in English, only a brief résumé is given for those readers who may not already be familiar with the names of these novelists; where pertinent, there is discussion of novels published after the completion of the critical works, or of works that have either been little noticed by critics or for which extant criticism is not easily available.

The First Postwar Best-Seller

Carmen Laforet, born in 1921 in Barcelona, was the first woman novelist to come to public attention in the postwar period. *Nada* (1944; *Andrea*, 1964), her first novel and greatest hit, became one of Spain's best-known novels for some two decades. Written in the form of an autobiographical memoir, it presents the narrator-protagonist's traumatic encounter with war-ravaged Barcelona after arriving from the relatively tranquil Canary Islands to study at the university. Living for a year with a group of relatives, nearly all of them with marked emotional disturbances or psychological abnormalities, Andrea loses many adolescent illusions and matures socially and emotionally in the process. Of interest for the feminist as a study of adolescent psychology and rites of passage to maturity, *Nada* ("Nothing") probably lacks the existential profundity attributed to it by enthusiastic readers during the 1940s. A full study of Laforet's life and works is available in Roberta Johnson's *Carmen Laforet* (Boston: G. K. Hall, 1981).

La isla y los demonios (1952; The Island and the Devils) received less attention but is in some ways superior to *Nada*. Again, the novelist explores an adolescent girl's experience, and again, the protagonist

119

lives with a collection of relatives suffering varying psychological abnormalities. Marta discovers adult sexuality, suffers her first disillusionments, and begins to mature, making this second work also a novel of passage. As it ends where *Nada* began (with the protagonist leaving for Barcelona and university studies), it might be termed a prelude. Both adolescent protagonists are isolated, alienated orphans (a frequent theme in Laforet's work), and both are interested in art, another reiterated theme. This time, however, the novelist does not employ the autobiographical form, and the resulting loss of immediacy attenuates narrative impact. Adolescence is not idealized: Laforet shows the occasional selfishness and lack of sensitivity of her young protagonists, their mistakes and moments of cruelty as well as their vulnerability. Most commentators consider Laforet's handling of adolescent psychology one of the principal merits of her fiction.

La mujer nueva (1955; The New Woman) is Laforet's first and only full-length novel having as its protagonist an adult, a married woman who repents of her "liberated" youth after a quasi-mystical religious experience. Much of the novel is told via a flashback to Paulina's university days during the era of the Second Republic (the early 1930s), constituting a link with the writer's tendency to treat adolescents (usually about to begin their university studies) in her other long fiction. Although allegedly the result of Laforet's "conversion," the novel also contrasts the regimented morality of the Franco regime with the freedom enjoyed by the youth of the previous generation, and the protagonist must contend with the change from the Republic's permissive attitude toward free love to the puritanical regulation and limitation of women's lives by government, church, and society in the postwar period. The first two novels can be considered a search for self, and in this aspect they resemble *La mujer nueva,* although Paulina's "maturation" is moral, a coming to terms with her conscience, rather than adolescent discovery of identity. Having lived with her boyfriend during the war and undergone a civil ceremony when she became pregnant, Paulina was left alone when her husband, Eulogio, went temporarily into exile; jailed, she and her infant son were rescued by her husband's cousin, Antonio, who fell in love with her. Rejected by her, Antonio finally entered a loveless marriage of convenience. When Eulogio returned after nine years from Central America (where he had also had an affair), he and Paulina had both changed, but she again became pregnant. Recovering from a miscarriage, she embarked upon an adulterous affair with Antonio, but escaped to Madrid suffering pangs of conscience after learning his wife was terminally ill. Working with a spiritual advisor in Madrid, she is peripherally involved in a crime, when her landlady's son uses Paulina's apartment as a hideout after a robbery and murder. The trial and sentencing to death of Julián bring Paulina to reflect upon her own guilt and selfishness and eventually she chooses to return to her husband and son, although Antonio is now a widower and her civil marriage to Eulogio leaves her free to remarry. She is also attracted by the tranquillity of the religious life, and as she has a university degree and teaching experience, could be independent. Interestingly enough, although she considers the convent, she does not ever really consider a "career," a reflection of the social values of the Franco regime.

La insolación (1963; Sunstroke) is Laforet's only full-length novel with a male narrator-protagonist.[1] Announced as the first part of a trilogy entitled "Three Steps Outside of Time," it has yet to be continued. Like *Nada,* Sunstroke focuses upon adolescence in the years immediately following the war, but both the time frame and ambience have changed: set in a Mediterranean summer resort, the novel takes place during the summers of 1940, 1941, and 1942 and contrasts the carefree atmosphere of childhood with the harsh realities of adult existence. Martín, the protagonist, fifteen when the novel begins, visits his father and new stepmother for the first time since the father's remarriage. The father, a military super-macho, expects his son to be like himself and is almost obsessed with Martín's masculinity. He is soon dominated by two neighbors, Carlos and Anita Corsi, of approximately the same age, who have been raised in a freewheeling, adventurous atmosphere (their father is a blackmarketeer, the late mother was a circus performer). In successive summers the trio mature physically, and Anita (one year older than the boys) becomes flirtatious and apparently promiscuous; her brother's latently incestuous desire to control her leads Carlos and Martín into a series of adventures. Resentment by Martín's stepmother of his father's seeming preference for male offspring (Adela had borne two daughters) creates tension, and to rid herself of her hated stepson, she takes advantage of a nocturnal visit by Carlos to Martín's room to insinuate to the father that the boys' relationship is homosexual. Severely beaten by his father, who considers sending him to a correctional institution, Martín returns to his maternal grandmother. Having become aware of his artistic vocation and of the superficiality of the Corsis, he is ready for a life of depth and commitment.

Laforet has published several collections of short fiction including *La muerta* (1952; The Dead Woman), nine short stories treating themes such as Christian charity, motherhood, childhood, hunger in postwar Spain, and at least two of feminist bent: "Rosamunda" presents an older woman whose lifetime aspiration of a stage debut, tardily realized, resulted in disaster, a variation upon the theme of the conflict between illusion and reality. "El veraneo" (The Summer Vacation) portrays the disillusionment of Rosa, a village schoolteacher whose family sacrificed her aspirations in favor of support for her brother, Juan Pablo. After ten years of sacrifice on her part, Juan Pablo is supposed to spend his vacation with her, but instead leaves the next day, finding village life unbearable. *La llamada* (1954; The Call) is a collection of novelettes, the title tale being an analysis of another stagestruck housewife. "Un noviazgo" (An Engagement) probes the psyche of an embittered spinster, examining her reactions to the marriage proposal by her widowed employer whom she had adored for years, but whom she rejects after the initial celebration, realizing that he merely wants a nurse in his old age. "El piano" is told from the viewpoint of a young wife whose piano—the last remaining tie with an earlier, more affluent life—is being sold as the pair struggle to exist independently. *La niña y otros relatos* (1970; The Child and Other Stories) is an anthology of novelettes and short stories previously included in other collections. In her brief fiction as in her longer works, Laforet is at her best in the presentation of feminine and adolescent psychology, and although she is seldom more than mildly feminist, her writing will be of interst to feminist scholars because of her choice of subject matter. During the last twenty years, Laforet has published nothing more than a few articles.

A Teacher, Journalist, and Social Novelist

Dolores Medio was born in Oviedo in 1914, of a family belonging to the commercial bourgeoisie. After her father's death in 1927 brought financial ruin to the family, she studied at the Normal School to prepare for a teaching career, and began her first teaching job in the Asturian village of Nava in 1936, in the highly politicized atmosphere following the outbreak of the Civil War. Imbued with her studies of contemporary psychology, the philosophy of Ortega, and experimental pedagogy, she attempted to initiate new methodologies which met with distrust and suspicion of Marxist taints, for which reason she was suspended the same year. Reinstated in 1940, she taught some five years until winning her first literary prize for a story in 1945, at which time she moved to Madrid to attempt to establish herself as a writer. For the next several years she studied journalism, supported herself by newspaper work, and undertook advanced studies in pedagogy. Her first major success came when her autobiographical novel, *Nosotros los Rivero* (1953; We Riveros) won the Nadal Prize. A complete study of Medio's life and works up to the early 1970s is available in Margaret Jones's *Dolores Medio* (New York: Twayne Publishers, 1974).

Funcionario público (1956; City Employee), one of the better achievements of the "social" novel, relates the plight of Pablo Marín, a poorly paid telegraph operator in Madrid, who lives with his wife Teresa in a sub-let room, suffering economic hardships and postwar shortages of housing and opportunity, until he is rendered impotent by the fear of having a child (the landlady will not allow children and they have nowhere else to go). He escapes from the grim realities of daily routine by fantasizing about a young woman whose diary he chances to find, overlooking the growing frustration of Teresa until finally she leaves him. Unlike most documentary social literature, this novel had a tangible impact, resulting in a pay raise for communications workers.[2] *El pez sigue flotando* (1959; The Fish Keeps Floating), Medio's third novel, presents a microcosm of Madrid via a vision of the tangential lives of characters in ten flats of a Madrid apartment building. The stories are fragmented, the reader's vision often not extending beyond what might be visible from one of the apartment windows. Essentially realistic, in spite of the experimental technique, this novel emphasizes once again the economic strictures of a majority of the characters, financial worries and deprivation, as well as isolation, loneliness, disillusionment, and emotional frustration. *Diario de una maestra* (1961: A Schoolteacher's Diary), considered one of Medio's most significant works, is frequently autobiographical, reflecting the novelist's own experiences, attitudes, personality, and philosophy, with a thin literary disguise. *Atrapados en la ratonera. Memorias de una novelista* (1980; Caught in the Mousetrap. A Novelist's Memoir) which covers many of the same years in Medio's life, allows the critic to compare autobiography with fictional disguise.[3] *Diario* spans a period from the protagonist's university studies and the beginning of her romantic liaison with her professor, Máximo Sáenz, until some eleven or twelve years later, when Max is released from political prison some eight years after the end of the Civil War. In the interim occurs the teacher's experience in the village, her conflict with the reactionary attitudes and suspension from her post, her attempts during the war to rejoin Max, and later her work in a war hospital in Oviedo. Surviving via a variety of jobs until restored to her teaching position, she continues to sacrifice in order to send tobacco and food to Max in prison, living for the day of his release. When at last the longed-for reunion arrives, Max is beaten, aged, disillusioned, and no longer interested in a life together. He stays barely long enough to inform her that he is going to America, leaving her stunned. On the verge of suicide, she is recalled to her pedagogical obligations by a handicapped child she had been helping.

Bibiana (1963), first volume of the trilogy *Los que vamos a pie* (Pedestrians), takes its title from the name of its protagonist, a rather simple, middle-class Barcelona housewife whose life revolves around her husband and children. Emphasis is placed upon daily routine, including many household chores—cleaning, cooking, marketing, doing the laundry—and Bibiana's relationships with her husband and adolescent offspring, who all somewhat look down on her, seldom realizing how they depend on her. There are few breaks in Bibiana's routine, except when she is inadvertently involved in a political meeting (a reflection of Medio's own experience, which landed her in jail), and another time when she is interviewed for a radio program. *La otra circunstancia* (1973; The Other Circumstance), a continuation of the trilogy, shifts its focus from Bibiana to her husband, Marcelo, and presents a later period of relative ease when economic hardships have given way to a certain prosperity and consumerism. Other problems appear, however, especially for Bibiana, with her daughter's corruption and husband's disaffection. To date, the trilogy has not been completed.

Also in 1973, Medio published *Farsa de verano* (Summer Farce), a novel resembling *El pez sigue flotando* (The Fish Keeps Floating) in its bringing together of a diverse group of unrelated people in the same space and time. Vacationers on a package tour are portrayed with their individual stories, preoccupations, and characters. Their realistic, everyday lives are interrupted unexpectedly by a tragic accident. *El fabuloso imperio de Juan sin tierra* (1981; The Fabulous Empire of Juan the Landless) is Medio's latest novel to date. Set in an Asturian village, it portrays the return of a long-absent former villager about whom many stories circulate. The emigrant's reappearance provides a pretext for re-creating memorable events of earlier years via conversations and recollections with residents Juan had known when an adolescent. Somewhat in the vein of Delibes' novel, *El camino,* with its evocative reconstruction of village personalities and relationships, anecdotes, and speech, this work of Medio's excels in its capture of colloquial, regional conversation and humble slice-of-life human interest stories. Medio has also published several collections of short stories, including *Compás de espera* (1954; Waiting Time), marked by its preoccupation with social inequities, class divisions and prejudices, economic injustices, and victimization of the weak by those more fortunate. *El bachancho* (1974), another story collection, includes many previously published in defunct magazines, mostly on social themes and depicting the problems of the poor from a realistic standpoint. Three novelettes or long stories—two published some years earlier—appear in *El urogallo* (1982; The Partridge). The title novelette relates the capture of a Republican guerrilla in the Civil War by baiting a trap with his fiancée (an allusion to a hunting technique in which the female is similarly used). *Mañana* (Tomorrow), first published in 1954, presents a young woman trapped in a monotonous existence who has her unexpected opportunity for a better life with a man ruined by ironic chance. *El señor García,* the third novelette of the collection, originally appeared in 1966, and like *Funcionario público,* depicts the plight of an underpaid office worker. García is led to believe that he will be promoted to office manager, resulting in the raise in the value of his personal stock and some limited adulation from co-workers. Ironically, the position goes to a relative of the boss and García returns to his dull existence with his deflated hopes.

Medio is not feminist by ideology, but with her emphasis on class and social issues, together with the female role model presented by her resolutely independent single protagonists in *Nosotros, los Rivero, El pez sigue flotando,* and *Diario de una maestra,* she makes more of a feminist statement than most of the women who precede her. Significantly, also, she is the only woman writer of her generation to transcend stereotyping of the "old maid" and to present the single state in a positive light.[4] Intellectual integrity and altruistic dedication to the collective good within the realistic critical tradition are hallmarks of Medio's career, followed by a keen appreciation of the ironics of everyday life, the contradictions of emotions and decision.

A Psychological Realist

Born in Santander in 1921, Elena Quiroga lost her mother at the age of two, and spent her early years with her father in a small Galician village (El Barco de Valdeorras [Orense]), two facts of great impact on her fiction. Educated for six years in a Catholic boarding school in Bilbao, she completed her high school education in Rome, but from very early in life read widely in her father's and grandfather's library, acquiring a literary culture most unusual for the times, the more so for girls. Quiroga's reading and her familiarity with developments in European and American fiction play an important role in her development as a novelist, especially in her successful adaptation of experiments initiated elsewhere, by William Faulkner in particular. Quiroga's self-discipline and will to excellence, her use of essentially different forms in each of her works, and constant self-improvement resulted in her being the second woman elected to the Royal Spanish Academy, in 1983. Her first novel, *La soledad sonora* (1949; Sonorous Solitude), an immature and sometimes melodramatic love story, is set against the background of the Spanish Civil War and the Spanish volunteers in the "Blue Division," who fought with the Nazis on the Russian front. A complete treatment of Quiroga's life and works through 1976 is available in Phyllis Zatlin Boring's *Elena Quiroga* (Boston: G. K. Hall, 1977).

Viento del norte (1951; Northwind) won the then-prestigious Nadal Prize (first awarded to Laforet for *Nada*). Set in rural Galicia during the pre-Civil War period, it presents a penetrating study of Marcela, a peasant girl abandoned at birth, and Alvaro, the wealthy landowner in whose home she was raised. A later May-September marriage (accepted by Marcela because she believes she must obey the master's wishes) produces a son but no communication between the couple, and further distancing occurs after Alvaro is confined to a wheelchair and Marcela begins to spend the afternoons with Alvaro's aunt and cousin, Lucía, on a neighboring estate, while he is visited by the doctor, priest, and judge. However, the latter follows Marcela in an effort to seduce her, and too late she realizes her love and respect for her husband and protector, rushing home to find that he has died, alone. Although flawed by a slightly melodramatic ending, Northwind is a better novel than many contemporary critics seemed to think. Well received in Galicia, it was termed anachronistic by many observers, who saw it as either a form of rural naturalism or influenced by romanticism. Quiroga herself was more than a little embarrassed by what she considered to be amateurish early efforts[5] and began investigations into narrative theory and structure. Her traditional beginnings thus afforded little warning of the experiments to follow.

La sangre (1952; Blood) is unique in being narrated by a tree, an ancient chestnut situated outside the ancestral home of a family of rural Galician nobility. Something of a family chronicle, the narrative traces the fortunes of several generations from the tree's limited perspective (only what it can "see," hear, and understand), meaning that when the characters move outside the tree's radius of observation, they disappear from the narrative and no conclusions are drawn about their activities in the interim. The culminating events, which include the end of the tree and the extinction of the family line, take place shortly before the outbreak of the Civil War.

Algo pasa en la calle (1954; Something's Happening in the Street) is experimental in that it has a dead protagonist, awaiting burial when the novel begins. The reader must reconstruct Ventura's personality and, in so doing, decide whether his death was an accident or suicide, by combining, comparing, and evaluating the partial perspectives of the other characters. Set in Madrid during the 1950s, the novel was daring in treating a taboo subject, divorce or the lack of it, through a retrospective evocation of the past of the major characters. Ventura, a university professor, had an incompatible marriage with Esperanza (so egotistical that she was jealous of her husband's affection for their daughter, and later behaved as her daughter's rival, flirting with her son-in-law). During the years of the Republic, when divorce was legal, he left (the novelist avoids mention of the word *divorce*, but presumably the marriage was terminated). The Franco regime reversed the reforms of the Republic, and held divorces invalid (arguing that only the "civil" aspect of the contract could be abrogated; the religious aspect continued in force and thus remarriage became impossible). Esperanza told their daughter, Agata, that Ventura had died and refused to let him see the child.

After some years, Ventura had an affair with one of his students, Presencia; they were "married" in a civil ceremony (considered concubinage under the Franco regime), and had a son, Asís, who is unaware of his parents' legal relationship until the "legitimate" family appears at the wake. Quiroga contrasts the two wives (Presencia seems calculated to be the exact opposite of Esperanza) and establishes a situation where the officially sanctioned marriage appears to have been far more immoral than the unrecognized one, which is a model of domestic and Christian virtues. The shifting, fragmented perspectives (presented in stream-of-consciousness fashion) require considerable effort and con-

centration by the reader who wishes to reconstruct events, and attention is drawn to the matter of the possible suicide (which is left
unclarified), two techniques allowing the novelist to distract the attention of the censors from the subtext.

La enferma (1955; The Sick Woman) is a variation on the technique
of the dead protagonist: Liberata, the sick woman, is confined to her
bed throughout the novel and never speaks (since a disappointment in
love years before, she has refused to say a word or leave her bed). Again,
the reader must combine several partial and incomplete perspectives
presented in stream-of-consciousness style and attempt to construct a
complete version of events, as well as reach a conclusion on the relative
rightness or wrongness of Liberata and her onetime boyfriend, Telmo
(who emigrated and married someone else). A second story line concerns the narrator, a woman from Madrid who is in the Galician fishing
village to settle an estate, who experiences something of an epiphany
regarding her own stagnant marriage and ritualized social life but is
unable to adhere to her resolve to change. Perspectives are polarized in
two factions, pro-Telmo and pro-Liberata, so that some of the "middle-
of-the-road" viewpoints present in the previous novel are missing here.

Quiroga again uses the stream-of-consciousness technique in *La careta* (1955; The Mask), a psychological analysis of the protagonist,
Moisés, alienated since the brutal killing of his parents during the Civil
War which he witnessed as a child of ten or twelve. Treated by relatives
as a martyr and hero, he is an amoral egotist whose dreadful secret is
slowly revealed as the novel progresses: although wounded, his mother
had not died when shot by the terrorists who killed his father. Instead,
she bled to death or was asphyxiated by Moisés in his efforts to keep
her from calling for help (out of fear the murderers would return and
find him). A hedonist whose search for pleasure is futile, he does not
manage even to enjoy his visits to prostitutes or his drinking. Beneath
a mask of innocence, he develops as a sadist who enjoys the subtle
psychological torture of his relatives, taunting one cousin who is childless with past complicity in an abortion, humiliating another admiring
cousin by forcing him to share his lover, goading the hapless "rival" to
kill him. Although Moisés apparently plans his own death as a form
of suicide, he changes his mind and kills the cousin in "self-defense."
The novel is imbued with existentialist philosophy, and the concept of
inauthenticity becomes a leitmotiv (the ironic significance of the title
is obvious). Several women are portrayed in the novel, but all data—
excepting conversations—reach the reader through the filter of Moisés's

consciousness. Thus, only his opinions are available, and given his psychological makeup, he is unlikely to be a reliable narrator.[6]

Plácida, la joven, y otras narraciones (1956; Young Plácida and Other Tales) includes two additional novelettes previously published separately, *La otra ciudad* (1953; The Other City) and *Trayecto Uno* (1953; Bus One). The latter, much like Medio's *El pez sigue flotando,* brings together a heterogeneous group of characters with no other relationship between them than their occupying the same space for a given time, in this case, a bus on the route passing Quiroga's house the afternoon of 15 January 1953. Her primary interest is depiction of the passengers, although the technique is less psychological this time than objectivist. *La otra ciudad,* also set in Madrid, is more subjective, concentrating on the development of four characters. The title alludes to a cemetery just outside the city limits, and the characters are Tomás, the groundskeeper, his two sons, Marcos (who has managed through study to become a pediatrician) and Esteban, and Cruz—the latter's fiancée—a telephone operator and an orphan, who has difficulty communicating her feelings. There is no plot in the traditional sense, although Marcos (the best developed character) undergoes a sort of religious conversion as a result of his suffering over patients he was unable to save. Young Plácida, an orphaned Galician peasant who dies in childbirth at the age of twenty, is the central figure of this third novelette, which begins with her death. Quiroga dedicates the novelette to Plácida (a real-life character) and all Galician women, thinking especially of their enduring patience and their difficult lives. No less than four characters, including the narrator, have lost their mothers at birth. Plácida was raised by neighbors, always had to work, never had possessions of her own, and married Salvador when already pregnant with his child. In order to support his family, he went to sea, and Plácida was alone when the baby came. Plácida does not summon help until she has been in labor for some time, and the village women do not call a doctor until alarmed by her pallor when she has almost bled to death. The doctor's diatribe is an indirect revelation of both the stoicism and self-sufficiency of the peasant women, accustomed not to seek help until it is a matter of life and death. Nora considers this Quiroga's best novelette; it is certain to be of particular interest to feminist readers.[7]

La última corrida (1958; The Last Bullfight) is unquestionably Quiroga's most "fictional" work, set outside the regions with which she is most familiar, her usual settings (Madrid, Galicia, Santander), and having as its protagonist a bullfighter—aged, unglamorous, injured at the end of a mediocre career. Although much of the novel is dialogue, or third-person, external description in the objectivist vein, Quiroga also gives attention to the internal subjectivity of her characters, principally three bullfighters who represent three ages, three approaches to the sport, and three stages in their careers. However interesting and successful as a literary exercise (by which Quiroga presumably demonstrated that she could handle a topic that was manifestly not a "woman's theme"), *La última corrida* has little relevance for the feminist critic, although there are portrayals of Manuel's relationship with Prado (a prostitute), and his marriage to Clementa.

Tristura (1960; Sadness) employs the Galician dialect for its title, rather than taking it from Castilian. Despite the importance of Galicia in her fiction, however, Quiroga has never written in Gallego. This novel won the prestigious Critics' Prize for the year of publication and, together with its sequel, constitutes what may be Quiroga's most significant contribution. Tadea the protagonist, may be considered in some aspects a mask of the author: they are the same age, raised partly by a father in rural Galicia and partly by a repressive grandmother in Santander, and attended, then withdrew from, Catholic boarding schools. The autobiographical substrata allows Quiroga to present with full accuracy and intensity the atmosphere in which Spanish girls of the upper middle class were raised and educated in the 1920s and 1930s. From the perspective of the protagonist—a little girl when the novelistic series begins—Quiroga depicts the social and religious conformity and hypocrisy of Spain's provinces in an impeccable style. The problems of growing up female are developed as part of the themes of absence and silence, interwoven into a larger bildungsroman formed by this novel and its sequel, *Escribo tu nombre* (1965; I Write Your Name), a title taken from a longer epigraph which reads in full, "On the private-school notebooks, Liberty, I write your name." A number of projected continuations of the Tadea series have not yet appeared. *Escribo tu nombre* is Quiroga's longest work. It provides a portrayal, as detailed and convincing as it is lengthy, of the ambient of a convent school and the community around it. The backlash provoked by the liberal tolerance of the Mother Superior provides a thumbnail sketch of the causes of the Civil War, and the school itself may be considered a microcosm of the society as a whole. Daring not only in its expression of a muted cry for freedom but as a hitherto nonexistent depiction of female sexuality, *Escribo tu nombre* may well be Quiroga's masterpiece, and its importance was fittingly recognized when it was selected to represent Spain in the first international Rómulo Gallegos contest for novels in Spanish.

Presente profundo (1973; Profound Present) is one of Quiroga's most philosophical works, influenced by ideas of all time as present, and Hegel's concept of reality (as seen by the readings of Rubén, sometimes narrator). Juxtaposing the stories of the suicides of two very different women, the novel provides a significant and probing analysis of their lives and of the feminine condition. So different are the women involved that it may well be that they were intended to be seen as a composite symbol of all women. Daría is an older Galician woman, a baker's wife neglected emotionally and physically and finally cast aside for a younger female, who one day simply walks into the sea when her children, too, forget her. Blanca, a cosmopolitan young divorcée, the daughter of international millionaires from Brazil, is separated from the child she loves, lives for a while in Madrid, and drifts into the drug culture, eventually dying from an overdose while staying in a hippie commune in Holland. These two extreme examples of the feminine condition are linked by the personality of a young doctor who happened to have contact with both of them. As an existentialist, he points out the vital significance of death, and meditates upon the complexity of time, the spirit, and the eternal scheme of things, relating them to the reality of the two women. Another philosophical element introduced by Quiroga comes from Oriental religions and the concepts of transmigration of souls or reincarnation. Daría's daughter-in-law, Amelia, is her continuation to such an extent that she seems to undergo a personality change after Daría's suicide and is taken over by her spirit, even taking on her physical appearance. Blanca's hippie lover is her continuation, as he carries out the plans she had made with him. Quiroga develops a narrative counterpoint between the two women, between Galicia and the urban world beyond, between present and eternity, that subtly underscores the all-inclusive nature of the symbolic extremes.

A Subjective Stylist with a Social Conscience

Ana María Matute was born in Barcelona in 1926 to an upper-middle-class family. Her father was a Catalan industrialist, her mother Castilian, and exposure to both linguistic cultures marked her childhood. The Civil War, which broke out when she was ten, deeply

scarred her psyche, and has left many traces in her fiction. Her schooling was interrupted by the war, and only two years after resuming
formal education in 1939, Matute left school to devote herself to the
study of painting and to write. She is primarily an intuitive writer,
often lyrical and intensely subjective, with occasional subtle expres-
sionistic touches. As is the case with many postwar writers, Matute
frequently makes orphans her protagonists, thereby symbolizing their
solitude, alienation, and vulnerability. Most of her major characters are
children or adolescents; the rare adult protagonists are usually engaged
in retrospective recall of childhood and adolescent episodes. The myth
of Cain and Abel, symbolizing the endemic causes of the Civil War
(conflict between brothers), is an obsessive motif in her fiction. Seldom
does Matute portray women in the role of wives or mothers, and when
she does, they are minor characters. Rarely, if ever, are they happily
married, and often they are widows. Motherhood is portrayed not as
fulfillment but the cause of endless sacrifice. The unbroken family is a
rarity in Matute's fiction, and happiness beyond the charmed fantasy
world of childhood is fleeting if it exists at all. Her typical protagonist
is an androgynous, half-tamed, and rebellious adolescent, usually with
a Peter Pan complex. Most often her narratives trace the passage to
adulthood, the loss of innocence, illusions, or idealism constituting the
essential core of a pre-adult mentality. The character who has surren-
dered to materialism, conventionalism, or practicality ceases to interest
Matute.[8]

Los Abel (1948; The Abel Family), her first published novel, uses a
diary format to update the biblical myth of the struggle between brothers (in this case, for the family lands and the same woman) as seen by
a sister. The girl's maturation parallels the growing rivalry and disintegrating family situation, culminating in a violent and bloody con-
frontation between the two oldest brothers, after which the narrative
is abruptly suspended. In *Pequeño teatro* (1954; Little Theater) written
earlier but delayed in publication, Matute utilizes motifs drawn from
the commedia dell'arte to suggest the Benavente theme of vested interests which allow people to be manipulated as puppets are moved by
strings. The plot involves the arrival of Marco, a bizarre but attractive
stranger to a Basque fishing village; only alienated Zazu is able to see
that he is a confidence man, and even she is hypnotized by his mag-
netism. By subtle suggestion it is intimated that Zazu is a nympho-
maniac, the town scandal (but tolerated because of her father's wealth).
Enslaved by her own sexuality, Zazu has kept her heart untouched;

when she senses the danger of being conquered by Marco, she walks off the end of the breakwater into the wild sea.

Fiesta al noroeste (1952; Celebration in the Northwest) is a symbolic novelette representing the conflicting forces in the Civil War via a Cain-Abel dichotomy. Juan Medinao, the elder, deformed, legitimate son, represents the landed aristocracy, church, and capitalism (the forces supporting Franco) as well as *caciquismo* (corrupt local political bossism), while his handsome illegitimate half-brother Pablo, the "disinherited," is associated with labor movements and nascent socialism. Most of the novel is presented as a confession by Juan (who suffers a latent homosexual attraction toward Pablo, an obsessive need to possess and control him). Wealthy Juan buys Pablo's sweetheart from her destitute parents, hoping to use her as bait to bring Pablo to his house but the strategem fails, and later he rapes Pablo's mother, thereby symbolically possessing him. The depiction of Juan's mother's desperate unhappiness, her helpless rage at his father's philandering, her loneliness, vulnerability, and ultimate suicide are among Matute's most memorable treatments of a minor character. Women appear merely as pawns in a game where all the stakes are held by men.

En esta tierra (1955; In This Land) is the revised, cut version of *Las luciérnagas* (The Fireflies), prohibited by censorship. Soledad, daughter of a bourgeois Barcelona family, sees their world destroyed by the Civil War. During a bombardment she is thrown together with Cristián, trapped in ruins, and later unable to locate any of her family. The two teenagers end up living together, and when the Franco forces arrive, they are jailed. In the censored third part Soledad gives birth to a son while in jail, and Cristián, unable to support them, is caught stealing to provide medicine for his son and sentenced to prison. Soledad moves near the prison camp with her son to be near Cristián, but suffers hunger and many hardships, reflecting a less-than-ideal world under the new regime (even for those who had been noncombatants, and in spite of the fact that Soledad's family belonged to a class that supported Franco). In this case (unusual for Matute's fiction) where marriage seems to have been freely chosen by the parties, external circumstances intervene to interfere with happiness.

Matute's longest and most ambitious novel, *Los hijos muertos* (1958; *The Lost Children*, 1965), is another attempt to explain some of the underlying causes of the Civil War in terms of individual passions and frustrations, placed in the context of a family conflict. Portraying three generations of the Corvo family (who acquire wealth in the nineteenth century but lose most of it in the twentieth), the novel embodies opposing sets of values in the characters. Especially important are the conflicts between youth and age, between conventionalism and authenticity, between materialism and idealism. The older generation is characteristically defeated, disillusioned, and sterile, while the promise of the younger generation is not realized, being crushed by the weight of tradition, inertia, circumstance. Matute creates a counterpoint between past and present, rural Castilla and urban Barcelona, youth and age, haves and have-nots, "Establishment" and the hope of renewal. Among a vast canvas of characters, especially important are Veronica and Daniel who elope shortly before the war (she is killed, together with her unborn child, in an air raid, while he spends many years at forced labor in the mines), and Mónica and Miguel, who represent the youth of the postwar generation (she belongs to the rural gentry, he to urban delinquents). The conversations between the aged Daniel and the chief of the penal colony where Miguel is a prisoner constitute an effort to go beyond the hurts and rancors of war, in which both had lost children (hence the title) and reach reconciliation. Meanwhile, injustice continues, and Miguel (who is a victim of the system) is killed in an escape attempt. Matute's most successful and lauded work, this novel won the Critics' Prize for 1958 as the best novel of the year and in 1959 was awarded the National Literary Prize "Miguel de Cervantes." Probably on the strength of this achievement, Matute received a grant from the Fundación March to work on her trilogy, "Los mercaderes" (The Merchants).

Matute wrote a good many works for children during these years, for which she received international recognition, and also published several collections of stories. *Los niños tontos* (1956; The Stupid Children) contains twenty-one lyric sketches, approaching the prose poem, frequently fantastic, and all dealing with children, many of whom die or disappear, often as the result of some traumatic disillusionment. *El tiempo* (1957; Time) is a heterogeneous group of previously published tales, many with social themes. *Historias de la Artámila* (1961; Tales of Artámila) is unified by the common geographical setting also portrayed in *Los Abel* and *Los hijos muertos,* the Castilian mountain village where Matute's maternal grandparents had an estate. The tales deal for the most part with the hard lot of the peasants, childhood discoveries of social inequity and injustice, or the loss of illusion. *Libro de juegos para los niños de los otros* (1961; Book of Games for the Others' Children) is not really for children: it concerns the "games people play" in society to perpetuate discrimination, class prejudice, divisiveness, and resentment. *Tres y un sueño* (1961; Three [Fantasies] and One Dream), a trio of novelettes, is Matute's least accessible work because of the often hermetic symbolism and the highly personal nature of the fantasy worlds portrayed. The protagonists have in common a childlike mentality and total alienation from the adult world, and illustrate Matute's conviction that childhood and adulthood are totally separate and distinct forms of existence. *El arrepentido* (1961; The Repentant One) also collects a number of tales published earlier, and reiterates Matute's obsessive themes: the Civil War, social injustice, the fantasy world of childhood, alienated adults. *Algunos muchachos* (1965; Some Kids) is her finest collection of brief fiction, with a great deal of variety on the level of plot and technique but a consistent repetition of her characteristic themes: the alienated individual (often set against the social structure), social injustice, the loss of childhood and/or innocence.

Primera memoria (1960; *School of the Sun,* 1963), the first volume of the trilogy "Los mercaderes," won the 1959 Nadal Prize. Returning to the Cain and Abel myth, it provides a symbolic and miniaturized portrayal of the Civil War from the distant and supposedly peaceful haven of the Balearic Islands. The adolescent narrator, Matia, whose father is in the Loyalist army, is living with her grandmother (a representative of the old order, reactionary and traditional, of wealth and *caciquismo*) and her cousin Borja, whose father is with the Franco rebels. In the form of a memoir written years later by the mature Matia, the protagonist retraces a number of discoveries: sordid adult sexuality, death, treachery and betrayal, and her own cowardice. The idealized figure of Manuel (who represents victims of exploitation and discrimination) has parallels with portrayals of Christ and His passion.

Los soldados lloran de noche (1964; The Soldiers Cry by Night) takes place shortly before the end of the war, beginning with Manuel's release from the reformatory to which Borja's treachery had sent him. In prison, Manuel has been influenced by the aura surrounding a man called Jeza, a Communist organizer who was executed and who comes to represent for Manuel real, uncompromising idealism. He seeks out Jeza's widow, Marta, to learn more of him, and in extended conversation hears of her sordid life with an abusive mother who ran a tavern and apparently dealt in drugs and contraband. Escaping from a lesbian admirer of her mother (who was apparently bisexual), Marta ran away with the mother's young lover, Raúl, Jeza's brother. When Raúl abandoned her, she was rescued from her depraved existence by Jeza.

Marta and Manuel agree to try to complete Jeza's last mission, taking certain documents to the mainland to be turned over to his comrades there, although both realize that it may be suicidal. Under cover of fog, in a small boat, they reach Barcelona only hours before the arrival of the Franco forces. Believing that it is better to die for an ideal, even someone else's, than to live without one, they occupy an abandoned machine-gun post on the road taken by the advancing army, where they are slain. Matute divides humanity into two groups in "Los mercaderes," the merchants (the vast majority) and the heroes (a few idealists). Marta and Manuel illustrate the latter category with their total reunciation of self-interest.

La trampa (1969; The Trap) returns to the island of Majorca and the original cast seen in *School of the Sun,* some twenty-five years later. Matia, fortyish and discontent after a life of futile searching for love, responds to the summons to her hated grandmother's centennial celebration (actually her 99th birthday). New characters introduced include Matia's university-age son, Bear, and Mario, the supposedly idealistic revolutionary who has recruited him for a mission on the island. To provide a hiding place for the terrorist until time to strike, Bear plants Mario in his mother's room, counting on their becoming lovers (as happens). Becoming fond of Matia, Mario repents of his plan to use her son in what is actually a personal vengeance (the intended victim is not a key politician but the man who killed Mario's father years before). Arriving unexpectedly, Bear overhears Mario tell his mother there will be no assassination, but leaves before learning why, carrying out the deed himself. He makes no effort to conceal his identity, as he intends to ruin the hated family of his mother (grandmother, Borja, and others). Contrasting youth and age, materialism and idealism once more, Matute seems somehow less dualistic than in the first two parts of the trilogy, for here the idealists are misguided and the cause is decidedly tarnished.

La torre vigía (1971; The Watch-Tower) is seemingly an enormous departure from Matute's established patterns, a neochivalric novel, set in the tenth century in an unnamed part of central Europe. A never-completed novel (announced for publication in 1976 or 1977) to be entitled *Olvidado Rey Gudú* (Forgotten King Gudu) also utilizes a tenth-century setting.[9] The Watch-Tower is narrated by a disembodied voice, belonging to the spirit of a young squire killed by his jealous older brothers on the eve of being knighted (a variation of the Cain and Abel theme). Once again, Matute traces the clash of idealism and materialism of the most sordid and degenerate sort. The young squire is sent to be raised in the baron's castle, a symbolic voyage of discovery, the discovery of evil. Slowly he realizes that the lord and lady are closer to ogres than knightly models: apparently they prey upon adolescents of both sexes. The abyss between chivalric ideal and human reality so disillusions the youthful protagonist that during his vigil in the chapel, he determines he will renounce knighthood and never be a warlord. It is as he leaves the chapel to talk to the enigmatic and visionary watchman in the tower (to which the title refers) that he is stabbed by his brothers. The novel has many apocalyptic motifs befitting its millennial chronology, the most important being an allegorical battle between the forces of good and evil, first in the spirit of the young protagonist, and second in the visions of the watchman. His visions seem to come straight from the Book of Revelations, with diabolic monsters and mighty, metaphysical combats between black and white armies, and many signs and omens of the end of the world. The apocalyptic thematics provide a link with Maria Aurèlia Capmany's *Quim/Quimà*, which begins in the tenth century and covers up to the Spanish Civil War. Matute perceives many similarities between the tenth century (as she envisions it) and the contemporary period, which explains her interest. Unfortunately, she has not been well for several years, and her writing has suffered.

Philologist, Scholar, Theorist, and Feminist

Carmen Martín Gaite was born in Salamanca in 1925, and obtained her doctorate in Romance Philology at the University of Madrid. She first became known as a member of the Mid-Century Generation of social realists, as was her former husband, novelist Rafael Sánchez Ferlosio. Her first literary success at twenty-nine came with the sophisticated and enigmatic novelette, *El balneario* (1954; The Spa), recognized by the Cafe Gijón Prize, an accolade of fellow writers and intellectuals. The narrator-protagonist, Matilde, a drab woman of indefinite age and timid manners, tells of arriving on a bus with her husband at a huge, labyrinthine, kafkaesque mineral spa, apparently far from town. Her perceptions of the building are confused, the husband's behavior contradictory, and she is so disoriented that the reader eventually begins to doubt the reliability of the narrator. Is she paranoid, hallucinating, perhaps drugged? Could the rambling corridors with rows of doors and uniformed personnel be a hospital, an asylum? Martín Gaite skillfully manipulates the transitions from one plane to another of the interior monologue as situations become increasingly surrealistic and bizarre, until at last it is revealed (when she awakes screaming) that Matilde has been dreaming. A second part narrated by an objective, omniscient voice allows the reader to contrast the dull, monotonous reality of Matilde's waking world with the adventure of the dream, the one opportunity she has to be a protagonist.[10]

Entre visillos (1957; Between the Blinds), which won the Nadal Prize, is an authentic depiction of the life of girls growing up in a provincial city in postwar Spain. The title refers to the jalousies covering the windows, symbolic bars on the cages in which females were confined. Martín Gaite utilizes a shifting narrative perspective, beginning with a young German who arrives to teach in the high school, and who permits her to bring to bear an objective and sometimes ironically bewildered viewpoint. Through him the reader visits the casino and meets the singer, a "liberated" woman for the times since she supports herself and defies convention, but she is ostracized by "decent" society, considered much worse than she actually is, for she dreams quite conventionally of marriage. The major focus is upon one of the German teacher's students (a secondary narrative consciousness) and her family. A girl of fifteen whose mother has died, she lives with her father, older sisters, and a maiden aunt. The aunt's life consists of going almost daily to Mass, and receiving visits from ladies her own age; the older sister, nearing thirty, perceives with horror that she may be condemned to the same kind of existence, and grows progressively more embittered and desperate. The middle sister has a fiancé who has gone to Madrid to establish himself professionally, whom she sees infrequently, always going to confession afterward, tormented by her response to his kisses and caresses. An ongoing argument revolves around her going to Madrid, to live with relatives and study at the university in order to be near him. Torn by ambivalence, she both wants to go and is terrified at the thought, at the risk it represents and what people will surely say. Afraid to broach the matter with her father, she quarrels with her fiancé who insists that if she loves him, she will make the effort to be together. Finally it is the little sister (her father's favorite) who dares to bring up the question, planning to join her at the university in another year when she has finished her secondary schooling.

The novel is especially revealing of provincial attitudes toward education for women, the negative extreme being the case of Gertrudis, another high school student, who becomes engaged to an aviator although she is only fifteen. He is delighted with her youth and naïveté, considering it a guarantee of her virginity (the most important qualities he seeks in a wife are physical beauty and innocence, defined as never having had a boyfriend). With her parents' approval, he insists on an early wedding and does not want Gertrudis to finish high school, saying that for what he wants, she has no need of algebra. An older sister who married against the parents' wishes appears at the wedding— badly dressed, pregnant again, and visibly aged: life has become a succession of childhood diseases and her husband has already tired of her (they quarrel, she is becoming unattractive, and her life is limited to other housewives whose conversation never transcends the bounds of hairdos and maids, husbands and manicures, children and clothes). Certainly, marriage is not idealized, no matter how desperately the unmarried females in the novel seek it. In addition to a fascinating and impressively real gallery of feminine characters, Martín Gaite sketches the daily life of the provincial city, especially its social customs and the regimented, ritualized relationships between the sexes. No overt criticism is made, nor is it necessary: the stifling, restrictive atmosphere speaks eloquently for itself.

Las ataduras (1960; Bonds) is a novelette that has been published separately and also in editions with several short stories. Exploring the possibilities open to women, it is presented from the perspective of a relatively "liberated" female, the only daughter of a teacher, who escapes a smothering provincial existence much like the one described in *Entre visillos,* and studies in Madrid where she becomes involved with a French intellectual and runs away to Paris. Having attempted to avoid dull domesticity and married life, she soon finds herself a mother of two, living much the sort of life she thought she was escaping—but far from her supportive family and without the security marriage might have provided. Early in the narrative there is a significant scene when a former friend and childhood playmate comes to say goodbye: he is emigrating to America, and she wistfully expresses a desire for similar freedom, only to be told that it is women's role to stay behind.

Ritmo lento (1962; Slow Motion) has as its protagonist a young man, David, who is out of step with contemporary society. An embodiment of the alienation of many intellectuals, he is frustrated, anguished by his solitude, unable to communicate. Unhappy and apathetic, he suffers from abulia, indecisiveness, and weakness of will. The action is internal, consisting of the thoughts of David, who has been confined to an asylum for the mentally ill. Other characters are seen from his perspective, via flashbacks (and he may be an unreliable narrator).[11] A complex, synchronic psychological exploration of a superior character, the novel manages to suggest that there is no place for such persons in society, and that uncompromising principles may be seen as insanity. Effects of the Civil War appear in David's recollections of the ruins of Madrid and allusions to poverty and hunger. Always conscious of the passage of time, he hates the haste of the rest of the world, and criticizes the tyranny of money and others' obsession with success (but he is obsessed with their obsession). The character does allow Martín Gaite to criticize contemporary values with a certain impunity (it could always be argued that he was crazy), and among things criticized are social customs, the army, the pedagogical methods in use, and various traditions.

Around the time she finished *Ritmo lento* Martín Gaite began to frequent the Madrid Atheneum, which has an excellent private library. She became interested in history, particularly of the eighteenth century. Out of her investigations came a number of essays, including *Usos amorosos del dieciocho en España* (1973; Amorous Behavior in Eighteenth-Century Spain) that would be relevant for a feminist history. During a prolonged narrative silence she published a number of critical articles and a collection entitled *La búsqueda de interlocutor y otras búsquedas* (1975; The Search for an Interlocutor and Other Searches), with especially interesting insights into her narrative theory. *A rachas* (1976), a slim volume of poetry, provides a very personal record of intimate thoughts, not originally intended for publication. Martín Gaite's short fiction (stories previously appended to the editions of *El balneario* and *Las ataduras*) appeared in paperback as her *Cuentos completos* (1978; Complete Stories). Rounding out the list of miscellany is the author's first novel for children, *El castillo de las tres murallas* (1981; The Castle With Three Walls), a lyrical fairy tale.[12]

Retahílas (1974; Threads) is one of Martín Gaite's most successful narrative achievements and was well received by the critics. Begun in 1965 and completed the last day of 1973, it repeats various constants of the writer. An introspective and retrospective novel in *tempo lento*, *Retahílas* reiterates Martín Gaite's interest in the feminine condition and her preoccupation with the destruction wrought by passing time, as well as exploring the potential for human communication. Like Juan Benet, she demonstrates an interest in the bases of individual consciousness, sensations, perceptions, sensorial data. Eulalia, a mature woman, educated, well traveled, and separated from her husband, drops in on her grandmother and finds her dying. She accedes to the old woman's last wish, to be taken to Galicia to her ancestral home (where Eulalia had spent her childhood). A message sent to her brother asking him to accompany her results in the arrival of her nephew, Germán. *Retahílas* is the story of a dialogue or, to be more exact, extended alternating parallel monologues held throughout an interminable night as they await the arrival of death. In their reconstruction of an irrecoverable past, exploring the dark corners of memory, a dialectic of silence and communication is developed, with the phenomenon of discourse itself occupying center stage.

Fragmentos de interior (1976; Glimpses of an Interior) depicts the environment of a middle-class family in Madrid at the time of writing. All members of the family, including Luisa, the new maid, have equal importance in this analysis of characters and their interpersonal relations. Each character has hidden problems: the emotional and professional frustrations of the parents, Luisa's deception in love, the generation gap in the case of the children. In this "modern marriage" the husband suspects his wife of infidelity but (far from the Calderonian concept of honor requiring that the stains of adultery be washed away with the blood of the guilty), he limits himself to treating her coldly, while going through her drawers in search of compromising letters (which he does not find), while she comments that he reminds her of a husband in the comedies of Benavente: lovers these days don't write letters. The relaxation of moral strictures that began in the twilight years of the Franco regime is evident in the changed attitudes portrayed, and Martín Gaite is among the first women writers to capture the change.

El cuarto de atrás (1978; *The Back Room*, 1983) is dedicated to Lewis Carroll and begins with the novelist's attempt to fall asleep while reading Tzvetan Todorov's work on the literature of the fantastic. She finally goes to sleep reading a letter from an unidentified man, but is awakened at midnight when a stranger reminds her of an appointment for an interview. The novel interweaves dialogue and the novelist's thoughts while discussing varied topics with the stranger, who strongly resembles a devil pictured on her bedroom wall, and dresses in black with a broad-brimmed black hat. Later she goes to sleep on the sofa, but when her daughter awakens her at five o'clock, she is back in her own bed, leading the reader to wonder whether the nocturnal visit and conversation were dreamed. In her dialogue with the stranger, constituting the bulk of the novel, the narrator recalls her experiences growing up during the Civil War and under the Franco regime. As autobiography, it is arranged not in traditional chronological fashion, but as a narration of past events viewed from a mature perspective, a free-association chain of flashbacks without regard for order. Circularity is achieved as the novel ends with the narrator beginning to read the opening lines of *El cuarto de atrás*—a stack of papers that grew as the interview progressed—and again finding herself about to fall asleep.

A blend of many novelistic sub-genres—autobiographical novel or memoir, metafiction (writing about writing), fantasy, mystery novel, social history, realistic fiction—*El cuarto de atrás* was awarded the 1979 National Prize for Literature and has provoked the greatest critical interest and enthusiasm of any of Martín Gaite's works. It led to the publication of a volume of critical studies, *From Fiction to Metafiction: Essays in Honor of Carmen Martín Gaite* (1983),[13] which includes five articles on *The Back Room*. Ten of the collection's sixteen essays are in English, making it an excellent source on this writer.

A Multifaceted Catalan Feminist

Born in Barcelona in 1918 of a totally intellectual family, Maria Aurèlia Capmany was the daughter of the Catalan folklorist, Aureli Capmany. Raised in a thoroughly cultured environment, she studied philosophy at the University of Barcelona, but stopped short of completing her doctorate. She taught at the university and other schools for several years before deciding to concentrate on literary pursuits. Together with Ricard Salvat, she founded the Adrià Gual School of Dramatic Art, where she acted and directed. She is currently Cultural Counselor of the City of Barcelona. A novelist, playwright, and essayist, she began to write at a relatively young age, strongly influenced by contemporary Anglo-Saxon writers: Joyce, Mansfield, Hammet, Hemingway, and especially Virginia Woolf. Capmany, well known as a lecturer and leftist politician, has published regularly for four decades. She is one of the leading figures of Catalan feminism, a champion of women's liberation, and has written extensively on feminist topics in magazines and newspapers, including *Serra d'Or* and *Presencia*, while her books on the subject are cornerstones of feminism in Spain. Most important are *La dona a Catalunya* (1966; Woman in Catalonia), *El feminismo ibérico* (1970; Iberian Feminism), and *El feminisme a Catalunya* (1973; Feminism in Catalonia), in collaboration with Carmen Alcalde. The social condition of women is Capmany's principal concern, and she has explored a semifictional, semiessayistic form as vehicle for her sociological critique in *Cartes impertinentes* (1971; Impertinent Letters). Ostensibly letters written by women from all walks of life to other women of all ages, each of these twenty-seven ironic epistles tells its own story, some constituting case studies, others utilizing irony to denounce the traditions and beliefs that have perennially circumscribed women. *Carta abierta al macho ibérico* (1973; Open Letter to the Iberian Macho) is part of a series of open letters by various writers to assorted Spanish groups and institutions. The author's name is given as Campmany (*sic*) for this publication, as well as another in the series, *Carta abierta a TVE* (Open Letter to Spanish Television). Addressing the Iberian macho, the writer attempts to determine whether a real Iberian male exists, and if so, whether he is exclusively Iberian or to be found in other industrialized societies, as well as whether he should be done away with in the interest of a more peaceful existence for women. Another amusing combination of ironic cartoons (by Avelli Artis-Gener) and incisive text is *Dona, doneta, donota* (1979; Woman, Little Woman, Big Woman), a satiric illustration of women's perennial fight to achieve their rightful place in society. Using laughter as a liberating weapon, the text attacks a series of false premises, stereotypes, and prejudices that have been used to restrict and suppress women.

Capmany turned to fiction four decades ago, completing her first novel in 1947. She has published some forty volumes of fiction and essays in Catalan, as well as several plays, including *Tu i l'hipòcrita* (1960; You and the Hypocrite); *El desert dels dies* (1966; The Desert of Days); *Vent de garbí i una mica de por* (1968; Headwind and a Bit of Fear); *Preguntes i respostes sobre la vida i la mort de Francesc Layret, advocat dels obrers de Catalunya* (1971; Questions and Answers on the Life and Death of Francesc Layret, Defender of the Workers of Catalonia), in collaboration with Xavier Romeu, researcher, and originally prohibited in Spain; *L'alt rei en Jaume* (1977; Old King James); and *Ca, barret!* (1984; Cabaret Theater), in collaboration with Jaume Vidal Alcover. She has also written radio and television scripts, and is an outstanding literary critic and essayist on sociopolitical subjects. Writings in the latter area are collected in *Pedra de toc I* (1970; Cornerstone I) and *Pedra de toc II* (1973; Cornerstone II). *Dietari de prudéncies* (1982; Prudent Diary) is written in modified diary form and consists of monthly entries or commentaries on current events in contemporary Catalan history— literary, social, political, cultural—from 1970 to 1980. Each entry becomes a sort of short narrative, intended to clarify some misunderstanding or area of vagueness.

Capmany's first novel, *Necessitem morir* (1952; We Must Die) had to wait several years for publication because of the Franco censorship. Georgina, the protagonist, is French, but has come to a large Basque country house where she lives from her early youth to the age of forty. The novel begins and ends with her gazing contemplatively at the sea, as she travels in an effort to free herself from her surroundings and the hereditary weight of cultural, religious, and family traditions that overwhelm and overburden her. From the mystery of her birth to the nebulous suggestion of her death, she feels the need to escape, but does not comprehend clearly how or from what. Her final journey, with mythic undertones, is to the Mediterranean. In one sense a journey to the past, it is a search for origins and repose, as well as a sort of new beginning.

L'altra ciutat (1955; The Other City) is a bittersweet counterpoint of past and present, youth and age, memory and reality. Rosa, the protagonist, a middle-aged teacher, returns with her students to the historic city of Tarragona, where she spent her youth. The "other city" of the title is the one of the past, alive again in her recollections, yet juxtaposed with a different reality that communicates the message that time past will never come again. *Betùlia* (1956) is a variation upon the previous theme, as the protagonist is a city, Betùlia (for example, Badalona). Rather than a physical and geographical description, however, what Capmany presents are the thoughts of its characters, not its real life or their real identities, but what they would like to be, their impossible dreams.

Tana o la felicitat (1956; Tana, or Happiness) is a short novel or novelette that centers upon Tana's wedding, presenting the marriage and years before it through the eyes of various family members. The varying perspectives serve as much to define the person holding that point of view as the event perceived, and each chapter presents the analysis of a member of the family, from the dominant, egotistical father, the incredibly self-effacing, submissive mother, and the assorted siblings. Tana is a very strong-willed young woman who gets what she wants, and when she wants a wedding, the groom is unimportant. *Véste'n, ianqui! o, si voleu, traduit de l'americà* (1959; Yankee Go Home, Or, If you Prefer, Translated from the American) has two possible levels of reading, one of them as a mystery novel or seeming adventure of international intrigue: A young American has disappeared in Albania, and a special agent is sent to trace him. Eventually found, he reveals his decision to forsake his family's wealth and remain there to build a new life. The second, deeper level of reading has to do with Albania's "third world" situation between two larger, powerful nations. *El gust de la pols* (1962; The Taste of Dust) is a complex narrative mosaic combining contemporary events with flashbacks in the lives of various characters, public happenings with private lives and reflections, intended to reveal the difficulty of distinguishing the "reality" of the individual behind appearances. Harsh criticism of bourgeois values—a frequent motif in Capmany's work—is interwoven with observations of the evolving status of the working class. Like *Cartes impertinentes,* this work belongs to an intermediate, hybrid genre, and is only partially fiction.

La pluja als vidres (1963; Rain on the Windowpane), another work withheld from publication for several years because of censorial prohibition, this novel was originally entitled "El cel no es transparent" (The Sky Is Not Clear), and in manuscript under this title it won the Joanot Martorell Prize for Catalan narrative. Written in 1948, it presents the intimate tragedy of characters the novelist affirms that she knew, in the barren lands of Murcia. *Feliçment jo sóc una dona* (1969; Fortunately, I Am a Woman) is the ostensible autobiography of Carola Mila, a woman of nearly seventy. Born in Barcelona the last day of 1899, she begins her memoirs in Majorca in the twilight of her life, allowing Capmany to retrace from a woman's perspective the development of varying levels of Catalan society in the first half of this century, from the anarchist dynamiters to the feudal aristocracy, the middle and upper-middle class, the prewar and postwar industrial entrepreneurs, the working class, and paupers. Capmany concentrates less on personal than collective experience, presenting political unrest, strikes, the war, and dictatorship for the primary purpose of demonstrating their effects upon women, exposing hypocrisy and injustice as they affected women at all social levels.

Un lloc entre els morts (1969; A Place Among the Dead) won the 1968 Sant Jordi Prize for the Novel in Catalan, a most prestigious award. This convincing, rigorously historical biography of a preromantic poet presents so much documentation and background research that it appears real, yet the young poet, Jeroni Campdepadros (1789–1821), translator of Southey and admirer of a variety of English and Continental poets, is completely fictitious. The novelist's mixed sentiments toward the "pure" poet (hands unsoiled by work, his work free of political commitment or utilitarian purpose) resulted in a figure who stands between two centuries, between two philosophical currents (eighteenth-century belief in reason, nineteenth-century romantic passion), between two loves and two social classes, a device that again permits her to criticize bourgeois society and the men and women belonging to it. The novelist brings to life the Barcelona of the Napoleonic occupation, with its lively streets, shrewd merchants and exporters, and bourgeoisie fearful that the new freedom may destroy their own economic edifice. Capmany is especially critical of certain types of women, the vain and venial sex object who uses eroticism for her own advancement, and the seemingly honest, religious woman who is in fact a hypocrite.

Although set outside Spain, *Vitrines d'Amsterdam* (1970; Showcaes of Amsterdam) is nonetheless another critique of facets of the Catalan industrial bourgeoisie in the persons of two of its members. Another mystery (somewhat in the vein of *Ves-t'en ianqui!* in that it too involves a disappearance in a foreign country), the novel presents the shock suffered by two wealthy Catalan shoe manufacturers in contact with the drugs, vice, and sordid life of Amsterdam's red-light district (the title allusion is to the display of prostitutes in windows). Tomás's strange disappearance is the point of departure of the narrative, and his brother Ignasi seeks him through the fringes of the underworld, sensing the vertigo Tomás must have experienced, on the verge of being annihilated himself, eventually reaching the conclusion that Tomás is dead. The idea is that one cannot swim with impunity in the waters of vice and crime. Capmany experiments with the structure of parallel or "bis" chapters, a device permitting her to contrast the thoughts of the protagonist at different moments, which is explained by analogy with a symphony whose major chords are echoed by a parallel sequence (only a small number of chapters have these "echoes").

One of Capmany's most original narratives is *Quim/Quimà* (1971), an apocalyptic and millennial novel which begins with an authorial prologue, a letter to Virginia Woolf acknowledging imitation of the latter's *Orlando*, both in the sex change of the hero and the thousand-year span, but here the similarities end. Beginning in the year 1000, when most of the Christian portions of the world expected the imminent end, the narrative follows Quim through the history of Catalonia up to the Spanish Civil War. The man Quim becomes Quima, a woman, but reverts to being a male when injustice is too much for him/her to endure. Not unrelated, since it involves use of history and legend, is *El malefici de la reina d'Hongria* (1982; The Enchantment of the Queen of Hungary), intended for juvenile readers, but with a message for adults as well. Set in the eighteenth century, it presents a struggle of world powers for control of the Mediterranean (and thus has a contemporary parallel). It focuses on three brothers, one of whom is nonviolent and peace-loving and thus favored by fortune (or the novelist).

El jaqué de la democracia (1972; The Dinner Jacket of Democracy) is a cross between detective fiction and political intrigue, mirroring the conflict between powerful conservatives and the forces of progress. Although the setting is fictitious, its parallels with reality are obvious. In the city of Salona, capital of Balvacaria, a tiny country belonging to the Admiralty of the Empire, two leading figures are assassinated: Jeroni Corona, a powerful industrialist, and a few days later, Esteve Coris, a lawyer for the labor movement. Malhakias Ryt, private detective from the "Gold Schell Agency," is charged with tracking down the murderers. The technique used by Capmany is again experimental: first some disordered fragments of the novel (pages numbered 36, 102, 234, etc.) are presented; next they are put in order, 1 to 20, and extended, and finally—as requested by the putative author of the fragments—Capmany integrates the fragments into a harmonious whole with her additions and so writes the novel.

Lo color més blau (1982; The Bluest Color [*La color más azul*, 1984]) reflects, as does so much of her fiction, the impact of the Civil War and its consequences for Catalonia. Presented as an epistolary novel concerned with the lives of two women, it is also concerned more profoundly with the experience of defeat and war's destruction. Oliva and Delia, co-protagonists and best friends, are both fifteen when the story begins with their separation in 1939. Delia goes into exile with her militant Communist parents, while Oliva remains in Barcelona with her wealthy family (who are quite relieved to have Delia's influence on their daughter interrupted). During the next twenty-nine years, the novel traces their parallel but vastly different lives, Delia's exile experience in France, Poland, and Mexico, and Oliva's adolescence and adulthood under the Franco regime. The use of letters is not new for Capmany, especially to put across a feminist message. In *Cartes impertinentes* as mentioned above, the device was used (including the specific exchange between a bourgeoise woman and a working-class woman), and again in *Liberación de la mujer: año cero* (1977; Women's Liberation: Zero Hour), she presents a similar exchange as a means of examining class consciousness and how class constitutes an obstacle to feminine solidarity. About a third of the letters are between Delia and Oliva, the remainder being their correspondence with others or letters between third parties, but it is the attempted dialogue between the two—both as individuals and as generic representatives of the proletariat and upper class—that holds most interest. Both Delia and Oliva are victims, and both subsequently look back upon their high school days in the open, progressive atmosphere of the Republic with idealization and nostalgic longing. The contrast between the girls' lives following their separation is enormous. Although they resume their correspondence after a ten-year hiatus, and eventually have a reunion in Paris in the historic, symbolic year of 1968, their long-awaited encounter is anticlimatic and disappointing, with no real communication or common ground. Through a strange chain of circumstances, Oliva has become a political activist, rejecting her bourgeois origins, while Delia has married a wealthy Mexican architect, adopting bourgeois values and rejecting her parents' revolutionary values. Each rather pities the other, although it would seem that Capmany intends Oliva's evolution to be seen as the more authentic: she has assumed command of her life, while Delia has always been submissive, an object, controlled by others.

Revolutionary, Journalist, Novelist, Feminist

Teresa Pàmies was born in Balaguer (province of Lleida) in 1919, the daughter of a poor farmer who soon became a militant leftist. She began to work in a sweatshop when she was eleven, and as a self-educated teenager became a correspondent for the revolutionary press. After the Spanish Civil War she and her family went into exile; she lived twelve years in France and twelve in Czechoslovakia, and approximately eight in Mexico, where she studied journalism at the Universidad Femenina. She returned to Catalonia in 1971, and most of her important works were published after that. Her fiction belongs to the documentary or personal testimony category, and is usually presented in the guise of memoirs, autobiography, or chronicles of the Civil War, exile, and clandestine activism, or as epistolary narrative re-creating important moments of recent history. Her literary honors include the Joan Estelrich Prize and the Josep Plà Prize, two of Catalan literature's most significant awards for journalism and the essay. Pàmies is one of the most original Marxist theoreticians of feminism. See especially

Maig de les dones (1976; Ladies' May) and *Opinió de dona* (1983; A Woman's Opinion).

Characteristically writing in the first person, Pàmies frequently employs what Möller-Soler[14] has identified as the tactical discourse of Communism, a conscious exploitation of voluntary ambiguity of vocabulary in order to avoid alienating the reader. A good deal of detail is provided on daily activities, often minutiae. Although Pàmies's experience is by no means typical of Spanish women generally, it is characteristic of women of her age who devoted themselves to the defense of the Republican cause and revolutionary ideas; presiding at meetings, delivering propagandistic speeches, visiting the front, and doing public relations work in foreign countries, followed by the sufferings of exile. Major works include *La filla del pres* (1967; The Prisoner's Daughter), and *Testament a Praga* (1971; Testament in Prague, in collaboration with her father, Tomás Pàmies), a controversial book that first brought her to public attention in postwar Spain. Inspired in part by a re-evaluation of socialist theory subsequent to the 1968 Russian invasion of Czechoslovakia, it is also an expression of the loneliness of exile. Divided into four parts, the first two containing fragments of her father's memories alternate with Pàmies's recollections of his death, a third part in which she is the only speaker, and a fourth consisting of two letters from the father, expressing both strength and longing for the native land he would never see again. Much the same thematics continue (minus the father-daughter relationship) in *Va ploure tot el dia* (1974; It's Going to Rain All Day), a three-part novel dedicated to exiles which presents the thoughts of a Catalan woman returning home after thirty years as a political exile. Present-tense action occupies only one day, with numerous flashbacks prompted by free association or questioning by the police. The motif of rain is effectively employed to suggest the passage of time and loss of youth in exile, together with the destruction of other equally irreplaceable intangibles.

Quan érem capitans (1974; When We Were Captains) is a memoir of the Spanish Civil War as viewed by an enthusiastically socialistic young woman, and includes portraits of important figures in letters and the arts, politicians of the day and other historic personalities, together with the anguish of the last days of the Republic, and rigors of the refugees' escape across the border into France. *Quan érem refugiats* (1975; When We Were Refugees) is equally dramatic, describing the terrifying situation of women in French refugee camps and prisons, and includes a graphic abortion performed in a jail cell. The five parts correspond to different locations, including glimpses of the suffering of those who remained in Catalonia, and the odyssey of those who manage to reach South America, with a picture of life in the Dominican Republic and Cuba under Trujillo contrasting with backward looks at the political situation in Spain. Continuing this theme, *Gents del meu exili* (1975; Unforgettable Characters From My Exile) is a down-to-earth documentary of some of the most tragic victims of war's pain and anguish that Pàmies has met, real people linked by despair and loneliness. A social document that emphasizes the universality of suffering as well as the inherent goodness of those portrayed, it is not bereft of humor. Very much in the same category is *Records de guerra i d'exili* (1976; Recollections of War and Exile), as is *Croniques de naufrags* (1977; Chronicles of Shipwreck Survivors) which, utilizing the epistolary format, presents letters from forty people of all ages who survive a terrible shipwreck (an allegory of the war) and chronicles their efforts to survive, whatever the difficulties of individual circumstances. Politics are kept very much in the background of this testimony of contemporary devastation.

Another aspect of Pàmies's life, political activism and clandestine revolutionary involvement, appears in *Romanticismo militante* (1976; Militant Romanticism) and *Amor clandestí* (1976; Clandestine Love). The latter presents the internal contradictions in the character of a strong woman militant. Using different typography, the novel contrasts the woman's innermost thoughts and feelings with her behavior and external events to emphasize the effect of the political atmosphere upon her private life. *Dona de pres* (1975; The Prisoner's Woman) is a study of a self-centered man imprisoned because of his political ideas, and his courageous, altruistic common-law wife who has something of a generic character, representing all women whose husbands became political prisoners and exemplifying their physical and moral anguish. Her existence is devoted to taking care of her son, born of her affair with the guerrilla, and to serving insofar as she can the father of her child and other political prisoners. Less fictitious, but belonging to this same thematic nucleus is *Una española llamada Dolores Ibarruri (La Pasionaria)* (1977; A Spanish Woman Called Dolores Ibarruri, The Passion Flower), a tribute to the most famous woman leader of the Spanish Communist party.

Surprisingly, perhaps, Pàmies has also written travel narratives, although not too surprisingly, they become vehicles for a social or political message. *Vacances aragoneses* (1979; Vacation in Aragon) is more than simply the description of a summer vacation in the mountains of Aragon: its true subject is the people living in the mountain valleys, and their sometimes tragic personal histories. *Busque-me a Granada* (1980; Seek Me in Granada) is centered around a journey of a Catalan woman to the south of Spain, fascinated by Granada with its traditions and political history and sentiment that are new and unfamiliar to her. Each character encountered is envisioned as a world of new possibilities, and the area's legends and historical anecdotes transform the trip into an intellectual journey, as well as a voyage back in time to study historical enigmas which are inset as intercalated tales. In *Rosalia no hi era* (1982; Rosalía Wasn't There) Pàmies travels to Galicia during the summer of 1981, searching for the area's famous poet, Rosalía de Castro, in places associated with Rosalía's tragic life. More than a biography, more than a travel memoir, it is also a feminist document with intense sentiment employed in the expression of Rosalía's anguish as a woman and mother, and her role as the voice of another oppressed minority culture. *Matins de l'Aran* (1982; Mornings in Aran) is a collection of ten stories set in the Valley of Aran high in the Pyrenees and linked by the person of the vacationing author who visits a variety of villages and landscapes, thereby providing the transitions from one tale to another. Again the subject is the life of everyday people, woodsmen and farmers, young and old, even summer visitors, and including emphasis on the flora and fauna as part of the pleasures of discovery.

More specifically political motivations underlie *Si vas a París, papá* . . . (1975; Daddy, If You Go to Paris), set in France in May 1968, and continuing an analysis of the contemporary crisis in French ideals, paralleling conflicts in Catalonia at the same time. The narrative combines history and fiction, real and imaginary characters. *Crònica de la vetlla* (1976; Old Timer's Chronicle), chronologically antedating Pàmies's other narratives, is set in her native city, Balaguer, during the final years of the dictatorship of Primo de Rivera, and describes local events up to the beginning of the Spanish Civil War. It can be considered a sort of study of backgrounds and causes of the conflict, exposing the differences between Right and Left, rich and poor, the hopes aroused by the Republic and the despair of its tragedy. *Aquell vellet gentil i pulcre* (1978; Those Nice, Clean People) uses multiple perspectives to develop a complex plot along several temporal planes, combining contemporary events and flashbacks to various periods. Set in postwar Barcelona, it portrays the degradation of defeat, in contrast with the power of Nazi refugees who have prospered in Spain. *Cartes al fill recluta* (1984; Letters to My Son, the Recruit) is, as the title suggests, an epistolary novel in the form of letters addressed by a woman to her son in military service, and including a fragmented narrative written during the night of 23 February with factual notes on the failed military coup. This crucial moment in post-Franco Spain's transition to democracy is narrated by a woman whose husband and son are situated in the crux of the action.

Memoria dels morts (1981; Memoir of the Dead) is more personal, beginning with a meeting between the author and her dead mother, in a fantastic, misty landscape of autumn in Balaguer. The first voices heard by the reader are those of the dead (a major premise is that the dead speak the truth, while the living must lie: only the deceased have true freedom of speech and nothing to hide). Via this encounter with her mother, Pàmies symbolically ends the Civil War which had disrupted the life of her family (in earlier books, the mother's death had aroused doubts, vague threats, thoughts of vengeance). The remainder of the narrative is realistic, and contrasts the world full of "necessary" lies told by the living, and especially those that victimize women, making the book an important exposition of feminist values. *Massa tard per a Cèlia* (1984; Too Late for Celia) is linked to the previous work by its emphasis upon a dead woman, but is something of a mystery novel, a search for clues to Celia's suicide through investigation of facts and opinions of characters who knew her: husband, son, neighbor, friends. One of Pàmies's most imaginative and purely fictitious works, it is set in contemporary Slovakia and makes extensive, adept use of the interior monologue.

Most of Pàmies's writings are heavily autobiographical, and their interest is more often sociological, political, and historical rather than literary, although she writes with lucidity, ease, and forceful, dramatic impact. Her narrative facility should be evident when one looks at the chronology of her works, all of them excepting *La filla del pres* published since 1971. Since her latest novel seems to take a new turn, Pàmies is a writer who may develop in other directions.

Chapter Eight
Recent Narrators in Castilian

Toward the end of the 1960s comes a crisis in the neorealist "social" literature cultivated by the mid-century generation. During the 1970s and 1980s the post-neorealist modes include neobaroque and neovanguardist, experimental styles and techniques. Language per se becomes a preoccupation, subjectivism intensifies, and intertextual allusions proliferate. Educational reforms of the early 1970s, which included new legitimization of the vernacular languages, stimulated publishing in the minority languages; abolition of the censorship at the end of 1978 provided further impetus, followed by intense interest in the regional cultures. In Castilian, the relaxation of controls during Franco's final years meant an increase of publications touching upon those areas previously censored, especially the political and erotic. Feminist writers would also take advantage of relaxed restrictions in these areas.

Two lesser transitional narrators are Luisa Isabel Alvarez de Toledo (Duchess of Medina Sidonia) and Carmen Mieza. Alvarez de Toledo focuses above all on social issues and humanitarian problems, the plight of the rural and urban lower classes. By contrast, and much in the vein of the dualistic writers of socialist realism in the 1950s and 1960s, her portrayal of the monied elite is critical. She moved from the indictment of economic inequities to activism in 1969 when she defended the villagers of Palomares after a nuclear bomb incident (an accident involving an American war plane). Jailed from March to November of that year, the duchess was powerfully affected by her prison experience, which is reflected in her subsequent writings, in an anticapitalistic stance, and in a more committed preoccupation with the problems of working-class women and the reform of women's prisons in Spain.

La huelga (1967; The Strike; trans. *The Strike. A Novel of Contemporary Spain,* 1971) is a thesis novel that intends to demonstrate injustice and brutality in the treatment of workers in Andalusia by the landowners and capitalists, in collusion with the authorities and the church. Although neither group is idealized, the upper classes fare

153

worse than the poor (a possible bias of the writer appears in her scorn for the landowners who are not true aristocrats but nouveau riche). Themes include corruption, promiscuity, and the forced emigration of Spanish workers to the countries of northern Europe where wages were incomparably more attractive (a perennial problem for the Franco regime during the 1950s and 1960s). Of sociological and sociohistorical interest, this work was followed by *La base* (1971; The Base), which is clearly related to the Palomares incident. It reflects the experiences of the Infantes family as a result of the establishment of a military base under the joint United States and Spanish treaty, resulting not only in the introduction of nuclear weaponry into the area, but opening the door to foreign and conflicting cultural values and a totally different economic system. The novelist studies especially the psychological repercussions when small farmers have their land appropriated for the base and are forced to become day-laborers there, with the resulting self-devaluation as they go from owners to a marginal labor force in an alien environment. The corruption produced by contacts with American affluence worsens the already materialistic local authorities, so that the earlier undesirable status quo comes to look rather idyllic by comparison. The novel concludes with a nuclear accident that destroys the region. *La cacería* (1977; The Hunt) uses as its point of departure the annual hunt staged by wealthy *madrileños* in an Andalusian village, exposing the moral decay of the traditional aristocracy and the parvenus. Several narrative threads are required to develop the relationships between representatives of the different social strata. Above all, the novelist concentrates on the social injustice that involved manipulation and exploitation of the lower classes.

Carmen Mieza (1931–1976) was born in Barcelona, and remained in Spain when her father fled to exile in Mexico immediately after the end of the war. Once she had completed her training as a teacher, she joined her father, and her experience in Mexico provides the basis for her only two novels, based upon her acquaintance with exiles and expatriates. *La imposible canción* (1962; The Impossible Song) presents Catalonian exiles living in Mexico City without ever either adapting to their new environment or making a commitment to it, dreaming of an impossible return to Spain. *Una mañana cualquiera* (1964; Any Morning) is clearly based upon a combination of autobiographical data and literary elaboration. A young woman comes from Spain to visit her exiled father in Mexico and meets his ignorant, vulgar Mexican wife. The father is a cultured man, a doctor, whose experience is a paradigm for the solitude and bitterness of exile. The daughter's expectations provide a contrast, for she looks forward to becoming a citizen of the world. Perhaps the novel intends to suggest that exile may look comparably attractive to those who have not experienced it, or that exile is a very different matter from voluntary expatriation.[1]

Lawyer, Feminist Leader, Journalist, and Novelist

Lidia Falcón, born in Madrid in 1935, a major intellectual and activist leader of Spanish feminism, is the founder of Spain's first Feminist Party (1979) and the feminist magazine, *Vindicación Feminista* (1976–79). She is the author of sociopolitical treatises on women and society, and has published fourteen works of fiction. Her autobiographical books and articles reflect the experience of growing up under Franco as a child of the vanquished Republicans, especially *Los hijos de los vencidos* (1979; Children of the Defeated), which documents her first fourteen years, picturing a sordid Spain with prevalent poverty, black marketeering, prostitution, and police oppression. Another fictional work with an autobiographical basis is *En el infierno (Ser mujer en las cárceles de España)* (1977; In Hell: To Be a Woman in Spanish Jails), a novelized account of conditions faced by women in jails, reformatories, prisons, and prison hospitals, written while Falcón herself was imprisoned. Still another autobiographical novel is *Viernes y trece en la Calle del Correo* (Friday the Thirteenth on Correo Street) that recounts the arrest and trial of activists and intellectuals accused of collaboration with ETA, the Basque terrorist organization (Falcón, arrested along with others in September 1974, remained in the women's penitentiary for nine months).[2]

Falcón has also employed humor in her irreverent critique of male exploitation of women, using the device of letters from a female lawyer (herself) to a friend, in *Cartas a una idiota española* (1974; Letters to a Spanish Idiot), presenting the stories of a broad range of women from university students to factory workers, peasants to typists, housewives to nuns, and prostitutes to diplomats' wives. *Es largo esperar callado* (1975; The Long Silent Wait) centers upon twenty years of clandestine activity by the Spanish Communist party, its internal conflicts, and power struggles. In addition to portrayal of such key political figures as Santiago Carrillo and Dolores Ibarruri, this novel re-creates the lives of Spanish exiles in France and various socialist countries. Significantly, it shows that women encounter difficulties not only in Spanish society, but within the supposedly more progressive context of leftist parties. *El juego de la piel* (1983; The Skin Game) reflects the European hippies scene in the 1970s, with drugs, delinquency, and near-death from addiction all viewed from the feminine perspective of Elisenda, a middle-class girl from Barcelona.

A Galician Professor, Critic, and Novelist

Marina Mayoral, born in Mondoñedo (Lugo) in 1942, is an authority on the poetry of Rosalía de Castro and professor at Madrid's Universidad Complutense. A major theme of her novels is personal liberty. *Cándida otra vez* (1979; Candida Again) is a mystery set in the early post-Franco years, but a mystery combined with sociohistorical problems. Cándida represents the more progressive Galician upper middle class, and together with others of the liberal segment of the province, views with some trepidation the indiscriminate sacrifice of Spanish tradition to modernization. Those who once constituted the opposition to Franco now face an identity crisis, as they have lost their raison d'être as the enlightened opposition. *Al otro lado* (1981; On the Other Side) refers to the unconscious dimension of everyday reality. Set in post-Civil War Spain, the novel portrays protagonists who exist in a society plagued by totalitarianism, dogmatism, and puritanical morality, where no discussion or questioning is possible. Many of them have their "other side," a world of insanity, fantasy, imagination, magic, and mystery. On a deeper moral level there is the problem of existential responsibility and guilt. *La única libertad* (1982; The Only Liberty) is set in Galicia with its magical, mysterious background, touched with Gothic overtones. A metaliterary novel within a novel is the "Historia de la Braña" which the terminally ill young narrator is writing, a reconstruction of the history of her family's country manor. Combining external narration with letters and various documents related to the Silva family history, the novel fuses realism and romanticism with aspects of mystery (found in all of Mayoral's narratives heretofore). The *pazo* of La Braña has been the setting of many tales past and present, shrouded in a mist of ambiguity and intrigue, and these are interwoven with the narrator's efforts to extricate her individuality from the web of ancestral tradition. *Contra muerte y amor* (1985; Against Love and Death) again fuses romantic and realistic elements. Set once more in Galicia, in a fishing village, the novel combines past and present, and suggests a parallelism between the earlier period and the moment of writing, so that the later story is a variation upon the one that went before. Esmeralda, the protagonist, and Daniel are linked with the village of La Tolda, rival of La Rosaleda, and drawn into the world of boxing when Esmeralda agrees to help a beginning fighter. Galicia and the Gallego language, always significant in Mayoral's writing, become even more visible.

A "New" Poet, Novelist, and Story-Writer

Ana María Moix, born in Barcelona in 1947, is a poet, journalist, translator, novelist, essayist, and short-story writer. The younger sister of the well-known novelist Terençi Moix, Ana María began as a writer of experimental poetry, in the vein of pop and op art, inspired by images, characters, techniques, and vocabulary of the mass media, exemplified in *Baladas del dulce Jim* (1969; Sweet Jim's Ballads) and *Call me Stone* (1969; title only in English). *No time for flowers* (1971; title only in English), a series of prose poems with a distinguishable narrative content, is her last book of poetry. A hybrid, it employs the interior monologue (used more extensively in her next novel) with many intertextual materials drawn from popular songs, Lorca, and other easily identifiable references. Her three books of poetry were republished as *A imagen y semejanza* (1983; In the Image and Likeness). Moix's first novel, *Julia* (1970), portrays the world of the Catalan bourgeoisie in the immediate postwar period—the world in which the author was born and raised. Some characters and events are autobiographical but have been subjected to considerable literary elaboration. A psychological mystery-intrigue, the novel is presented as the interior monologue of the emotionally disturbed and sometimes suicidal young protagonist. During a sleepless night Julia relives the main events of her last fifteen years, and most particularly her quest for personal freedom. The roots of her self-destructiveness are traced to the decadent, oppressive, and ambivalent atmosphere in which she was raised.[3] Julia's tortured remembrance of the past includes her relationship with her two brothers (Rafael who died in adolescence, and the homosexual Ernesto), her adored, egotistical mother, despised grandmother, and anarchist grandfather. An overdose of drugs, an almost-successful suicide attempt, intensifies the process of Julia's alienation. Her phobias, superstitions, and the presence of a double, Julita (her five-year-old self), are further symptoms of Julia's problem. Moix presents a distinctly feminine viewpoint, indicting traditional values and institutions as she

examines the impact upon her persona of a society in transition, adolescent and student rebellion, and the question of lesbianism broached
when a schoolmate makes sexual advances.

Moix has translated Beckett, Aragon, and Marguerite Duras from
French to Castilian, and a possible influence of the first two may be
perceived in her sometimes-absurdist, sometimes-surrealist imagery.
She has also translated Rodoreda and other Catalan narrators into Castilian. *Ese chico pelirrojo a quien veo cada día* (1971; That Red-headed
Boy I See Every Day) is a collection of ten stories exploring the same
repressive and warping environment portrayed in her novels, with its
negative repercussions upon the vulnerable younger generation.
Themes include sexual initiation, the seduction of an innocent, madness, metamorphosis (of adolescents unable to adapt to life who ultimately turn into animals). The writer's obvious liking for a parody here
results in the story of a vampire who is turned into a human by too
much contact with people. In her tales of rites of passage, especially,
Moix displays an exquisite knowledge of adolescent psychology, and
her difficult themes are treated with tenderness and skill, as well as
with occasional subtle irony and false ingenuousness. Her indictment
of the social system, while implicit, is inescapable.

Moix continues her satire of the Catalan bourgeoisie in *¿Walter, por
qué te fuiste?* (1973; Walter, Why Did You Leave?). While this novel
is not strictly a sequel to *Julia*, some members of the same family
appear again, together with episodes from some of the writer's earlier
stories. Moix attempts to trace the social, ethnic, and moral crisis of a
class as part of an ambitious and complex novel with multiple narrative
voices (first, second, and third persons), doses of fantasy, and several
time planes. Set in Barcelona during the 1960s, the novel plumbs the
psyches of three major characters to develop their individual conflicts
with the Establishment. Sexually explicit and daring for its date of
publication, *Walter* treats homosexuality, lesbianism, sodomy, and bi-
sexuality within a context that varies from the parodic and comical to
the serious. Ostensibly a search for Walter, the novel is also an inquiry
into the meaning of life. Ismael, a thirty-year-old circus performer
returns to their summer place called "T" in search of cousin Lea, to
deliver a packet of letters from Julia, now dead. The house, filled with
ghosts of the past, was the vacation home of an extended family, with
Julia and her brothers among the cousins, including prudish María
Antonia, intellectual Ricardo, rebellious, defiant Lea, and the mysterious Walter, introduced via Lea's glamorous descriptions as her suitor

but in reality only a dull seminarian that Lea perversely delights in seducing. A recurring motif in Moix's fiction is escape, whether by drugs, madness, suicide, alcohol, sex, metamorphosis, or—in Ismael's case—life in the circus. Paired with the difficulty of adaptation, it serves to underscore the loss of innocence, purity, ideals, and eventually youth. Childhood is both paradise and prison, and its tragic aspects are lucidly reflected in Moix's second novel.[4]

Although she wrote fiction for children and an essay on a Catalan artist in the interim, Moix did not continue her adult fiction until twelve years later. *Las virtudes peligrosas* (1985; The Dangerous Virtues) is a collection of five novellas or short stories whose tones range from melancholy to cruel irony, and that coincide in presenting characters whose state of mind distances them from their surroundings. Memories, sadness, fatigue, disappointment, radical solitude, and lack of communication, as well as a paralyzing fear of the present or the future are among the factors contributing to their alienation. The probable influence of Faulkner or Juan Benet, mentioned in connection with earlier works, is particularly evident in the style of the title tale, and the third one, "El inocente" (The Innocent One). At times, also, Moix's stories recall those of Virginia Woolf or Katherine Mansfield. "Erase una vez" parodically adopts the "Once upon a time" beginning of fairy tales as the name of a problematic character distinguished by her golden curls, and her brother "Uno para contarlo" (One to Tell), a burlesque of the cliché language, characters, and situations of the genre.

Publisher, Novelist, Feminist

Esther Tusquets, born in Barcelona in 1936, is like Moix, a Catalan writer whose creative work has been done in Castilian. Her studies in the Colegio Alemán (German private school), which gave her an atypical formation for the time, were followed by work in history at the universities of Barcelona and Madrid. For a quarter-century she has been director of Editorial Lumen, one of the most venturous publishing houses of the experimental vanguard. Her fiction is the product of her maturity, beginning in 1978 with *El mismo mar de todos los veranos* (The Same Sea of Every Summer). This first novel exploits a wealth of intertextual allusion to literary texts and myth as part of the delineation of the process of loss (of love, beliefs, emotional reserves). The novelist concentrates upon the search of E., a middle-aged woman, for fulfillment beyond traditional marriage and motherhood. A text that requires a plurality of readings, *El mismo mar* traces the nameless female university professor through her narrative of her lonely childhood, and later the disillusioning and painful suicide of the sweetheart who had made her aware of life's potential for happiness. Her meaningless marriage, followed by motherhood equally devoid of intimacy and communication, leave her vulnerable to mid-life crisis as she faces maturity aware of the hollowness of her existence. Rebelling against the constrictions and values of her social class, and seeking her own self-realization and expression, she initiates a brief but intense love relationship with Clara, a student who in various ways represents herself at the same age. After a month the idyll is terminated by the narrator's family. Tusquets drew immediate attention, not only for the maturity and artistry of her narrative, but for the sensuousness with which she presents feminine sexuality, the frankness with which lesbianism is treated, and her focus upon the disintegrating family as seen not only in the failed marriage but in the expressive mother-daughter relationships.[5]

El amor es un juego solitario (1979; Love is a Solitary Game) appeared one year later and constitutes the second portion of a trilogy, linked not by the identity or continuity of characters but of theme and sentiment. The tightly intertwined love triangle formed by Elia, Clara, and Ricardo is the central focus of what is essentially a psychological analysis of the three characters' emotions. Elia is an archetypal figure, the primal female seductress with an elemental animalism that impels and enables her to attract and seduce an unknown mate through biological allure. Simultaneously, however, she is almost overcivilized, the idle and parasitic ultramodern female who views love less as adventure than as a relief for ennui. She controls the lives both of her naive younger homosexual partner, Clara, who gives her total devotion, and Ricardo, the heterosexual lover who still suffers adolescent insecurity. Again, the protagonist is a middle-aged female dissatisfied with her role as wife and mother, anguished by the aging process, who desperately seeks fulfillment in eroticism while also attempting to recapture her lost youth through possession of the younger lover. Neither affair, however, suffices to solve her existential dilemma of being-towards-death, nor allows her to achieve authenticity.

Varada tras el último naufragio (1980; Beached after the Last Shipwreck) completes the trilogy that explores facets of the alienation of the middle-aged woman. Again, the protagonist experiences a crisis precipitated at least in part by her unsatisfactory marriage, although in this case the problem arises as the result of the disintegration of a marriage she had once believed to be ideal. Love, sexual relationships, and roles are important throughout the trilogy, and once more the roles are tangled and the relationships complex. Elia (not the protagonist of the previous work, despite certain coincidences of character) is timid and introverted, and has customarily expressed herself through writing. Abruptly abandoned by her husband, she must struggle with her undesired liberty. Her friend, Eva, a feminist lawyer involved in labor issues, is also plunged into crisis by the extramarital affair of her husband, Pablo. Elia and Pablo, though very different, share an interest in writing, and are somewhat passive, plagued by self-doubt, and both at least temporarily undergo a personality change or role reversal, becoming more assertive and active. Tusquets explores the existential self-other relationships and the formation of identity concepts, showing how one becomes a prisoner of roles or the expectations of others, as well as questioning the distance between the true or existentially authentic self and the public image. Existence of differences, the awareness of a façade or of involvement in role-playing, leads to a sense of farce or falseness shared by a number of Tusquets's characters. Both faces of the problem are equally important: distance between true self (existential authenticity) and facade(s), and distances between self and others, particularly in relationships supposed to be intimate. Parallelism and repetition (of characters, dialogue, and situation) are employed by the novelist as a subtle underscoring of the problems of role, façade, self, and authenticity.[6]

Siete miradas en un mismo paisaje (1981; Seven Glances at the Same Landscape) is a collection of short stories grouped around the personality of Sara and portraying significant events in her life from the age of nine to the age of eighteen. Although not arranged chronologically, the vignettes do trace Sara's course from childhood through adolescence and across the threshold of adulthood. Tusquets's insightful penetration of adolescent psychology is evinced via interior monologues and Sara's retrospective reconstruction of childhood relationships with playmates, older cousins, and her upper-middle-class family. Sara's first encounters with the rigidity of the class system, adolescent love, and her hero worship of a prima ballerina are the subjects of other episodes. Two of the tales are related to Sara's first grown-up love at seventeen and eighteen, with its disappointments and joys. Via Proustian flashbacks and objective correlatives, Tusquets endows Sara's rememberings with a density of texture and universality.

Para no volver (1985; Never to Return) takes its title from the well-known verse of Rubén Darío, "Juventud, divino tesoro, / ya te vas para no volver" (Youth, divine treasure / you're going, never to return). The cover is illustrated with a photograph of Freud's couch, whereon the protagonist (another Elena) undergoes psychoanalysis some four days a week. Having passed forty, she is preoccupied by aging and death, especially death as an existential given, and shows some symptoms of being a manic depressive. The wife of a prominent moviemaker, now suspected of deceiving her, she is on the verge of menopause and suffering from "empty nest syndrome," with tears and depression whenever she enters her sons' vacant rooms. The world of the cinema is a constant intertextual presence, most of the allusions being used ironically. Elena's analysis quite logically serves to evoke her past, especially her childhood and adolescence in the postwar years, and the environment of the enlightened bourgeoisie in the pedestrian and mediocre culture of Barcelona in the early Franco era. As the protagonist re-creates her life and her marriage, she also sketches the typical life-style of the wealthy Catalan and middle-class intellectuals, including the periodic trips to Perpignan (across the French border) to cram into a weekend half a dozen movies not permitted in Spain, buy foreign newspapers and magazines, pharmaceuticals, contraceptives, and articles of plastic, all unavailable in Spain. Such concrete details have the solidity of bricks and function to strengthen the historical edifice of the epoch reconstructed by Elena's free associations throughout the course of her treatment. Ironically, while her psychiatrist impassively listens to her day after day, Elena is in reality psychoanalyzing her husband.

Journalist and Feminine "New Novelist"

Rosa Montero, born in Madrid in 1951, has worked in independent theater, studied journalism and psychology, and is one of Spain's best-known media interviewers. She is closely associated wth *El País,* one of the country's major newspapers, and for a time edited its Sunday literary supplement. She won the National Prize for Journalism in 1981. Two collections of her interviews have been published, *España para ti* (1976) and *Cinco años de País* (1982), in which are reflected the first five years of democracy in Spain (pursuant to the general elections of June 1977). The twenty interviews selected for the latter collection range from politicians (defeated and in power) to movie stars, a publisher, bullfighter, minister, prince, and philosopher, and provide ample evidence of Montero's ability to obtain a story. *Crónica del desamor* (1979; Chronicle of Falling out of Love), her first novel, follows an autobiographical format and concentrates upon feminist issues, many of them taboo during the Franco regime: contraception, abortion, homosexuality, and the unwed mother, among others. Problems of the working woman, and especially the issue of fair and equitable salaries, are also raised. Many types of relationships are explored, from male-female to friends of the same sex and parent-child, particularly one involving a feminist daughter. A series of women appear, whose common denominator is their unhappy relationships with males. They are women who are alone, or lonely, who separate from one man, idealizing another, or who attempt to find self-realization in work or eroticism, who grope toward liberation. The strictly up-to-the-moment chronology is reflected in references to the "supposed democracy" and a rather cynical attitude toward political parties as no longer functional. Many of the characters seem to function as much as embodiments of current attitudes as authentic individuals, and there are occasional touches of contemporary *costumbrismo*.

La función Delta (1981; The Delta Function) is mildly experimental in technique, employing the structure of two interrelated diaries, or chapters headed by chronological references (in one case, names of days of the week, in the other, dates). The dated entries are shorter and more numerous than those headed by names of days, which total seven and give very little sensation of being written as portions of a diary. Lucía, a woman in her sixties, terminally ill with cancer but undergoing radiation therapy, is the author of both diaries, one of them dealing exclusively with her reaction to her existential situation, her feelings about old age, death, and the one friend who still visits her. The second diary, more fictitious in its retrospective concentration on a crucial week in her life some three decades earlier as well as more self-consciously literary in its elaboration, concentrates upon the premiere of the movie in which she made her debut as a director at the age of thirty, and also explores her relationships with two lovers. Both feminist and existential in its orientation, the novel treats women's problems from a standpoint of obvious acquaintance with sociological and psychological theory. An absorbing testimony of the complex situation of women in Spain at the time of writing, it is of special interest for its tackling of another subject seldom treated, the problems of dying.

Te trataré como a una reina (1983; I'll Treat You Like a Queen) portrays the decadent, run-down, and degrading atmosphere of a Madrid nightspot in the red-light district, surrounded by cheap apartments, seamy clubs, and a general commerce in drugs and prostitution. The "Tropicana" bar sign, an illuminated postcard totally out of place, symbolizes the desire to escape to an exotic tropical paradise as suggested by the neon palm trees and boats (to Havana, in the case of Bella, a fiftyish barmaid). As a metaphor, it indicates the artificiality or impossibility of the escape offered, while drawing attention to the desperate limitations of the existences around it, characterized by solitude and poverty both spiritual and economic. The only escape is madness, death, or prison, or at best, a return to the miserable, backward village from which the characters first fled.

Journalist, Professor, Critic, Narrator

Born in Nava (Asturias) in 1930, Marta Portal has been a journalist and professor of literature, and has written essays, short stories, and literary criticism, as well as novels. She holds a doctorate in Information Sciences from Madrid's Universidad Complutense, where she teaches, and in 1975 was awarded the Adelaida Ristori Prize in Rome. Portal's first novel, *A tientas y a ciegas* (1966; Blindly, Gropingly), won the Planeta Prize, and has been a best-seller with some thirty editions. Her protagonist, Sara, a married woman of thirty, is something of an anomaly for Spain in the 1960s because she decides to return to the university to complete her degree. A frigid beauty who has resented her faithless husband's exhibition of her as an object, she has an affair with her professor and discovers her own sensuality. Nonetheless, she is too conventional to leave her husband, determining instead to give herself more completely to the marriage and have children. As a tentative expression of a woman's attempt at independence and finding self-fulfillment outside matrimony, the novel interests, despite the completely moralistic resolution. It is a curious commentary upon social mores that Spanish officialdom of the epoch (represented by the censorship) could find adultery a more acceptable solution than divorce. Portal's next work of fiction, *El malmuerto* (1967; The Wrongly Killed) is a group of novelettes. A second novel, *A ras de las sombras* (1969; Level with the Shadows), was followed one year later by *Ladridos a la luna* (1970; Barking at the Moon), which returns to the theme of adultery, once more given a conventional resolution. During a night of insomnia, the protagonist makes a decision to end the illicit love affair.

During much of the next decade Portal involved herself in study of the Mexican novel and of semiotics, receiving at least two fellowships from the Fundación March for study in Colombia and Mexico, as a result of which she published studies on the narrative of the Mexican Revolution and on *Pedro Páramo,* as well as a short-story collection, *La veintena* (1973; A Score [of Tales]). Approximately half the stories are fairly traditional, the remainder more experimental, such as "De orbe novíssimo," which approaches science fiction and concerns a world where nothing has names, and "La princesa y sus atributos" (The Princess and Her Attributes), a semiburlesque myth in which an Oriental princess is endowed with three breasts instead of two. Portal's most recent novel, *Un espacio erótico* (1983; An Erotic Space), refers in part to the "space" of fantasy, but is a tale of passion, loneliness, and rarefied love. Elvira, a Spaniard married to a Mexican and living in relative luxury in the capital, leaves her husband to return to Spain because of the husband's semipsychotic treatment of her as a representative of the Spanish conquerors and the outrage perpetrated against his Aztec ancestors— a treatment that is undermining her health. To retain her, the husband attempts to blackmail her with pornographic photos in which her face has been superimposed via double exposures on bodies in every imaginable sexual posture; when she refuses to be dissuaded, he uses the "proof" to prevent her gaining custody of their son or even having visitation rights. Elvira's work as a journalist and translator in Madrid permits some exploration of the problems of the female professional from a mildly feminist standpoint and depiction of her patronizing, patriarchal boss. Her work and writing alternate with a heterosexual love affair with a younger colleague, Montoro, and a lesbian relationship with her cousin, Elena, which she breaks off when Elena becomes too possessive. A disembodied female voice, which could be the novelist or an external narrator, begins and ends the novel with expressions of desire to know Elvira completely (sexually, psychically, spiritually).

Drama Teacher, Translator, Critic, and Narrator

Born in Madrid in 1943, Lourdes Ortiz is a prolific and versatile writer who has published children's books, written articles for newspapers and magazines on sociology, art, and literature, published essays on literary criticism, and translated books from French, in addition to writing three experimental plays (*Las murallas de Jericó, Penteo* and

Fedra) and at least five novels. *Luz de la memoria* (1976; The Light of Memory) is an experimental narrative beginning in the second person, but including the depositions of the protagonist's mother and wife, his reactions to them, and the associated recollections. Enrique García is confined to a psychiatric hospital after an emotional crisis in which he killed a dog (his wife is convinced he meant to kill her). Enrique, introverted, antisocial, and profoundly alienated since early youth (as is evident in his recollections which alternate with the present tense), feeling himself rejected by his parents for whom he expresses scorn, has a long history of frustrated relationships, failure as a writer, problems within a radical political organization and apparent expulsion, and imprisonment. His marriage became a ménage à trois (or more) in an endless round of alcohol, marijuana, hard drugs, and casual sex. Most of the novel is devoted to Enrique's treatment in the hospital. Shortly after release, when his liberated wife rejects his proposal that they retire to some solitary spot to live completely alone, he drunkenly decides to imitate Saint Simeon the Stylite by spending the remainder of his life in a tower, from which he falls to his death after a few hours when his wife has apparently just convinced him to descend.

Picadura mortal (1979; A Fatal Sting) is billed as a "novela negra" (crime or detective novel) and has the novelty of a female detective, who is retained to investigate a businessman's disappearance in the Canary Islands. Bárbara Arenas, the detective, is also the narrator, an intelligent, liberated woman whose casual sexual encounters form part of the narrative. The case is reconstructed subjectively, but with effective use of suspense which conceals the identity of the guilty party until the very end. Quite a different approach is employed in Ortiz's next novel, *En días como éstos* (1981; In Days Like These) which treats the theme of terrorism and violence. Toni (the protagonist), Carlos, and Jorge are terrorists and fugitives, whose flight from the law is the major event of the novel, narrated in large part by means of Toni's interior monologues. The contrast provided by the tranquil life of those on Toni's family's farm in the central portion of the novel makes even more shocking the conclusion: Toni is convinced by police agents to contact Carlos to allow him to clear himself with the police, but instead both are gunned down.

Urraca (1982) is a historical novel about Queen Urraca of Castile and Leon (1109–26), the mother of Alfonso VII. The narrative is structured as a dialogue between the imprisoned queen and the monk who brings her food, and employs archaic language in an effort to re-create the medieval atmosphere, as well as to portray the strong, ambitious character of the protagonist. *Arcángeles* (1986; Archangels) is a meditation upon the passage of time, and an ironic backward glance at those who were protagonists of the epoch twenty years ago (i.e., the 1960s in Spain). Simultaneously, the novel is a voyage of initiation on two levels, the initiation of young Gabriel in a quest for knowledge, via an itinerary involving a descent to a Dantesque inferno, and at the same time, a parallel initiation of the novelist who accompanies Gabriel on his journey as she searches for adequate means of narrating his new perspective and knowledge. The language attempts to reflect the rapidity of life in the 1980s as well as the conglomerate of sensations and colors of the typical televideo sequences, employing simultaneity of dream and waking impressions, an accumulation of aggressive imagery and telegraphic syntax.

Journalist, Narrator, and Critic

Soledad Puértolas, born in Zaragoza in 1947, studied journalism and later received an M.A. in Spanish literature at the University of California. She writes literary criticism for Spanish newspapers and, in addition to a study of Pío Baroja, has published *El bandido doblemente armado* (1980; The Doubly Armed Bandit), a novel narrated by a young man who serves as the link between ten independently constructed short stories (that could be read separately, but that are unified by the figure of the narrator and his relationship to the Lennox family, to which many other characters belong). The narration emphasizes the contrasting personalities of two youths, the narrator and his friend, Terry, the first a passive observer of life, the other a risk-taker increasingly involved in criminal activity.[7] An exploration of the themes of trust and friendship, the novel is also an attempt by the narrator to liberate himself from the "myths" of his youth—those who had impressed and influenced him—by converting them to literature. They are more mysterious and literary than realistic individuals. *Una enfermedad mortal* (1982; A Mortal Illness) is a short-story collection with pieces set in many places and times but unified by a common concern with moral problems, especially existential authenticity, responsibility for others, and sincerity. *Burdeos* (1986; Bourdeaux) is written in a markedly different tone from the writer's first novel, from the perspective not of adolescence but characters whose problem is maturity. Pauline, whose life has unfolded within the narrow confines of her family apartment and who long ago lost her illusions, begins slowly to accept the present and finally understands the fascination of life and its passing current. René, who has been different and solitary since his mother's departure, doubts his own ability to be brave and worthy, due to his radical mistrust of others. Lilly travels through Europe as a reporter, discovering her own weakness and solitude, for which her only solution is work and a problematic relationship with men. All three—united by comparable searches and losses, linked by intimate and invisible connections—share subtle similarities more than specific relationships. Their lives are symbolic of the lives of many, of a larger whole of which they are fragments, and are intended to reveal both the painful complexity of existence and its mysterious harmonies.

Minor Contemporary Narrators in Castilian

Elena Santiago, a journalist residing in Valladolid, has published several novels. *Acidos días* (1979; Acid Days) depicts the rural social organization and mentality by means of a circular structure and narration by the protagonist, Nino, who recalls his life and family and the women who mothered him rather than loved him as he wished. *Una mujer malva* (1981; A Mauve Woman) is protagonized equally by Maximina and nostalgia. Two faces of womanhood—childhood and old age—appear in the two halves of Maximina's name, the child Mina, and the aged woman, Doña Maxi, inhabitant of an asylum for senior citizens. José, the inseparable companion of her childhood, reappears in the asylum of the novelistic present, unleashing a chain of recollections but also leading to acceptance of old age and the aspects of life it represents. Since gerontological themes are very seldom central in novels, this work holds a special interest. *Gente oscura* (1981; Obscure People) employs a closed spatiotemporal frame of reference to present a few days in the life of Antonia, a very young woman who seeks more tenderness and warmth than what is offered by the egotistical persons around her (the "obscure people" of the title). Limited to life in a village and work in the family store, thinking of escape, she is drawn to two boys, representing love and friendship, and the idealized memory of a man, an emigrant, but opts to remain when she learns she is to be a godmother. *Manuela y el mundo* (1983; Manuela and the World) begins with the unexplained kidnapping of Manuela's husband, Teodoro, for what may be political reasons, and while she awaits news in a state of shock, Manuela relives her lifetime of contacts with men, from adolescence to maternity, and she is periodically recalled to the present by visits from the police or reporters.

Sara Suárez Solís, born in Oviedo, a teacher and critic, previously published two books of criticism on the novelists Camilo José Cela and Pérez de Ayala. Her first novel, *Camino con retorno* (1980; Road with Return), portrays the vicissitudes of a provincial family in the Franco era, with its atmosphere of intolerant religiosity, exalted patriotism, black marketeering, the hypocritical educational formation of women, the prejudices and social ambitions of the epoch that determine the destiny of Carmina, a figure representative of innumerable other women of her age, futilely sacrificed. *Juegos de verano* (1982; Summer Games) is written in the form of an extended letter from an aging Don Juan to a friend, in which he requests his assistance in extricating himself from the scandal in which his pursuit of women has involved him. The suicide of one victim led to entrapment as vengeance planned by a younger woman, and his wife seeks divorce as a result.

Josefina R[odríguez] Aldecoa, born in La Robla (León) in 1926, holds a doctorate in Philosophy and Letters from the University of Madrid. From the 1940s onward, together with her late husband, novelist Ignacio Aldecoa, she was associated with literary circles, especially the magazines *Espadaña* and *Revista Epañola* in which she published articles, stories, and translations (including the first story of Truman Capote to appear in Spain). She taught in Spain and in the United States, and in 1960 published *El arte del niño* (The Art of the Child), a pedagogical study. *A ninguna parte* (1961; To Nowhere) is a collection of short stories, and *Los niños de la guerra* (1983; Children of Wartime) a personal and generational memoir, includes biographies and literary commentaries on ten narrators of the Mid-Century Generation. Her first novel, *La enredadera* (1984; The Clinging Vine), is an artistically mature narration of the parallel lives of two women, separated by almost a century but united by a house, by their struggle against second-class citizenship, and their desire for self-affirmation. Using the round of the four seasons as its basic structure, the novel depicts in counterpoint two very different instances of the feminine condition. Julia, a present-day university professor, recently separated from her husband and facing the combined responsibilities and uncertainties of independence, contrasts with Clara, who in the nineteenth century was abandoned by her husband when complications after the birth of their daughter rendered her sterile. The country mansion in the mountains, surrounded by botanical luxury (gardens, greenhouse, and mountain wilderness), is the stage for the drama of conscience and memory in which the image of the clinging vine is used to considerable effect to represent woman's economic and emotional dependence. Despite the parallels between the two, the outcomes are different, for Julia has the benefits of education and the change in attitudes that the intervening century has produced. *Porque éramos jóvenes* (1986; Because We Were Young) employs three time planes, the present and a remote past being narrated in third person, and a more recent past in the first person as part of a series of letters written from New York to Ibiza. The converging times combine to provide different aspects of a collective itinerary, sections of the chronicle of a generation; and thus this second novel is in some ways a fictionalized version of Aldecoa's personal and generational memoir, *Los niños de la guerra*. Beginning with the suffocating restrictions suffered in the provinces during the postwar years and including the moments of liberty enjoyed in foreign countries, this novel re-creates the painful process of maturation of those who were young in the difficult early days of the Franco era, with the themes of love, disillusionment, existential alienation, and vital or political disenfranchisement. Despite the late date at which she became part of the novelistic scene, Aldecoa promises to figure among the more important women novelists of her generation.

Cristina Fernández Cubas, born in Arenys de Mar (Barcelona) in 1945, has published two short-story collections, *Mi hermana Elba* (1980; My Sister Elba) and *Los altillos de Brumal* (1983; The Highlands of Brumal), and one novel, *El año de Gracia* (1985; The Year of Grace). *Mi hermana Elba* includes four stories, the first of which is "Lúnula y Violeta," a contrasting portrait of two friends, one introverted and sensitive, passive and dependent, the other very much the opposite: extroverted, energetic, talkative. Mystery surrounds Violeta's identity and to some extent her sanity, as well as her death.[8] "La ventana del jardín" (The Window on the Garden) presents an unsettling encounter by the narrator with two former friends whom he visits at their isolated farm, only to discover little by little that their son lives in a sort of quarantine imposed by the psychotic parents, who have taught him a private language in which all words have their conventional connotations altered. The title story includes another abnormal child and evokes little Elba's death, but the focus of the story is the elder sister and narrator, who concentrates on the more normal world of her own passage from childhood to adolescence. The final story, like the others, presents the physical or moral degeneration of a life that ends in death or ruination. Eduardo discovers that his seemingly docile and submissive wife has in fact analyzed him most cleverly; this drives him to drink.

Fernández-Cubas published *El vendedor de sombras* (The Seller of Shadows), apparently children's fiction, in 1982, and followed a year later with her collection of stories, *Los altillos de Brumal*. The title tale presents the attraction of the remote village of Brumal where time becomes liquid and unreal, and language, clothes, and perceptions are inside out or backwards. Ambiguity exists, as in several of this writer's works, as to the character's sanity. Mirror symbols and various psychological abnormalities are manipulated to increase the interpretative possibilities, and several alcoholic characters and incomprehensible languages appear throughout Fernández-Cubas's work. Intertextual references are frequent, and occasional passages seem parodic.[9] *El año de Gracia* is an adventure story in the classic vein of *Robinson Crusoe* and *Sinbad the Sailor* (to which it makes frequent intertextual allusions). Daniel, the protagonist and narrator, a young seminarian who is skilled in Latin and Greek, is absolutely innocent and naive concerning things of the secular world. His voyage of initiation and adventure includes tempests, shipwreck, a desert island with a very peculiar savage who speaks Celtic. Daniel writes his memoirs during the progress of his experiences, and comments upon the process of writing as part of the memoir. The novel has a circular structure, the voyage ending where it began, but Daniel does not remain in the seminary, returning only long enough to notify the director of his decision to marry. The oneiric atmosphere throughout, the constant interplay of the normal or realistic with the marvelous or fantastic, the problems of communication and perception, as well as the extensive intertextual fabric, add depth and density to the novel, an adventure for intellectuals and connoisseurs.

Carmen Gómez Ojea, born in Gijón in 1945, has published at least three volumes and has some eight novels, fifty stories, and a book of poetry as yet unpublished. *Cántiga de agüero* (1982; Canticle of Omens), a complex family saga with mythic overtones, magic, and history, is set in Galicia and resembles in its atmosphere the works of Valle-Inclán, Torrente Ballester, and Alvaro Cunqueiro in their portrayal of magic, superstition, and capture of the special language and spirit of Galicia. Constanza, the protagonist, lives in an environment of witches, diabolic possession, madness, suicide, resuscitation, curses, mystery, and expiation. Reality is dual and ambivalent, as the imagi-

native versions of the characters contrast with the more prosaic interpretations of the narrator. Numerous intercalated tales occasionally
recall the Byzantine narrative. Constanza's arranged marriage, her husband's seeming indifference, her own moods of despair and isolation
are offset by her love affairs with her uncle's administrator and husband's brother. Isol, Constanza's daughter, runs away at fifteen and
becomes a gypsy; later she organizes a fanatic religious cult and dies at
the hands of her followers. Constanza dies as a blind saint in a small
Mexican village shortly after the Revolution, and her body is allegedly
cut into bits, the "relics" being sold to her followers, who later learn
that they have actually received chicken parts. And finally, Constanza
is the subject of a book by a foreign professor, suggesting the need for
a revision of history (a subject insinuated frequently by references to
Jewish ancestors, miracles, and other matters of dispute). Gómez Ojea
employs a feminist perspective to indicate the need for a rereading of
Spanish history from a feminist viewpoint.

   Otras mujeres y Fabia (1982; Other Women and Fabia) narrates the
daily lives of women in a lower-middle-class neighborhood from the
viewpoint of the schoolteacher, Fabia. A panoramic vision of feminine
activity is suggested when Fabia's evocations of famous women in history, her own female forebears, and an upper-class cousin are interspersed with her perceptions of the sights, smells, and sounds of
domestic chores of her neighbors. *Los perros de Hecate* (1985; Hecate's
Hounds) has a timeless atmosphere, in spite of an almost contemporary
time frame. The magical atmosphere of Galicia, witchcraft, and enchantment evoked in *Cantiga de agüero* reappear in the persons of Tarsiana, the protagonist and her wise maid, Regalina, both of whom have
not a little of the supernatural at given moments (Tarsiana believes or
imagines that she has lived a millennium). Both have the power to
contact spirits and act as mediums between the visible, normal world
and an interfacing world just beyond the lighted windows. In all three
novels Gómez Ojea's language is enormously rich, sometimes archaic,
deliberately medieval or hermetic and esoteric, unfailingly personal,
and fascinating.

   Clara Janés, born in Barcelona in 1940, is a novelist, poet, translator, essayist, and biographer. She has a degree in history and, according
to varied sources, has studied literature at the universities of Perugia,
Grenoble, and Oxford, and comparative literature at the Sorbonne.
With more than a dozen books to her credit, she has published a short

novel, *La noche de Abel Micheli* (1965; The Night of Abel Micheli), and a longer novel, *Desintegración* (1969).

Magdalena Guilló, born in 1940, holds a degree in mathematics, and since 1972 has resided in Salamanca where she teaches. Guilló writes both in Catalan, in which her first book was published *(En una vall florida al peu de les espases* [1977]) and in Castilian, in which she has published two novels, both dealing with Judaic themes. *Entre el ayer y el mañana* (1984; Between Yesterday and Tomorrow) is inspired by the life of Theodor Herzl and the foundation of Zionism, while *Un sambenito para el señor Santiago* (1986; Penitent's Garb for Santiago) is set in Sevilla at the end of the Renaissance, in the atmosphere of the Inquisition, but emphasizes the heterodoxy that abounded before the inquisitors had functioned long. The novel focuses upon the figure of the "heretical" doctor Arias Montano (a historical figure, also mentioned by Lope de Vega) and the inquisitorial process of this enlightened and ascetic humanist whose "sin" was his Jewish origin (he was a convert to Catholicism like many others investigated by the Holy Office).

Adelaida García Morales, born in Badajoz, was raised in Sevilla and studied at the University of Madrid. A teacher of Spanish language and literature as well as of philosophy, she has also served as a translator for OPEC, and worked as a model and actress. She has written poetry and short stories, and one of her unpublished novels, "Archipiélago," was a finalist for the Sésamo Prize in 1981. *El Sur* (1985; The South) is published together with another short novel, *Bene. El Sur* is a very original love story, powerful in its simplicity, which emphasizes (as does the companion piece) the mysterious aura surrounding the masculine characters who form the narrative centers. In a phantasmagoric reality, moving in a territory bordering upon incest and evil as contemplated from the amoral purity of adolescents, both tales take the reader to regions seldom treated by Spanish literature. *El silencio de las sirenas* (1985; The Silence of the Sirens) has been very successful commercially, and won both the Herralde Novel Prize and the Icaro Prize given by the periodical *Diario 16* to the literary discovery of the year. In the mysterious atmosphere of a forgotten, isolated village in Las Alpujarras (where the author has resided for five years) in the province of Granada and where the presence of the ancient Muslim conquerors still floats in the air, a young woman from far away lives a strange, excessive, and desperate love story with a man she barely knows, who resides in Barcelona. Again, the protagonist and central passion are totally romantic, although García Morales narrates this novel via the voice of María, the village schoolteacher, which allows her to establish a sense of distance.

Ana María Navales was born in Zaragoza (n.d., circa 1945) and wrote her doctoral thesis on the Spanish epistolary novel. She became known first as a poet, publishing several books of verse: *En las palabras* (1970; In the Words), *Junto a la última piel* (1973; Next to the Last Skin), *Restos de lacre y cera de vigilias* (1975; Remains of Lacquer and Wax from the Midnight Candle). She received gold medals in the international Silarus contest for poets in the Spanish language held in Italy and in the International Poetic Contest of Terni. *Cuatro novelistas españoles* (1974; Four Spanish Novelists) is a critical study of Delibes, Aldecoa, Sueiro, and Umbral. Later books of poetry attributed to Navales include *Paternoy, Del fuego secreto, Mester de amor, Los espías de Sísifo,* and *Nueva, vieja estancia.* She has also done two anthologies, one of poets and the other of narrators, focusing on contemporary Aragonese writers: *Antología de la poesía aragonesa contemporánea* and *Antología de narradores aragoneses contemporáneos.* Her first work of fiction is a short-story collection, *Dos muchachos metidos en un sobre azul* (1976; Two Kids in a Blue Envelope). The twelve tales cover a wide variety of themes and vary considerably in style from a frankly experimental mode resembling some of the poetry of the *Nueve novísimos poetas españoles* included in Castellet's 1970 anthology, to an attenuated surrealist interior monologue and a more recognizably neorealist mode, modified by the suppression of many verbs and frequent use of telegraphic syntax or very brief sentences. Navales's first or perhaps second novel is *El regreso de Julieta Always* (1981; The Return of Juliet Always). An aged and psychotic painter who signed her paintings with the pseudonym of Julieta Always is the center of narrative interest. Julieta is first imagined by the author after she reads a brief news report of the painter's death and then, moving backward and forward in time, various episodes provide a multiple perspective on the character: the childhood of a country girl, whose life is darkened by a crime; the Civil War coinciding with her young adulthood; flight to Cervère, across the French border, and the penury of the refugees; a later bohemian existence in Paris with other artists and her painting, as well as poverty and decadence. Using an open-ended structure and poetic language, the novelist presents Julieta's confinement to an insane asylum, unable to learn of the exposition of her paintings and her success, the fate of a woman who has vanished and is preserved only in another painter's portrait, and the novelist's invention. *El laberinto de Quetzal* (1985; The Laby-rinth of Quetzal) is Navales's third novel. An experimental narrative, it presents the vagaries of a labyrinthine ego or narrative consciousness via mythical "excursions" to different centuries and distant lands. The pagan god, Quetzal, with his eyes still new and ready for fabulous discoveries, transmits a novel image of objects, countenances, and life, always different and the same.

Chapter Nine
New Novelists in the Vernacular Languages

The Franco regime's early prohibition of publication in (and public use of) the vernacular languages began slowly to give way to de facto tolerance after the first two decades. The educational reforms of the 1970s, which included provision for teaching of the regional languages, restored official legitimacy and added impetus to vernacular publishing (especially in Catalan and Gallego), which began to increase, together with other cultural activities in the vernaculars, that is, theatrical festivals, song festivals, and folk programs. With the death of Franco and the transition to democracy came the regional autonomy movements, closely linked to their respective languages and cultures, and literary production in the minority languages boomed. A certain "backlash" for a time even saw expressions of hostility against those writers who failed to use their regional languages. Although there are numerous regional autonomy movements with their associated cultural manifestations, some of them cannot be considered languages: Bable (Asturian), Andalán (Aragonese), Andalusian, and Leonese, to mention some of the better-defined and more aggressive, belong more properly to the category of dialects. At least three—Euskera (Basque), Catalan, and Gallego—are sufficiently differentiated linguistically to merit separate treatment and have their own literary traditions.

A Basque Poet, Novelist, and Journalist

Arantza Urretabizkaia, born in Donostia (San Sebastián) in 1947, served her literary apprenticeship as a poet, contributing to the anthology *Euskal Literatura* (1972), and winning the City of Irun Prize with *Maitasunaren magalean* (1982; In the Lap of Love), her second volume of poems. She published her first novel, *Zergatik Panpox?* (1979; Why, Little One?), a lyrical interior monologue expressing the loneliness and pain of abandonment felt by a young mother. Struggling to support herself and her son, still yearning for the husband she has begun to outgrow, she expresses her unhappy groping toward liberation and a dawning awareness of her own capacities. A collection of three stories entitled *Aspaldian espero zaitudalako, ez nago sekulan bakarrik* (1983; Since I've Waited for You so Long, I'm Never Alone Any More) exhibits the same lyrically intimate tone, sensitivity, and tenderness of her novella. Urretabizkaia also collaborated with Antton Olariaga in writing a historical epic, *Albaniaren Konkista* (1983; The Conquest of Albania), which was made into a movie.

A Galician Poet, Novelist, Actress, and Radio Journalist

Xohana Torres, born in Santiago de Compostela in 1931, has written all of her work in Galician. Very involved both in feminism and the Galician cultural movement, she created the first totally Galician radio program, *Raiz e tempo* (1963; Root and Time), and during the same decade acted in an avant-garde theater group working in Gallego, Teatro-Estudio. Torres received the Pedron de Ouro Award in 1972 for her contributions to Galician culture, especially her novel *Adiós, María* (1971), which deals with one of the region's most significant endemic ills, the perennial emigration from the poor and overpopulated area to other countries. Torres has also written poetry, drama, and children's literature, and has adapted the works of several other writers to Gallego. She is a critic and essayist, writing particularly on ethnography and drama. Her major themes are love of Galicia, nostalgia, passing time, loneliness, desolation, and memories of family. Additional works include *A outra banda do Iberr* (On the Other Side of the Iberr), *Polo mar van as sardinas* (1967; The Sardines Go by the Sea), *Un hotel de primera sobre o rio* (1968; A First-Class Hotel on the River), and *Estacions ao mar* (1981; Seasons/Stations of the Sea).

A Galician Writer, Teacher, and Feminist

Born in Vigo in 1938, María Xosé Queizán teaches Galician language and literature and is a politically involved feminist. Her essay collections include *A muller en Galicia* (1977; Women in Galicia) and *Recuperemos as mans* (1980; Recovering Our Hands). *A nova narrativa*

galega (1979; New Narrative in Galicia) is literary criticism. Queizán
has long participated in theatrical projects and has written an unpublished play, *Non conven chorar mais* (No Point in Crying Any More). The
author of numerous uncollected poems and short stories, she also has
published at least three novels, beginning with *A orella no buraco* (1965;
By the Shore of a Hole), written under the influence of French objectivism and the *nouveau roman*. A more or less direct outgrowth of the
author's sojourn as a student in Paris and her encounter with Heideg-
ger, Jaspers, Sartre, and other existential philosophers, the novel presents a fundamental human problem, liberty, and, without attempting
to resolve it, does suggest the need for seeking solutions. The novelist's
youthful quest, her restlessness, intellectualism, and vitality are insinuated, along with hints of existentialism. In each chapter a cold, objective evocation establishes the minute or hour, the sociological
tempo, in counterpoint with the time of a man's life. *Amantia* (1984)
is a feminist novel whose action is set during the Roman colonization
of Galicia in the fourth century. The egregious figure of Priscillian
stands out in the epicurean atmosphere of the decadent empire, as does
a circle of cultured women, connoisseurs of Roman poetry. Some of the
poetry in question resembles the "concrete poetry" experiments of the
late 1960s and early 1970s (in which the words or letters of the poem,
in addition to a message, had to picture an object). Thus, a poem to
Maximila forms a lyre (although very bad lyrics). The heroine, Amantia, a tireless reader and excellent, intuitive critic, is unpretentious,
sensitive, simple yet elegant. More than an active force, however, she
is an observer of historical events (including important happenings in
the early Christian church). The author has done a good deal of ar-
chaeological research, and the pages are liberally sprinkled with the
names of ancient items of clothing and objects of adornment, archaic
articles once in daily use, and references to personages and events of
the epoch. The text is followed by a glossary of names of historical
characters and pre-Roman gods of Galicia, with identifying data. *O
segredo da Pedra Figueira* (1985; The Secret of Figueira Rock) is a semi-
mythological, semifantastic novel in the vein of *The Lord of the Rings,*
illustrated with stylized paintings that recall both fairy tale and myth.
Possibly evoking the Celtic period of Galicia, the novel is a blend of
primitivism and sophistication (and although presumably intended for
adolescents, could be read by adults). Treasure, dragons, seafaring adventure, pagan gods and priestesses, a secret cave, a magic stone, and
cabalistic language all form part of what is on a deeper level a bil-

dungsroman, the growing up of a girl to womanhood beneath the matriarchal tutelage of older women.

A Catalan Novelist and Poet

Maria Angels Anglada, born in Vich in 1930, specialized in Classical Philology—which is often reflected in her creative writing—and won the Josep Pla Prize (one of the most important awards for prose in Catalan) with her first novel, *Les closes* (1979; The Enclosed). Anglada has also written critical essays on Italian poetry and themes from Greek mythology. A historical novel, *Les closes* is set against the background of nineteenth century Catalan society, re-creating the personal history of Dolors Canals in the difficult years immediately prior to the liberal Revolution of 1868 which ushered in the First Republic. The novel is narrated by Dolors's great-granddaughter, and experiments both with nonlinear narrative and multiple perspectives. Translated to Castilian with the title *Los cercados,* it appeared in 1986. This is not Anglada's first excursion into Catalonia's past, as she had published *Memòries d'un pagès del segle XVIII* (Memoirs of a Peasant of the Eighteenth Century) in 1978. Previously, she had collaborated with Núria Albò in producing a poetry collection entitled *Díptic* (1972). In 1980 she returned to poetry as a solo writer, producing a collection characterized by its constant references to the Mediterranean and the classical world, as perhaps may be suggested by its title *Kyparissia.* People, landscape, language, and atmosphere are equally important, although if a major theme must be identified, it is love of country (Majorca).

No em dic Laura (1981; My Name Isn't Laura) is a collection of stories, characterized (like the previous work) by emphasis upon things Greek, containing three subdivisions that may be considered long short stories or novelettes (each is further subdivided in two, three, or four titled parts). The first is set in Greece under the military dictatorship, switching to the fifteenth century before its ending, and provides a poetic re-creation of various archeological incidents and the Greek landscape. The second, "Flors per a Isabel" (Flowers for Isabel) is based upon historical fact and returns to themes already enunciated in Anglada's first novel, as well as treating the same setting(s) and members of the same family, although the time frame has been moved back to the period of the Napoleonic wars at the beginning of the century. The last tale is set in Vich in the postwar epoch (during the childhood of the writer), but it is more than a simple re-creation of the past; above all, it is an imaginative piece of fiction that combines lyricism and intrigue.

Viola d'amore (1983; Viola of Love) differs from Anglada's earlier fiction in no longer depending upon history or archeological reconstruction. Anglada now calls upon the world of music as external intertext for her fiction, and much as her previous work had a tripartite structure, she returns to the principle of threes here, introducing the Trio Izvorul, whose first two members (Gerda and Virgili) subtly recall Thomas Mann, while the third member, who comes from an opposing ideology, constitutes a link with Anglada's prior works. In combination, the group functions in the lyric climate of the work to provide a sense of counterpoint and internal rhythm.

Novelist and Poet

Born in Tarragona in 1936, Olga Xirinacs has been very active in the cultural life of her native city. Although she began writing in her childhood, she did not become known until 1971, and since then has won numerous prizes. Her poetry collections include *Botons de tiges grises* (1977; Gray Stem Buttons), *Clau de blau* (1978; Key to the Blue); *Llençol de noces* (1979; Bridal Sheet), and *Preparo el te sota palmeres roges* (1981; I Prepare Tea beneath Red Palms). The first significant prose work is *Música de cambra* (1982; Chamber Music), described by the author as a book of memories interwoven with strange adventures. The format is a modified diary form, covering three years (1979–1981), but inasmuch as what is involved is thoughts, the chronology is actually much ampler and more diffuse. A volume of old periodicals from 1850 found in a half-forgotten house mentions curious facts that are re-created in *Música de cambra* as a counterpoint to the present-day narration. *Interior amb difunts* (1983; Interior with Cadavers), winner of the 1982 Josep Plà Prize, treats of the insistence of the dead on resuscitating, their desire to live again. Drawing in part upon the turn-of-the-century impressionist painters for background, the novel delineates the period (especially the years around 1906–1907) as a passionate time, telling the story of young lovers whose letters form part of the narrative and date from those years. Again using a modified diary format combined with the epistolary form, Xirinacs extends the narrative to the end of the 1920s, but the primary emphasis is on the first decade of this century. *Al meu cap una llosa* (1985; A Gravestone at my Head) won the Sant Jordi prize, and again re-creates a bygone time, but a more recent one: the early part of World War II and the atmosphere of wartime England. However, Xirinacs is more interested in another historical and literary occurrence, the suicide of Virginia Woolf in March 1941, and to this end she employs the shade or spirit of Woolf, creating a counterpoint between the shadow's thoughts and the crisp, official version of the war's progress as broadcast on the BBC.

Cartoonist and Fiction Writer

Nùria Pompeia was born in Barcelona of a well-to-do family in 1938 and raised during the Franco era. Initially a journalistic cartoonist, she contributed regularly to the radical periodical *Triunfo* and later became managing editor of the weekly *Por favor*. Pompeia has the somewhat unusual distinction of being the only woman in the Peninsula to become nationally known as a cartoonist. Working both in Castilian and Catalan, she produces works of a hybrid nature, neither simply cartoon nor fully verbal: text and sketch are equally important. Her best-known creation is the "brat," Palmira, who dominates a sort of comic strip collected or anthologized in *La educación de Palmira* (1972; Educating Palmira). Pompeia's most famous character is a sort of Lucy from the "Peanuts" comic strip with the important difference introduced by an even stronger feminist emphasis. In this integrally conceived volume Pompeia demonstrates how traditional education deforms the female child's natural impulses and intellect, setting the stage for future conflict and alienation. *Maternasia*, an earlier volume of cartoons (1967), relies heavily upon visual effects in the re-creation of a graphic history of the "second sex" which stresses the changes in a woman's body and life-style that motherhood produces.

In *Mujercitas* (1975; Little Women), a compendium of themes from four earlier collections of cartoons plus text, Pompeia combines incisive satire with more innocent hilarity in an indictment of those sectors and attitudes of society that in various ways play a part in changing the active, creative, adventurous, spontaneous, rebellious girl-child into a passive, inhibited, submissive, and boring conformist. Against Victorian morality and biblical defenses of male dominance, the emphasis on physical beauty and sexuality, sexist role-typing, and the ably parodied "happily-ever-after" plot, Pompeia juxtaposes traditional stereotypes with contemporary feminist reality, making her points with penetrating humor and insight. This author's first exclusively verbal text, *Cinc cèntims* (Five Cents), appeared in 1981, a collection of twelve short stories dominated by their common narrator, Lucy. The same characteristically satiric sense of humor and critique of upper-class life-styles and conformity are expressed in vivid, precise, and colloquial Catalan. Utilizing a feminist viewpoint without exception, the stories cover such subjects as a drunken dinner party, weekend rituals and outings of the well-to-do, pseudo-intellectual pursuits, sexist educa-tion, and the pretense of would-be art collectors. Strongly feminist notes are struck by the portrayal of politics within marriage, and the disappointment of women's hopes for liberation under one regime after another (Spanish marriage emerges as a paternalistic despotism). Be-neath the humor and probing analysis lies an intense experience of the disappointments and trials of marriage and motherhood.

Inventari de l'ultim dia (1986; Inventory of the Last Day) belongs, by virtue of its title, to the not-insignificant literature of apocalyptic themes that has appeared in the second half of the present century. A woman returning to the abandoned ancestral home of her family (al-ready expropriated by the local city government and on the point of being auctioned off to pay outstanding debts) provides the pretext for most of the book, or at least for those situations having decisive scenes set in Barcelona. The female narrator humorously depicts the doubts and vicissitudes to which her generation was subjected. With passing years, it becomes clear that her words refer as much to the international as the national scene, to postimperial America as to Spain. Examining life among the Barcelona bourgeoisie, the novelist introduces other ex-plicit or implicit life-forms somehow linked to previous ones. "Inven-tory of the Last Day" is a lucid personal reflection upon the values of the bourgeoisie of immediately before and after the war. The female protagonist relates from considerable ironic distance her reflection on the values and life-styles of certain contemporary figures whose choices during these politically difficult years of transition appear based less upon competition and personal competence than upon chances for ob-taining lasting security. Above all, this novel constitutes an exposé of relations between the government and the principals, family, and as-sociates of those groups out of popular favor. The novelist is especially interested in revealing relationships between twentieth-century spe-cialists and their constituencies or public dimensions (i.e. contrasting decisions and determinations made on the family and social levels). *Inventari de l'ultim dia* is based upon historical events, upon recent (post-Franco) history in Spain, and has both a sociological and political science component. The narrative personality implicitly rejects established principles based upon relationships of power, family groups, and authoritarianism, as well as intellectual fashions, and questions authority in various significant ways, most particularly within the family. In this highly personal novel Pompeia returns to a point before time or outside meaningful contemporary time, examining the types that are perceived as worthy members of the family dynasty. The narrative constitutes a searching reflection upon the social and economic philosophies of Marxism, as well as a meditation upon the mechanisms of power. Without the appearance of an autobiographical novel, it clearly reflects the writer's reactions to events in Spain during the transition to democracy and the several power shifts, as well as the shortcomings of the various ideologies, interwoven with meditations inspired by fluctuations and ideological uncertainties in the writer's personal life. *Inventari de l'ultim dia* provides a lucid and sometimes tragic reflection upon a generation disoriented and struggling to cope with freedom, wavering between nostalgia for past certainties and a present of drug-induced mysticism, frenetic hedonism, and utter despair. Transcending feminist concerns without abandoning them as she broadens her focus to the period as a whole, Pompeia is clearly a writer to watch.[1]

Painter, Novelist, and Feminist

Born in 1937 to a conservative bourgeois family in Barcelona, Nùria Serrahima lived her early years under traditional auspices and received her elementary education at a convent school. She decided at age fourteen upon a painting career, leaving school for five years of intensive study. Before fully embarking upon an artistic career, however, she decided that her true interest was literature, and shortly before her father's death in 1958, she began to prepare herself as a writer. After an apprenticeship served in journalistic pursuits, she produced her first novel, *Mala guilla* (1973; The Bad Sprout), written in Catalan at a time when very few women were choosing to produce literature in the vernaculars. In this very personal account of passage to adulthood the autobiographical content is considerable, both on the sociohistorical and personal levels. The adolescent's experience is portrayed in the context of tense postwar readjustment under the Franco regime. Her relationship with her late father emerges as especially significant. Like the author, the fourteen-year-old protagonist decides to quit school, but before she does so, the novel portrays formative influences that combined to repress and limit female students and abort artistic or literary interests, independence, and self-expression: continual insistence on sin and confession, the distant echoes of World War II, fear aroused by her totalitarian grandparents, and a labeling of the girl as bad because of innocent mischief, energy, and spontaneity.

L'olor dels nostres cossos (1982; The Odor of our Bodies) is a collection of three novellas united by common feminist themes, the use in all of a first-person narrative perspective, and a feminine protagonist. The narrative consciousness of each is a woman, and the attitudes and tone are feminist. In the title novella Gloria (the married protagonist) spends a sleepless night beside a snoring husband, reflecting upon conjugal life, anguished by her low self-esteem, the disillusionment with romantic love, her economic dependence, Rafael's paternalistic tyranny, and her love for their children, which is the primary factor in her rejection of separation and suicide. Both Gloria and Rafael have had numerous affairs, their marriage having become a matter of habit and maintaining appearances. The style is rather matter-of-fact, in contrast with the lyrical, occasionally surrealistic effects in the second story, "Negres moments d'Emma" (Emma's Black Moments). Instead of a single, unbroken unit of time and a single monologue, Emma's disordered memories constitute many brief "moments," recollections of significant incidents arranged without regard to chronology. Emma is brilliant, but insecure, neurotic, suicidal, alcoholic, claustrophobic, asthmatic, hysterical, and radically alone in a fantastic, hallucinatory world. Her numerous affairs have not satisfied her many needs and longings, and a doctor who sees her several times estimates that she needs at least five years of psychoanalysis. Emma suffers occasional overwhelming homicidal urges and, like Gloria, longs to escape responsibility. She appears to be temporarily separated from a lesbian lover, but the extrication of reality from fantasy and hallucination is very difficult. "Amants" (Lovers), the third tale, is also a collection of memories, but in a lighter vein, as the narrative consciousness has assigned a letter of the alphabet to each of her former lovers (thirty in all) and recalls them in alphabetical order. Fragmentary, nostalgic, and evocative, the recollections resemble prose poems in their lyric brevity.

Liberated Expatriate and Intellectual

Born in Barcelona of bourgeois family in 1940, Helena Valentì grew up in postwar Spain in the Franco era, experiencing the repression and restrictions that were typical of the period. Escaping this narrowness, she lived and studied in England, obtaining her Doctor of Literature degree from Cambridge University. Her marriage to an Englishman ended in divorce, and Valentì lived a bohemian existence in London for some five years in which she observed the women's liberation movement there. She returned to Catalonia in 1974, living for a time in Barcelona. Her first book, *L'amor adult* (1977; Adult Love), is a collection of thematically related stories in which feminist and autobiographical substrata are frequently important. The fictional collection is replete with motifs based upon personal experience: the foreign female in England, the enlightened and tolerant British husband, posters with women's lib subjects, quantities of gin and unwanted pregnancies, an abundance of hostilities within matrimony where there seems to be no communication but instead frequent separations and aggressively unconventional sexuality, the feminist movement per se, and the "liberated" but not therefore satisfied female. If there is a common denominator to this collection of eleven stories, it is the liberated woman (protagonist or central consciousness of various tales); the remainder present an unsatisfactory marriage or love relationship. A dominant note is the battle of the sexes, a conflict from which neither motherhood nor infancy appear to be exempted. More decisive than sexual license would be the enchantment of nearly all characters with the mystique of their respective sexes and the foreseeable inability to mature. The feminism of Valentì is judicious, neither unduly agressive nor defensive.

In *La solitud d'Anna* (1981; Anna's Loneliness) the existential preoccupations already implicit in the previous fictional work are amplified. Anna, the protagonist, as the title might suggest, is practically an incarnation of existential solitude (in this novel, primarily the feminine lot). Masculine characters appear only in secondary roles and are portrayed as insensitive, indifferent, and impotent (but necessary for procreation). Brutal or ineffective, infantile or criminal, they are exploiters so self-centered as to be all but devoid of emotion and so, lacking in understanding, they are almost completely unaware of their offenses against womankind. Anna, after three years of living with her lover Lluis, decides to have an abortion, which spells the end of their relationship. Lluis disappears leaving a fistful of large bills, while Anna is in the clinic. There is a general atmosphere of absurdity and despair, particularly concerning the character of Raquel, who becomes a mother while still amost a child, repeating a perennial cycle wherein the male disappears once fecundation is completed, leaving the female to cope alone. Valentì holds out little hope for marriage as an institution, or for heterosexual love. In *La dona errant* (1986; The Errant Female) Valentì presents a novel without beginning or end, in which the action is directly melded to the daily adventure of people in the street, so well known yet so mysterious. The novel is compared to a giant chess game without players, in which the pieces are moved regardless of what those present might wish, as if impelled by unknown cosmic forces. The younger generations, searching for their niche in the world, have inherited from the immediately preceding generation certain modes of conduct that they intuit are mistaken, and so are concerned with the "gap" between their scales of values. Valentì has translated the writings of Doris Lessing, Virginia Woolf, Katherine Mansfield, and Robert Graves to Catalan and Castilian.

An Academician, Librarian, and Novelist

Joana Escobedo, born in Barcelona in 1942, has produced a number of erudite articles and books related to her librarianship of special collections at the Biblioteca de Catalunya. She also is a teacher of the Catalan language to foreigners and has collaborated on texts for this purpose. Her novels include *Silenci endins* (1979; Silence toward the Center) and *Amic, amat* (1980; Friend, Beloved). *Silenci endins* employs different viewpoints to relate a nonlinear history of passions, intuitions, frustrated desire, ontological insecurity, and powerlessness. During a seemingly endless night of insomnia, in which the protagonist moves between sleeping and waking, reality and half-dreaming, she becomes increasingly aware of the imprint left by years of rigid, formal education and a morally repressive environment. A persona of the author, with whom she shares several points in common—both are from Barcelona, approximately the same age, scholars of linguistics, acquainted with several languages, fond of travel, and addicted to the movies as well as poetry—the protagonist experiences an intellectual awakening (as the author did about 1962 under the influence of new European philosophical currents), an existential awareness and consciousness of nothingness. The novel analyzes the consciousness of an entire group of middle-class intellectuals. In *Amic, amat* the female protagonist, Magda, is engaged in a search for identity and self-expression within the confines of a difficult relationship. Struggling against her need for and dependence upon love, she begins to question conventionalism while defending herself from pain, both physical and psychic. The masculine protagonist also undergoes an identity crisis (the love relationship is to a certain extent the axis around which each revolves), experiencing the pain of falling out of love and attendant fears. The love relationship is analyzed against the background of daily life in Barcelona that forms a counterpoint with a contrasting socio-cultural ambience, that of New York, which is first visited, then remembered. The nonlinear chronological sequence is combined with a use of dialogue alternating with interior monologue.

A Difficult, Independent, Neglected Narrator

Antonia Vicens, another Majorcan narrator, born in Santanyi in 1942, won the important Sant Jordi prize for the novel with her first attempt at the genre, *39 graus a l'ombre* (1968; 39 Degrees [centigrade; 102 degrees Fahrenheit] in the Shade). This was followed by *Material de fulletó* (1971; Material for a Soap Opera), in which—as in the earlier work—the author presents a concrete, clearly delimited world, profoundly examined, filled with turbulence and intuitions and seen largely through adolescent eyes. The final pages both surprise and disconcert the reader, opening up a world of magic filled with unexpected dramatics and a bit of horror. Vicens evokes the beginning of that escape to the limits of a dream, an oneiric landscape where things are and are not, simultaneously, where the narrative moves from objective reality to contradictory interior worlds, blurred or absurd. This same sort of vision of the world or of reality occurs in other narratives by Vicens, *Primera comunió* (1980; First Communion, a story collection) and *Quilòmetres de tul per a un petit cadaver* (1982; Miles of Tulle for a Little Cadaver). These works also exhibit the rupture of temporal planes, breaks in the language, and changes of narrative forms, intended to emphasize the dichotomy between reality and illusion and evoke other forms of irreality, being and nonbeing. One of Vicens's key works is *La festa de tots els morts* (1974; 2d ed., 1982; The Feast of the Dead, i.e., All Souls Day), a novel with rare vigor and fantasy, that opens the eyes of the reader to see that what is "normal" is also strange, desperate, sad, poetic, risky, and beautiful. Some of the episodes in *La festa de tots els morts* are strongly reminiscent of Kafka, although the plot of this hauntingly poetic narrative revolves around the impenetrable solitudes of Coloma and Victor, two essentially isolated beings, conscious of their aloneness yet unable to achieve a saving, redeeming capacity of communication that would allow them to break through the shell surrounding them. Vicens's love of words and of language, of Catalan and Majorcan, reaches a particularly fervent expression in this novel, which the critic Josep Llompart in the prologue to the second edition considers to be a key work in Vicens's evolution. *La santa* (1980; The Saint), like several of this writer's works, portrays her native area of Majorca, a small town on the eastern coast of the island with its streets and plazas, atmosphere and inhabitants. The village acquires generic properties, despite its clear individualization, and begins to exhibit aspects of the universal of which it is a social microcosm. Vicens thereby manages a lucid critique of society with universal implications, without venturing beyond that area that she knows best.

A Valencian Writer, Philosophy Teacher, and Translator

Isabel-Clara Simó, born in Alcoi (Valencia) in 1943, was for ten years director of the journal *Canigó,* to which she also contributed many articles. In addition to her teaching, she has translated from the Italian. Her fiction is always accessible, making brilliant use of everyday language and anecdotes, motivated by a strong social consciousness and sense of commitment. Simó is concerned above all with the oppression of women, workers, and Catalan-speaking peoples. She examines problems of women of various ages, especially adolescence and old age, in her short-story collection, *Es quan miro que hi veig clar* (1979; It's When I Look that I See Clearly). Another concern is the emerging feminine independence. *Júlia* (1983), Simó's history based first novel, portrays the struggles of industrial laborers in Valencia at the turn of the century. The protagonist, Julia, is a former factory worker who suddenly married into the upper class as the result of a capricious old man's whim that breaks unwritten laws against class mobility. The resultant turbulence within the household allows the novelist to examine bias as well as Julia's inner strength. The narrative covers some twenty-two years, although part of the historical background extends at least twenty more years into the past. Julia's case is clearly exceptional for the epoch, and her mentality in some ways more resembles the twentieth-century feminist. *Bresca* (1985; Honeycomb), a new story collection, examines some difficult social problems, particularly suicide and violence (even among children), but these are handled with reasonable optimism and occasional humor. Another novel, *Idols* (1985), masterfully combines feminist concerns with the writer's denunciation of the neglect of Catalan literature, utilizing a counterpoint between the language with its artistic manifestations and the strong, nurturing woman who may be seen as an allegory of popular culture. Bru, the male protagonist, a lucid young student, is entrapped for a time in a passionate relationship with disturbing Ruth, but eventually chooses Maria Dolça. The title is drawn from Francis Bacon's *Novum Organum,* from which a paragraph is cited to illustrate the prejudices (idols) that function to cloud one's thinking.

A Major Journalist, Feminist, and Narrator

Born in Barcelona in 1946, Montserrat Roig is a well-known journalist and television interviewer who also has taught at the University of Barcelona. The daughter of the Catalan writer, Tomas Roig i Llop, she participated in the 1966 anti-Franco student occupation of the Capuchin monastery in Barcelona, a demonstration that signaled the open resurgence of Catalan nationalism that marks her generation. Roig has published at least six collections of her interviews as well as a study of Catalans in Nazi concentration camps, a report on Leningrad during World War II, and a volume of feminist essays, mostly in Castilian, including *Rafael Vidiella, l'aventura de la revolució* (1974; R.V., The Adventure of Revolution); *Els catalans als camps nazis* (1977; trans. to Castilian as *Noche y niebla: los catalanes en los campos nazis,* 1978); *El feminismo* (1981); *Mujeres en busca de un nuevo humanismo* (1981; Women in Search of a New Humanism). *¿Tiempo de mujer?* (1980, A Woman's World?) is a collection of Roig's previously published articles on women.[2]

Between 1970 and 1980 she published a collection of short stories and four novels in Catalan, all of which appeared in Spanish translations between 1980 and 1983. Her literary style reflects the influence of her journalistic apprenticeship, and her fiction communicates a strong sense of the contemporary chronicle. Older Catalan authors (Oller, Villalonga, Pla, and Rodoreda) are her principal models. Her first important literary success came with her short stories, with prizes in 1966 and 1969. In 1970 her short-story collection won the important Victor Català prize for fiction; *Molta roba i poc sabó . . .* (Lots of Clothes and Little Soap [and So Clean They Love It]). Translated into Castilian as *Aprendizaje sentimental* (1981; Sentimental Apprenticeship), these stories have also been rendered into Russian. The central theme of the collection, if there is one, is an initial consideration of the world attempted by an adolescent, a mixture of sarcasm and idealization. The protagonists of the several tales represent one generation of the Franco era in Barcelona. Their confusions with Marx and Engels, sex and God, comprise one aspect of the stories. They are contrasted with another group that considered them merely laughable caricatures. The combined cast of characters includes many fictional residents of the "Ensanche" (Expansion) area of Barcelona, a conservative bourgeois section built at the turn of the century, who reappear in Roig's trilogy which explores the thorny problems of Catalan identity in the modern world.

Ramona, adéu (1972; Goodbye, Ramona), first volume in the trilogy, explores the evolution of the Miralpeix and Claret families between 1894 and 1979, concentrating on the women. Using a third-person external narrator in combination with the diary format, Roig presents three generations of women with the same name. Their thoughts, their lives, their perceptions of local and international history are given more significance than those of the masculine members of the family. Really three stories in one, the novel recounts significant episodes in the loves and lives of the grandmother, mother, and daughter, all called Mundeta (a nickname for Ramona), members of the petite bourgeoisie of Barcelona between 1894 and 1969. The mother's oft-repeated account of her search for the body of her husband among the Civil War dead serves as a framing device. Neither an easy novel nor a pleasant one, this work presents close relationships without closeness, emphasized by the use of different forms of narration (the grandmother's disappointments in love are communicated through a first-person diary, the mother's story is a standard omniscient narration, and the daughter's inability to distinguish love from politics is presented via extensive use of dialogue). Nonetheless, each has essentially the same illusions and must lose those misconceptions concerning life and love through personal experience without being able to benefit from the lessons of the others. Use of the family as a structural framework facilitates the recording of various periods of contemporary Catalan history, as well as examination of similarities, change, and contrast among the individuals. The youngest, Ramona, rebels against social class conventions, but must struggle with the new problems that such emancipation brings. There is a good deal of sociological documentary in this novel, and throughout the entire trilogy.

The second novel of the trilogy, *El temps de les cireres* (1977; The Time of Cherries, translated into Castilian and Greek) won the 1976 Sant Jordi Prize. Pursuing the saga of the same families, the author concentrates upon the return of a forty-year-old woman to the family she ran away from some twelve years before. Experiencing ambivalent feelings, she suffers from apprehension and affection as she observes the distant behavior of the various family members who have become strangers to her. The title alludes to a happy time long past, a group of people who are psychologically lost. *L'hora violeta* (1980; English trans., *The Violet Hour*/forthcoming from Virago Press), undoubtedly the most feminist portion of the trilogy, presents fictional biographies of the same families blended with political and feminist considerations. The title is drawn from the "violet hour" mentioned in *The Waste Land,* as indicated by T. S. Eliot's lines cited on the title page. Imbued with feminist preoccupations and thematics, the novel reflects the "testimonial" orientation of a reporter-novelist who is also a contemporary historian. The novel is divided into five parts, the first ("L'hora perduda," The Lost Hour) presenting the triangle involving Natalia, a successful photographer; Jordi, a writer; and Agnes, mother of his children. Natalia's confidante, Norma (protagonist of the third part, "L'hora dispersa"), is a mask of the author. The central section, "Novel of the Violet Hour," set a generation earlier, focuses on Natalia's mother Judit (a frustrated concert pianist), alternating sections of her diary 1942–48 with action set in 1958 and viewed by an omniscient narrator. The diary re-creates the complex relationship of Judit and her husband Joan following his return from a Nazi concentration camp, the birth of their mongoloid son Père, and the child's death at the age of five. Portions are narrated from the perspective of Joan's sister Patricia in 1964 upon Judit's death, and others emphasize the perspective of Kati, Judit's intimate friend who died a suicide. The panorama of unfulfilled and frustrated females that results is grim, as their lives seem to differ only in minor degrees of intensity of anguish.

L'opera quotidiana (1982; The Daily Opera) exploits the analogy with a musical opera as the characters deliver arias and cavatinas or initiate duets in the attempt to retell their life stories or communicate their intimate feelings. For most of them, love is largely an attempt to escape from their boring daily lives. Roig again uses characters and ambients drawn from her trilogy, as Patricia Miralpeix, ancient but seemingly eternal, patiently listens to the narrative recounted by Horaci Duc. The characters are dreamers, disoriented or disconcerted, who attempt to invent a life beyond the limits of the drab, unsatisfactory reality they know. Roig creates one of her best-developed masculine characters, able to love completely and with full devotion (unlike her female creations). The novel is structured as a series of conversations between Horaci Duc and his landlady, Patricia Miralpeix.

Feminist Novelist, Translator, Journalist, Scriptwriter

Born in 1946 in Manacor (Majorca), Maria Antònia Oliver is known for her fantasy creations, an especially imaginative style of writing that owes something to the magical heritage of her native island. She has written both short and long fiction, criticism, travelogues, and TV screenplays, in addition to newspaper work and translating from English and French to Catalan (including works of Virginia Woolf, who has had a significant impact on Oliver's own creative writing). Her first novel, *Croniques d'un mig estiu* (1970; Chronicles of a Half Summer), is concerned with the rites-of-passage theme and presents the sexual awakening of an adolescent boy, against the background of a similar (symbolic) loss of innocence by his homeland, as the formerly somnolent, rural area of Majorca where he has been raised is radically transformed and threatened with environmental chaos by commercial development and the tourist invasion. *Cròniques de la molt anomenada ciutat de Montcarrà* (1972; Chronicles of the Oft-Named City of Montcarra) is concerned with the same theme, the destruction of Majorca, but approaches it in a different manner, employing the form of a family chronicle (three generations of connected families that form concentric circles). The family is representative of a proletarian segment that frequently emigrates. Oliver employs the fantastic Majorcan folktales known as "rondalles" together with popular sayings and songs, which are incorporated into the fragmented narrative. Fairies, giants, and mythical creatures from the "rondalles" are the agents of destruction in a somewhat apocalyptic ending that is intended to indict the false progress of the tourist boom via a symbolic disappearance of the island.

Coordenades espai-temps per quardar-hi les ensaimades (1975; Time-Space Coordinates for Keeping Pastries) is a long short story, later reprinted in the collection *Figues d'un altre paner*). Inspired by a dream of the author, a return to her childhood in Manacor, the narrative features a dreamlike prose. *Figues d'un altre paner* (1979; A Horse of a Different Color) contains a very important prologue by Oliver in which she explains facets of the development of some of her fiction. Another important aspect of the collection is that some stories contain the germs of later works, developed into novels and screenplays. *El vaixell d'iràs i no tornaràs* (1976; The Ship That Never Returned) again incorporates elements from folk and fairy tales, beginning with a rhyming motif and proceeding to the magical adventures with giants, rose-colored robots, and other similarly fanciful beings. However, the novel is considerably more than just an entertaining fantasy, for Oliver employs the literary topos of the voyage as symbolic of life and includes philosophical monologues as counterpoint to the narrative. One of her more feminist works from the earlier period, this novel creates a social microcosm wherein problems are solved by a strong woman. The conformist attitudes of the majority are satirized, especially their unquestioning actions. *Punt d'arròs* (1979; Knit-Purl) is fully feminist, and begins with a quotation from Virginia Woolf together with an acknowledgement of Oliver's indebtedness to Woolf. A variation upon the theme of the search for identity, this story stresses the need for solitude in order for the woman to find herself. The title alludes to a major structuring image (knitting is symbolic of the repetitive routines of daily life, especially of the monotony of domestic chores).

Vegetal i Muller qui cerca espill (1982; Vegetable and Woman in Search of a Mirror) are different approaches to much the same problem of a woman's identity and self-realization. Two TV screenplays subsequently published in book form, these works are preceded by an authorial prologue explaining Oliver's view of the relationships between the screenplay and fiction writing. *Vegetal* presents a middle-aged widow whose paternalistic husband had totally dominated her life, without allowing her to do anything on her own (her having plants became a bone of contention because she bought them herself). After his death she indulges herself by buying more and more plants, which are her only company, and—unable to cope with her sudden freedom— she ends by becoming a plant herself (a metamorphosis explained by an earlier monologue in which she compares herself to the decorative foliage plants, lacking freedom of movement and intended primarily to look pretty).[3] *Muller qui cerca espill* also addresses the problem of the limited options available to women, presenting the history of a lack-luster engagement: the bride-to-be has dreamed unrealistically of a career as a movie star, but her conventional and traditional parents have furthered the suit of a dull yet solid candidate for her hand. The counterpoint between the bride's imagining of herself as a triumphant artist and the prosaic reality of her wedding, which effectively marks the end of her dreams, makes understandable her final smashing of her mirror.

Crinères de foc (1985; Manes of Fire) also employs a contrapuntal technique, weaving together two parallel stories, the growing up of the protagonist along with her hometown (recalling the first two novels with their concern for the social and environmental consequences of economic growth and change). This novel also explores the need for self-identification, in women and in social groups, and depicts the menace to visions and identities that rapid growth entails. Combining several sub-genres—science fiction, fantasy, psychological novel—with an occasionally epic sweep, the narrative transcends traditional classifications. *Estudi en lila* (1987; *Study in Lilac*) makes experimental use of the genre of detective or crime fiction as a vehicle for feminist concerns, investigating the problem of rape and its aftermath. All of the major characters are female, the detective as well as the two very dissimilar victims, a young and vulnerable Marjorcan and a fashionable middle-aged antique dealer. Oliver's characteristic reliance upon counterpoint techniques appears again via the detective's interrelating the victims who both struggle with their feelings of shame, guilt, helplessness, and fear, their outrage and desire for vengeance.

Writer, Critic, and Professor

Carme Riera, born in Majorca in 1949, writes novels and short stories in Catalan, essays and criticism in Castilian, and is a professor of Castilian literature at the Universidad Autónoma in Barcelona. Her emergence as a writer belongs almost entirely to the post-Franco era: recognition first came in the form of a prize for her short story, "Te deix, amor, la mar com a penyora" (I Leave You, Love, the Sea as Token) in 1974. A collection of Riera's stories in Catalan and in the Majorcan dialect was published under this title the following year, and although overlooked by professional critics, rapidly became a bestseller, with nineteen printings in nine years. A second and comparably successful collection of brief fiction appeared in 1977 with the title *Jo pos per testimoni les gavines* (I Call the Seagulls as My Witness). The title tale is a sequel to the title tale of the previous collection. Riera herself translated most of the stories from the two collections into Castilian, where they appeared with the title *Palabra de mujer* (1980: A Woman's Word). The collection was translated into Greek, and four pieces were translated into Russian for an anthology. The fictional world of Carme Riera is populated in a semi-Kafkaesque fashion by beings who lose at playing a game whose rules are unknown. Her characters are frequently those who have been unable or unwilling to assimilate to everyday "normality," who ignore or reject the passwords for togetherness and coexistence, often seeking unusual means of relating to the world.

Other works of Riera which appeared in the same year include *Els cementiris de Barcelona* (1980), a narrative tour of Barcelona's historic cemeteries, and *Quasi be un conte, la vida de Ramon Llull* (1980; Almost a Story: The Life of Ramon Llull), a biography intended for juvenile readers of a multifaceted writer and thinker from the thirteenth century, the first great European intellectual to abandon Latin for writing in the vernacular (in his case, the Majorcan dialect, which he shares with Riera).

Riera was awarded the important Catalan literary prize, Prudenci Bertrana, in 1980 for her first novel, *Una primavera per a Domènico Guarini* (A "Primavera" for Domenico Guarini), translated into Castilian in 1981. Complex in its structure and style, the novel is especially concerned with linguistic experimentation. Predominantly neobaroque language, frequently learned or even esoteric, alternates with language of a markedly different nature and tone—colloquial, conversational, and sometimes vulgar. Juxtaposed to this is another linguistic mode, "journalese," the standard newspaper idiom, interspersed with passages of a more impersonal, academic essay style. Most of the novel is written in standard Catalan, but there are also passages in the Valencian and Majorcan dialects. Not merely a linguistic exercise, the novel presents a case for the reader to solve: why did Domenico Guarini attempt to destroy Botticelli's famous painting, *Primavera*? The narrative is presented from the perspective of a Catalan (Majorcan) newspaperwoman who attends the trial of Guarini in Florence. There is in effect a double search for truth, as the journalist searches not only for Guarini's motivation but also for enlightenment into her own very personal and private dilemma (presented as a metanovelistic parallel or counterpoint). Meditating before the restored painting, she experiences an epiphany in which some of the numerous points that her own situation has in common with that of Guarini are crystallized. That mystic revelation remains enigmatic (the reader is not privy to the details), as it is linked to some hermetic message in the painting itself that can only be apprehended via a transformation of the viewer.[4]

Epitelis tendríssims (1981; Exquisite Epithelia) is Riera's third collection of brief fiction, but unlike her previous collections these stories are geographically or spatially linked: all are set in the same small Majorcan hotel, at least initially. Each story deals with a different guest of the hotel and purports to discover his/her secret life, and that vital secret is usually erotic in nature. The reader thus encounters a new facet of Riera, or at least a different emphasis: by contrast with the strong linguistic emphasis of earlier works, the present stress is on the erotic, or at least on erotic language, but not the frequently clinical terminology found in the works of the usual author of erotic literature. Riera attempts to find a more suggestive means of communicating pleasure and stimulation by incorporating the imagination.

Historian, Philologist, Novelist

Margarida Aritzeta, born in Valls in 1953, holds a degree in history and philology, has participated in a radio cultural program and taught at the Escola Universitaria de Tarragona. Her first novel, *Quan la pedra es torna fang a les mans* (1981; When Stone Turns to Mud in One's Hands), was awarded the Victor Català Prize. *Un febrer a la pell* (1983; February Under the Skin) won the Sant Jordi Prize and portrays a man's unexplained disappearance, set against the background of the attempted coup in the Cortes on 23 February 1981. The protagonist tries to solve the disappearance by reconstructing the events leading up to the vanishing point. Something of a spoof on the *novela negra* or crime novel, the narrative includes a baffling assemblage of characters and incidents and maintains the mystery until the end. The potential for a seemingly average individual's complete personality change provokes humor but also serious reflection. *Vermell de cadmi* (1984; Cadmium Red) is even more fantastic, although it blends fantasy with realism, reflecting the politics of the day with misinformation, goofs, and cover-ups, while more fanciful aspects include a sort of metamorphosis whereby people become invisible beings, undergo gender changes, and age at an accelerated rate. Incorporating certain motifs of science fiction, the novelist investigates governmental invasion of privacy and subtly demonstrates attitudinal changes that occur when people play two gender roles.

Chapter Ten
Summary and Conclusions

The weight of extraliterary factors in determining the direction and development of the twentieth-century novel in Spain increases incalculably when the scholarly focus is narrowed to the narrative written by women. Social conditioning and the education of women, circumscribed roles and the limited options available, feminine political and legal status, the temperamental and psychological configurations attributed by Spanish society to the female, all are logically reflected in what is written by women, shaping and constraining their views of themselves, others, and the world. Those aspects of collective feminine experience—the family, marriage, motherhood, divorce, prostitution, and work—that illustrate the social condition of Spanish women and constitute an essential frame of reference are colored by the socioeconomic context in innumerable shadings. These render the body of narrative written by women in Spain both different in historical flavor and detail and yet the same in underlying concerns.

The achievements of nineteenth-century women narrators, although traditionally undervalued, constitute a solid basis upon which those who follow can build. The essentially critical realist stances of Pardo Bazán and Monserdà de Macia and the social concerns of García de la Torre are echoed by many of the women who come after them. The rural naturalism present in Pardo Bazán's best-known masterpieces is developed to a new art form by Caterina Albert through her incorporation of fragmented structures and modernist aesthetics, while the former's feminism is taken up by Carmen de Burgos with her strong social conscience and crusading zeal. Concha Espina, although less liberal, brought increased acceptance for women writers through her own popular success and achievement of national and international recognition. Notwithstanding her aesthetic and cultural conservativism, this prolific regional realist possessed undeniable narrative vigor, and the strengths of her best efforts added solidity to the corpus of Spanish women's fiction. Her winning of the National Prize for Literature (even if awarded to an aesthetically defective work) attests to modifying "es-

tablishment" attitudes. Unobtrusively but persistently, María Martínez Sierra portrayed women in extramarital and extradomestic roles,
actively seeking their own fulfillment. No matter how virtuous her
heroines, they are also independent, intelligent, moderately liberated,
and unvaryingly superior to the men. Avoiding polemics, she com-
bated stereotypes (especially the embittered spinster) and created role
models engaged in pursuits previously reserved to men. Ably seconded
by a number of lesser women writers, the turn-of-the-century generation improved upon the legacy received from their predecessors without surpassing the greatest achievements of Pardo Bazán. Generally
more conservative in their aesthetics than their male counterparts in
the Generation of 1898, they experimented very little with genre and
novelistic structure, but thematically they were more innovative, incorporating a broad spectrum of social, academic, philosophical, and
psychological problems, spiritual and ecological concerns, psychosexual disturbances, and denunciation of the feminine lot.

The contemporaries of the *Novecentistas* and Generation of 1927, less
known and less prolific than their predecessors, continue to be preoccupied with social issues and display slightly more critical attitudes,
as well as increased interest in the use of children and adolescents as
protagonists. War and exile emerge as significant generational themes
in later writings of this group, and problems of the divorced or separated woman also receive more frequent fictional treatment. The feminist movement per se appears in this group's fiction, resulting in a
more specific formulation of the conflict between domestic toil and
self-realization, and works demythologizing family relationships begin
to make their way into print. In the writings of the most talented
narrators of this group—Crusat, Mulder, and Chacel, especially—a
frankly subjective and nonmimetic orientation parallels the development of the "dehumanized" psychological narrative associated with the
Generation of 1927. Influences of Joyce and Proust are coupled with
other echoes of European modernism in these writers' works. Intense
introspection and concentration upon problems of the ego are counterbalanced, however, by the collective orientation of León and the feminist preoccupations of Campo Alange. At the same time, a subdued
but determined nonconformity results in more audible expressions of
dissent and rejection of many patriarchally and societally inscribed
boundaries.

Intellectualism, increased concern with formal elements, and neobaroque experimentation pervade Chacel's highly aestheticized texts,

while Conde makes further incursions into terrain previously considered the domain of male writers. Chacel's candidacy for the international Cervantes Prize and Conde's admission as the first woman member of the Royal Spanish Academy evince the slow but continuing progress of Spain's female writers in gaining recognition. Similarly, the posthumous accolades accorded Mercè Rodoreda pay tribute to an extraordinary woman narrator whose talent was but little rewarded during her lifetime, but whose progressively increasing stature benefits the status of feminist narrative in the peninsula as a whole. Rodoreda's penetrating and haunting vision of women at odds with their environment, her skill at re-creating peculiarly female aspects of existence, her sensitivity to loneliness, anguish, and financially induced desperation are special strengths. This writer's treatment of identity problems provoked by woman's circumscribed existence, presentation of the destructive potential of eroticism, and versatility in use of a broad spectrum of styles ranging from the bleakest realism to hallucinatory surrealism makes her both unmistakable and unforgettable.

Censorship and political strictures in the postwar period complicate the already difficult task facing women wishing to write in Spain, yet they rise to the challenge in unprecedented numbers. Despite a measure of recognition accorded a handful of especially well known novelists (Laforet, Quiroga, Matute, Medio, and Martín Gaite), the majority remain in relative obscurity. Many of these are comparably prolific and have enjoyed some popular success (Kurtz, Alós, Salisachs), while others such as Soriano and Fórmica have produced a less extensive work of superior quality which is known only to a handful of connoisseurs. Curiously, perhaps, the writer who is emerging in the final analysis as the most significant of Castilian narrators of the older postwar generation, Carmen Martín Gaite, has become more experimental and more feminist, while the remainder of the group has evolved less. The younger generations of postwar writers have been able to benefit from the earlier group's advances and successes in creating subtexts that express their nonconformist attitudes and protests in spite of the Franco censorship. A distinguishing feature of the postwar groups is the presence, in numbers, of women writing in the minority or vernacular languages, especially Catalan, and their rapidly increasing visibility and significance. Preoccupations of a primarily sociopolitical nature in the early postwar years give way slowly to more personal, psychological, and feminist themes with the progressive vitalizing of the Spanish economy and rapid social change. By and large, the Catalans (Capmany, Pàmies, and their younger counterparts) are more radically feminist, more aggressively activist, and more to the left on the political continuum than those writing in Castilian.

Among the younger writers, the best known and most studied of those writing in Castilian are Moix and Tusquets, while the most interesting and significant of those writing in Catalan include Oliver, Vicens, Riera, Roig, Valentí, and Serrahima. The first three, curiously, are Majorcan. Montero, Ortiz, Guilló, and García Morales are currently among the more promising and talented of the latest group of Castilian narrators, although many others have produced works of merit. As a chronological grouping, the youngest writers share birth dates well after the end of the Civil War, and their writings are seldom marked by the shadow of the conflict, although many portray the difficulties of growing up in the repressive Franco era. An ascending curve of intensifying feminist consciousness and expanding feminist thematics characterizes their works, and their attitudes are both more egalitarian and more aggressive than those of their predecessors. As beneficiaries of battles won by prior generations, they enjoy an enviable opportunity that should be reflected in a literary corpus of truly European proportions.

Notes and References

Chapter One

1. Chronologically, the three series of articles on women writers are M. Ossorio y Bernard, "Apuntes para un diccionario de escritoras españolas del siglo XIX," *La España Moderna* 9 (1889): 169–94, 10 (1889):188–207, 12 (1889):181–92; 14 (1890):202–12, and 17 (1890):183–202; J. Pérez de Guzmán, "La mujer española en la Minerva literaria castellana bajo los Austrias," *La España Moderna* 114 (1898):111–29, 116 (1898): 84–110, 117 (1898):50–80, and 118 (1898):90–120; and María Victoria de Lara, "La cultura feminina en España," *Bulletin of Spanish Studies* 7 (1930):82–84, and "De escritoras españolas" 8 (1931):213–17, 9 (1932):31–37, 168–71, 221–24.

2. María del Pilar Oñate, *El feminismo en la literatura española* (Madrid: Espasa Calpe, 1938).

3. Ibid., 9, 11, 21.

4. Quoted by Oñate, 160 (my translation).

5. Amar y Borbón, an early, noble voice for Spanish feminism, contributed two important treatises to the debate on the intellectual capacities of women, *Importancia de la instrucción que conviene dar a las mujeres* (Zaragoza, 1784) and *Discurso en defensa del talento de las mujeres y su aptitud para el gobierno* (Madrid, 1786).

6. Perhaps there is some ironic poetic justice that Gregorio Martínez Sierra is remembered in this book only as a "man who defended women," although he is also given credit for María's *Feminismo, feminidad, españolismo* (Madrid: Renacimiento, 1917), originally signed by both of them. Her name is not mentioned.

7. Concha Fagoaga, *La voz y el voto de las mujeres* (Madrid: Editorial Icaria, 1984). This work reflects the political atmosphere at the time of publication (the Parliamentary Assembly of the European Council called upon member states to foment the participation of women in politics and recognized the existence of continuing sexual discrimination in Europe, including women's underrepresentation in political parties, unions, and national assemblies).

8. Reprinted by CVS Ediciones, Madrid, 1975.

9. For historical background, see Gabriel Jackson, *The Spanish Republic and the Civil War, 1931–1939* (Princeton, N.J.: Princeton University Press, 1967); Max Gallo, *Spain Under Franco* (New York: E. P. Dutton & Co., 1974).

10. Alejandra Ferrandiz and Vicente Verdú, *Noviazgo y matrimonio en la burguesía española* (Barcelona: Cuadernos para el Diálogo, 1974).

11. A collection of articles published in Barcelona by Cuadernos para el Diálogo, 1974.

12. The subtitle of *El miedo a la igualdad* is *Varones y mujeres en una sociedad machista* (Male and Female in a "Macho" Society) (Barcelona: Grijalbo, 1975).

13. Nuria Beltrán, *¿Muerte civil de la española?* (Barcelona: Plaza y Janés, 1975).

14. See Richard A. Nuccio, "The Socialization of Political Values: The Context of Official Education in Spain," Ph.D. dissertation, University of Massachusetts, 1977.

15. I have studied various manners in which contemporary Spanish women novelists depict the single female in "Portraits of the *Femme Seule* by Laforet, Matute, Soriano, Martín Gaite, Galvarriato, Quiroga and Medio," *Feminine Concerns in Contemporary Spanish Fiction by Women,* edited by Robert Manteiga, Carolyn Galerstein, and Kathleen McNerney (forthcoming from University of North Carolina Press). With the exception of Dolores Medio, they use stereotypes, often verging upon caricature.

16. Additional information may be found in the interviews with Charo Ema in Linda Gould Levine and Gloria Waldman, *Feminismo ante el Franquismo: entrevistas con feministas de España* (Miami: Ediciones Universal, 1980). On the foundation (1979) and development of the Spanish Feminist Party, see also the essays and novels of Lidia Falcón, a guiding force in establishment of the party and founder of the feminist magazine, *Vindicación feminista* (1976–79). Her sociopolitical treatises on women and society (e.g., *Los derechos civiles de la mujer* [Barcelona: Nereo, 1963], *Los derechos laborales de la mujer* [Madrid: Montecorvo, 1965], *Mujer y sociedad* [Barcelona: Fontanella, 1969], and the two volumes of *La razón feminista* [Barcelona: Fontanella, 1981, 1982]) include invaluable analyses of the repression of women in Spain and elsewhere. Additional information is provided by her autobiographical works, especially *En el infierno. (Ser mujer en las cárceles de España)* (1977).

17. Further details are provided by Lidia Falcón, Eva Forest, and Elisa Lamas in their interviews in Levine and Waldman, *Feminismo ante el Franquismo.*

18. An anthology that contains fascinating documentation on working conditions for Spanish women, including those employed as domestics, is Mary Nash, *Mujer, familia y trabajo en España, 1875–1936* (Barcelona: Anthropos, 1983). It is unfortunate that the cutoff date is 1936, although conditions did not improve measurably for the next three decades.

19. *La integración de la mujer en la economía* (Informes OCDE. Madrid: Ministerio de Trabajo y Seguro Social, 1986) cites the rapid increase of percentage of women in the work force in Spain and the resultant bettering of economic status, as well as suggesting strategies for equal employment opportunities.

20. William Chislett, *The Spanish Media Since Franco* (Washington, D.C.: Writers and Scholars Educational Trust, 1979), in a xerox publication distributed by the Index on Censorship, devotes the first part of his report to

"The Press Under Franco" and provides a working journalist's perspective on conditions for writers in Franco Spain. His views develop insight into the circumstances in which women writers had to work, and provide an accurate idea of the degree of governmental control over everything published in Spain. The relatively early date at which he treated the post-Franco period (the report was written two and a half years after the dictator's death) did not allow him to observe more than the early stages of transition to democracy. In fact, the report appears to have already been in press when the censorship was abolished 31 December 1978.

Patricia W. O'Connor has also studied the mechanisms of censorial functioning in a series of articles.

For the methods whereby writers managed to circumvent censorship, see Janet Pérez, "The Game of the Possible," *Review of Contemporary Fiction* 4:3 (Fall 1984):22–30.

21. Though it is still relatively soon for evaluations, several reports written in the 1980s bear upon changing conditions in Spain and provide updated perspectives on the situation there. See especially David S. Bell, *Democratic Politics in Spain* (London: Frances Pinter, 1983); T. D. Lancaster and G. Prevost, eds., *Politics and Change in Spain* (New York: Praeger, 1985); S. Lieberman, *The Contemporary Spanish Economy: A Historical Perspective* (London: Allen & Unwin, 1982); José Maravall, *The Transition to Democracy in Spain* (New York: St. Martin's Press, 1982); and John M. McNair, *Education for a Changing Spain* (Manchester, England: Manchester University Press, 1984).

22. Lawrence H. Klibbe, *Fernán Caballero* (New York: Twayne Publishers, 1973) offers the first book-length study in English on this author. For the best references in Spanish, see Javier Herrero, *Fernán Caballero: un nuevo planteamiento* (Madrid: Editorial Gredos, 1963), a study emphasizing the relationships between the writer's life and her writing; and José F. Montesinos, *Fernán Caballero, Ensayo de justificación* (Mexico: El Colegio de México, 1961) for the best evaluation of the importance of this writer, her literary virtues, and defects.

23. Extensive information on Avellaneda's life, her novels, and her works in other genres may be found in Hugh Harter, *Gertrudis Gómez de Avellaneda* (Boston: G. K. Hall, 1981).

24. In *Women in Hispanic Literature: Icons and Fallen Idols,* 201–14.

25. The first life-and-works study of this writer in English is Walter T. Pattison's *Emilia Pardo Bazán* (New York: Twayne Publishers, 1971). It follows an earlier consideration of her novelistic aesthetics in D. F. Brown, *The Catholic Naturalism of Emilia Pardo Bazán* (Chapel Hill: University of North Carolina Press, 1957). A good many articles have been published on this author in English, several by Ronald Hilton. One of the major biographies in Spanish is Carmen Bravo-Villasante's *Vida y obra de Emilia Pardo Bazán* (Madrid, 1962). She has also made available to scholars the intimate personal correspondence between this novelist and the other great writer of the period

in *Cartas a Benito Pérez Galdós (1889–90)*, ed. Carmen Bravo-Villasante (Madrid, 1975).

26. Maurice Hemingway has recently published another book-length treatment of this novelist, *Emilia Pardo Bazán: The Making of a Novelist* (London and New York: Cambridge University Press, 1983). He attempts to trace her growth to maturity as a novelist in the 1880s and 1890s, and deals only with that period. For his discussion of *Los pazos,* see pp. 27–41.

Chapter Two

1. Further biographical data is available in Josep Miracle, *Victor Català* (Barcelona, 1963) and Joan Oller i Rabassa, *Biografia de Victor Català* (Barcelona, 1967). In Catalan.

2. Arthur Terry, *Catalan Literature,* in the series *A Literary History of Spain* under the general editorship of R. O. Jones (London and New York: Barnes & Noble, 1972), 109.

3. *Guia de literatura catalana contemporania,* ed. Jordi Castellanos (Barcelona: Edicions 62, 1973).

4. Jaume Vidal Alcover, *Sintesi d'historia de la literatura catalana* (Barcelona: Edicions de la Magrama, 1980), 2:65.

5. Ibid., 47–48.

6. The only book-length study of this writer is Elizabeth Starçevic, *Carmen de Burgos, defensora de la mujer* (Almería: Editorial Cajal, 1976). Primarily a biography, it contains an investigation of the situation of women at the beginning of this century in Spain, citations from various documents, and interviews with some contemporaries of the author.

7. Eugenio de Nora, *La novela española contemporánea* (1927–39), 2d ed. (Madrid: Gredos, 1968), 2:49–53.

8. See the introductions to the editions by Rosa Romá of *El hombre negro* (Madrid: Emiliano Escolar, 1980, 13–28) and *Villa-María* (Madrid: Emiliano Escolar, 1980, 13–28).

9. Josefina de la Maza, *Vida de mi madre, Concha Espina* (Madrid: Magisterio Español, 1969) gives an intimate, insider's view of the novelist's life, but has a predictable bias on the significance of her work.

10. Alicia Canales, *Concha Espina* (Madrid: E.P.E.S.A., 1974) publishes previously unavailable letters that are of scholarly significance.

11. Nora, *La Novela española contemporánea,* 1:329.

12. Ibid., 1:330.

13. Ibid., 1:332.

14. Ibid., 1:334.

15. Patricia O'Connor, *Gregorio and María Martínez Sierra* (Boston: G. K. Hall, 1977). See especially pp. 59–67 and extracts from Gregorio's letters to María, "establishing beyond any doubt María's active authorship" (60). Nevertheless, those interested in doing research on María's work will probably

not find her name listed in card catalogs; in most libraries it will be necessary to look under the name of Martínez Sierra (Gregorio).

16. Ibid., 122.

Chapter Three

1. Nora, *La novela española contemporánea,* the most complete survey of the twentieth-century Spanish novel yet attempted, treats the *novela rosa* in 1:426–28 and on 430 devotes a paragraph to Icaza, considered the "dean" of female cultivators of the genre.

2. Ibid., 3:247.

3. Ibid., 3:248.

4. Ibid., 3:249.

5. Ibid.

6. Ibid., 3:250.

7. For a more complete analysis, see Estelle Irizarry, "*Cinco sombras* de Eulalia Galvarriato: Un novela singular de la postguerra," in *Novelistas femeninas de la postguerra española,* ed. Janet Pérez (Madrid: Porrúa, 1983), 47–56.

8. Janet Pérez, "Spanish Women Writers and the Essay," *Siglo XX/ 20th Century* 1–2 (Winter 1986):43–54, includes a more complete discussion of *Raíces bajo el tiempo.*

9. Nora, *La novela española contemporánea,* 3:384.

10. Ibid., 3:381.

Chapter Four

1. Carmen Conde, *Por el camino, viendo sus orillas* (Barcelona: Plaza y Janés, 1986), a series of memoirs currently in three volumes. The citation is from 3:261. Conde's autobiographical materials are not ordered sequentially, but the memoirs are predictably revealing of formative influences, significant acquaintances, and decisive experiences. The section on Juan Ramón Jiménez (3;61–81) illuminates this poet's influence on Conde's lyrics, but a similarly clear source of poetics for her prose is lacking (despite her confessed admiration for Miró, and the editorial counsel of her husband).

2. Nora, *La novela española contemporánea,* 2:386.

3. Ibid.

4. Very little has been published on Conde's prose, as most critics have concentrated on her poetry. However, there is an introductory essay by Milagros Sánchez Arnosi in her edition of *La rambla* (Madrid: Magisterio Español, 1977, in the collection Novelas y Cuentos) that studies Conde's fictional ties to her native Cartagena. Eunice Myers has written on Conde's children's fiction: "Four Female Novelists and Spanish Children's Fiction," *Letras femeninas* 10:2 (Fall 1984):40–49.

5. Translated from remarks by Rosa Chacel reported in *Hoja informativa de Literatura y Filología,* Fundación Juan March, 37 (April 1976), 1–7.

6. See Rosa Chacel's explication, "Respuesta a Ortega: La novela no escrita," *Sur* 241 (July–August 1956):97–119. Additional information on the formative influences of Ortega and Unamuno upon the work of Chacel may be found in Julián Marías, "Camino hacia la novela," in *Ensayos de convivencia* (Madrid: Espasa-Calpe, 1962).

7. Rosa Chacel, "Sendas perdidas de la Generación de 27," *Cuadernos hispanoamericanos,* nos. 322–23 (April–May 1977):13.

8. Eunice Myers, "*Estación, Ida y vuelta,* Rosa Chacel's Apprenticeship Novel," *Hispanic Journal* 4:2 (Spring 1983):77–84. José R. Marra-López, in *Narrativa española fuera de España (1936–1960)* (Madrid: Ediciones Guadarrama, 1963), 133–47, considers *Estación, Ida y vuelta,* together with Francisco Ayala's *Cazador en el alba,* one of the two most interesting works of the period.

9. Eunice Myers, interview with Chacel, *Hispania* 67 (May 1984):286–87.

10. See Eunice Myers, "Narcissism and the Quest for Identity in Rosa Chacel's *La sinrazón,*" *Perspectives on Contemporary Literature* 8 (1982) 85–90. See also José Blanco Amor, "Rosa Chacel entre Madrid y Buenos Aires: Cuarenta años madurando *La sinrazón,*" *La Estafeta Literaria* 617 (1 August 1977):20–21.

11. Rosa Chacel, *Saturnal* (Barcelona: Seix Barral, 1972).

12. Ibid., 42–49, 52, 61.

13. Ibid., cf. 152–58.

14. Julián Marías, quoted in Blanco Amor, *La Estafeta Literaria,* 21.

15. Given the disparity of published dates of birth, I have chosen the more recent one (I interviewed Ballesteros in Madrid in August 1985, and it is impossible that she was then ninety-four).

16. Nora, *La novela española contemporánea,* 3:368.

17. Mercedes Ballesteros, *La cometa y el eco* (Barcelona: Planeta, 1956), 276.

18. Nora, *La novela española contemporánea,* 3:368.

Chapter Five

1. *Guia de literatura catalana contemporania* (Barcelona: Edicions 62, 1973), 403.

2. Carme Arnau, *Introducció a la narrativa de Mercè Rodoreda: El mite de la infantesa* (Barcelona: Edicions 62, 2d ed., 1982), 11.

3. Ibid., 46–47.

4. Ibid., 50.

5. José Ortega, "Mujer, guerra y neurosis en dos novelas de Mercè Rodoreda," *Novelistas femeninas de la postguerra española,* 71–84.

6. Arnau, *Introducció a la narrativa,* 95–97.
7. Ibid., 256.
8. Mercè Rodoreda, *Cuánta, cuánta guerra* (Barcelona: Edhasa, 1982), 16.

Chapter Six

1. From a letter-questionnaire from Kurtz to the author, dated 13 May 1964.
2. For a discussion of some of Kurtz's stories, see Eunice Myers, "Autotextuality and Intertextuality in *El desconocido* by Carmen Kurtz," *Hispania* 71, no. 1 (March 1988):43–49.
3. A fuller exposition and analysis of this novel appears in Myers, *Hispania* 71, no. 1 (March 1988):43–49.
4. Correspondence cited in note 1.
5. Carmen Kurtz, *Al lado del hombre, La vanguardia española* (20 September 1961), 9.
6. Carlos Murciano, "Carmen Kurtz," an interview, *La Estafeta Literaria* 582 (15 February 1976):16–18.
7. Alfonso Martínez Mena, "Carmen Kurtz: *El viaje,*" *La Estafeta Literaria* 568 (15 July 1975):2169.
8. Fuller treatment appears in Janet Winecoff, "Existentialism in the Novels of Elena Soriano," *Hispania* 47, no. 2 (May 1964):309–15.
9. Nora, *La novela española contemporánea,* 3:103.
10. Ibid., 3:104–5.
11. Ibid., 3:104.
12. Letter from Salisachs to the author, dated 27 June 1962.
13. Nora, *La novela española contemporánea,* 3:393.
14. Ricardo Huertas, "Mercedes Salisachs," an interview, *La Estafeta Literaria* 530 (15 December 1973):16–18.
15. María Dolores Lado, "Mercedes Salisachs y la novela católica," *Letras Femeninas* 12, nos. 1 & 2 (1986): 114–20, concentrates essentially on *La gangrena.*
16. Mercedes Salisachs, *La presencia* (Barcelona: Argos Vergara, 1979), 299.
17. Letter-questionnaire from Alós to the author, dated 18 September 1963.
18. Elizabeth J. Ordóñez, "The Barcelona Group: The Fiction of Alós, Moix, and Tusquets," *Letras Femeninas* 6, no. 1 (Spring 1980):38–49. Approximately half the article is devoted to Alós. A cited dissertation of use to those who read Spanish is Fermín Rodríguez, "La mujer en la sociedad española en la novelística de Concha Alós," Ph.D. dissertation, University of Arizona, 1973.

Chapter Seven

1. A recent analysis of this novel is Roberta Johnson's "Light and Morality in Carmen Laforet's *La insolación*," *Letras Femeninas* 12 nos. 1 & 2 (Primavera-Otoño 1986):94–102.

2. Interviews with Dolores Medio by the author in Madrid, winter 1962 and 1965.

3. Recent studies of *Diario de una maestra* and of the autobiographical substrata in Medio's fiction are Carolyn Galerstein, "Dolores Medio's Women in Wartime," *Letras Femeninas* 12, nos. 1 & 2 (1986):45–51; and Elizabeth Ordóñez, "*Diario de una maestra*: Female Heroism and the Context of War," *Letras Femeninas* 12, nos 1 & 2 (1986):52–59.

4. Fuller examination of this theme may be found in Pérez, "Portraits of the *femme seule*," in *Feminine Concerns in Contemporary Spanish Fiction by Women*.

5. Quiroga interview by author in Madrid, spring 1962.

6. Albert Brent, "The Novels of Elena Quiroga," *Hispania* 42 (1959):210–13, discusses Quiroga's first six novels as an introduction.

7. Nora, *La novela española contemporànea*, 3:171.

8. A full treatment of Matute's fiction to 1969 can be found in Janet Díaz, *Ana María Matute* (New York: Twayne Publishers, 1970); and Margaret E. W. Jones, *The Literary World of Ana María Matute* (Lexington: University Press of Kentucky, 1970).

9. Matute in conversations with author in Lubbock, Texas, December 1978.

10. Joan Lipman Brown, "*El balneario* by Carmen Martín Gaite: Conceptual Aesthetics and 'L'étrange pure,'" *Journal of Spanish Studies: Twentieth Century* 6, no. 3 (Winter 1978):163–74.

11. See Joan Lipman Brown, "*Tiempo de silencio* and *Ritmo lento*: Pioneers of the New Social Novel in Spain," *Hispanic Review* 50, no. 1 (Winter 1982):61–73, for additional discussion of this work and its significance.

12. For a full analysis of this fairy tale written for the child in everyone, see Ruth El Saffar, "Carmen Martín Gaite and *El castillo de las tres murallas*," *Letras Femeninas* 8, no. 2 (Autumn 1982):46–53.

13. Mirella Servodidio, ed., *From Fiction to Metafiction: Essays in Honor of Carmen Martín-Gaite* (Lincoln, Neb: Society of Spanish & Spanish American Studies, 1983). In addition to three panoramic thematic studies, there are one or more essays on each of Martín Gaite's novels and novelettes except *Las ataduras*.

Two additional essays on *El cuarto de atrás* appear in a special number of *Letras Femeninas* devoted to women novelists and the Spanish Civil War: Catherine G. Bellver, "War as Rite of Passage in *El cuarto de atrás*," *Letras Femeninas* 12, nos. 1 & 2 (Primavera-Otoño 1986):69–77; and Jean S. Chittenden, "*El cuarto de atrás* as Autobiography," *Letras Femeninas* 12, nos. 1 & 2

(1986):78–84. An earlier study is available by Joan Lipman Brown, "A Fantastic Memoir: Technique and History in *El cuarto de atrás*," *Anales de la literatura española contemporánea* 6 (1981):13–20.

Besides the commemorative volume cited, there are two other articles in English on specific aspects of Martín Gaite's writing: Joan Lipman Brown, "*A rachas:* The Poetry of Carmen Martín Gaite," *Letras Femeninas* 5, no. 2 (Autumn 1979):13–21; and Catherine G. Bellver, "Carmen Martín Gaite As A Social Critic," *Letras Femeninas* 6, no. 2 (Autumn 1980):3–16. The latter aspect has also been studied by Joan Lipman Brown in "The Nonconformist Character as Social Critic in the Novels of Carmen Martín Gaite," *Kentucky Romance Quarterly* 28, no. 2 (1981):165–76.

14. For more on this sort of writing, see Lourdes Moller-Soler, "El impacto de la guerra civil en la vida y obra de tres novelistas catalanas: Aurora Bertrana, Teresa Pàmies y Mercè Rodoreda," *Letras Femeninas* 12, nos. 1 & 2 (Primavera-Otoño 1986):34–44.

Chapter Eight

1. Mieza has also published a collection of interviews entitled *La mujer del español* (Barcelona: Ediciones Marte, 1977). For critical studies, see Carolyn Galerstein, "Spanish Women Novelists and Younger-Generation Writers in Exile and Return: Outsiders or Insiders," in *European Writers in Exile in Latin America*, ed. H. B. Moeller (Heidelberg: Winter Verlag, 1983), 137–48; also, Carolyn Galerstein, "The Second Generation in Exile," *Papers on Language and Literature* 21, no. 1 (Spring 1985):220–28.

2. Another novel of Falcón is studied by Elizabeth Starčevic in "*Rupturas*: A Feminist Novel," *Anales de la literatura española contemporánea*. *Reading for Difference: Feminist Perspectives on Women Novelists of Contemporary Spain* (Boulder: University of Colorado, 1987).

3. Studies on *Julia* include Geraldine Cleary Nichols, "*Julia:* 'This is the way the world ends . . . ' " *Novelistas femeninas de la postguerra española*, ed. Pérez, 113–24; Sara Schyfter, "Rites Without Passage: The Adolescent World of Ana María Moix's *Julia*," *The Analysis of Literary Texts: Current Trends in Methodology* (Ypsilanti, Mich.: Bilingual Press, 1980), 41–50; Michael D. Thomas, "El desdoblamiento psíquico como factor dinámico en *Julia*, de Ana María Moix," in Pérez, ed., *Novelistas femeninas*, 125–34.

4. For an overview of Moix's first several works with good discussion of the novels, see Margaret E. W. Jones, "Ana María Moix: Literary Structures and the Enigmatic Nature of Reality," *Journal of Spanish Studies: Twentieth Century* 4, no. 2 (Fall 1976):105–16.

5. Two excellent studies of this novel are Geraldine Cleary Nichols, "The Prison-House (and Beyond): *El mismo mar de todos los veranos*," *Romanic Review* 75, no. 3 (May 1984):366–85; and Elizabeth J. Ordóñez, "A Quest for Matrilineal Roots and Mythopoesis: Esther Tusquets's *El mismo mar de todos*

los veranos," *Critica Hispánica* 6, no. 1 (1984):37–46. Another approach to the same novel is Mary Vázquez, "Image and the Linear Progression Toward Defeat in Esther Tusquets's *El mismo mar de todos los veranos,"* in *LA CHISPA '83: Selected Proceedings,* ed. Gilbert Paolini (New Orleans: Tulane University, 1983), 307–13.

6. For an overview of language in Tusquets's trilogy, see Catherine G. Bellver, "The Language of Eroticism in the Novels of Esther Tusquets," *Anales de la Literatura Española Contemporánea* 9, nos. 1–3 (1984):13–27.

7. This novel is further discussed by Catherine Bellver in "Two New Women Writers from Spain," *Letras Femininas* 8, no. 2 (1982):3–7.

8. *Mi hermana Elba* is the other work treated by Bellver in the article cited in note 6.

9. The most complete study of Fernández-Cubas to date is Phyllis Zatlin, "Tales from Fernández Cubas: Adventure in the Fantastic," *Monographic Review/Revista Monográfica* 3, no. 1–2 (1987):107–18.

Chapter Nine

1. The one book available to date on the Catalan women writers is logically enough in Catalan: Patricia Gabancho, *La rateta encara escombra l'escaleta* (Barcelona: Edicions 62, 1982).

2. For more on Roig and three other young Catalan women writers, see Geraldine C. Nichols, "Mitja poma, mitja taronja: Génesis y destino literarios de la catalana contemporánea," *Anthropos* 60–61 (1986):118–23.

3. A long discussion of Oliver's use of metamorphosis in *Vegetal* may be found in Janet Pérez, "Plant Imagery and Feminine Dependency in Three Contemporary Women Writers," *In the Feminine Mode: Essays on Hispanic Women Writers,* ed. Noël Valis and Carol Maier, forthcoming from Bucknell University Press.

4. A feminist analysis of this novel is presented by Elizabeth J. Ordóñez, "Beginning to Speak: Carme Riera's *Una primavera per a Domenico Guarini,"* in *LA CHISPA '85, Selected Proceedings,* ed. Gilbert Paolini, (New Orleans: Tulane University, 1985), 285–93.

Selected Bibliography

PRIMARY WORKS

Albert i Paradis, Caterina [pseud. Victor Català]. *Drames Rurals, Caires Vius.* Barcelona: Edicions 62, 1982. Prologue by Carme Arnau.
———. *Obres completes,* Biblioteca perenne vol. 28. Barcelona: Selecta, 1951; 2d ed., 1972.
———. *Solitud.* Barcelona: Selecta, 1983. Prologue by Manuel Montoliu.
Alós, Concha. *El caballo rojo.* Madrid: Circulo de Amigos de la Historia, 1976.
———. *Las hogueras.* Barcelona: Planeta, 1964; 30th ed., 1982.
———. *La madama.* Barcelona: Ediciones G.P., 1974.
Ballesteros de Gaibrois, Mercedes. *El chico.* Barcelona: Destino, 1967.
———. *La sed.* Barcelona: Destino, 1965.
———. *Taller.* Barcelona: Destino, 1960.
Böhl de Faber y Larrea, Cecilia [pseud. Fernán Caballero] *The Sea Gull,* translation and introduction by Joan Maclean. Woodbury, N.Y.: Barrons, 1965.
———. *The Castle and the Cottage in Spain.* Translation of *La familia de Alvareda* by Lady Wallace. London: Saunders, Otley, & Co., 1861. Also *The Alvareda Family.* Translated by Viscount Pollington, London: Newby, 1872.
Burgos Seguí, Carmen. *Quiero vivir mi vida.* Madrid: Biblioteca Nueva, 1923.
Capmany Farnès, Maria Aurèlia. *Cartes impertinentes.* Palma de Mallorca: Francesc de B. Moll, Raixa, 1971.
———. *Lo color mès blau.* Barcelona: Planeta, 1982.
. *Dona, donuta, donuta.* Barcelona: EDHASA, 1979.
———. *Feliçment, jo sóc una dona.* Barcelona: Nova Terra, 1969; 3d ed. 1977.
Chacel, Rosa. *Acrópolis.* Barcelona: Seix Barral, 1984.
———. *Barrio de Maravillas.* Barcelona: Bruguera, 1980.
———. *Memorias de Leticia Valle.* Barcelona: Bruguera, 1980.
Conde Abellán, Carmen. *Creció espesa la yerba . . .* Barcelona: Planeta, 1979.
———. *Soy la madre.* Barcelona: Planeta, 1980.
Espina, Concepción [also Concha Espina]. *Agua de nieve.* Translated by Terrell Louise Tatum, *The Woman and the Sea.* New York: R. D. Henkle, 1934.
———. *Dulce nombre.* Translated by Frances Douglas, *The Red Beacon.* New York: Appleton, 1924.
———. *La esfinge maragata.* Translated by Frances Douglas, *Mariflor.* New York: Macmillan, 1924.

211

————. *El metal de los muertos.* Madrid: Afrodisio Aguado, 1941.

Falcón, Lidia. *En el infierno. (Ser mujer en las cárceles de España).* Madrid: Ediciones del Feminismo, 1977.

————. *El juego de la piel.* Barcelona: Argos-Vergara, 1983.

Fórmica Corsi, Mercedes. *A instancia de parte.* Madrid: Cid, 1954.

Galvarriato, Eulalia. *Cinco sombras.* Barcelona: Destino, 1947; 4th ed., 1967.

Lafitte y Pérez del Pulgar, María de los Reyes [Condesa de Campo Alange]. *La flecha y la esponja.* Madrid: Arion, 1959.

————. *La mujer en España, Cien años de su historia 1860–1960.* Madrid: Aguilar, 1963–64.

Laforet, Carmen. *Nada.* Translated by Charles F. Payne, *Andrea.* New York: Vantage Press, 1964.

Martín Gaite, Carmen. *El cuarto de atrás.* Translated by Helen R. Lane, *The Back Room.* New York: Columbia University Press, 1983.

————. *Retahílas.* Barcelona: Destinolibro, 1979.

Matute, Ana María. *Los hijos muertos.* Translated by Joan MacLean, *The Lost Children.* New York: Macmillan, 1965.

————. *Primera memoria.* Translated by Elaine Kerrigan, *School of the Sun.* New York: Pantheon Books, 1963.

————. *Los soldados lloran de noche.* Barcelona: Destino, 1964; 1982.

————. *La trampa.* Barcelona: Destino, 1969; 1980.

Medio, Dolores. *Bibiana.* Barcelona: Destino, 1967.

————. *Diario de una maestra.* Barcelona: Destino, 1976.

————. *La otra circunstancia.* Barcelona: Destino, 1973.

Moix, Ana María. *Julia.* Barcelona: Seix Barral, 1972.

————. *Walter, ¿por qué te fuiste?* Barcelona: Barral, 1973.

Montero, Rosa. *Crónica del desamor.* Madrid: Debate, 1979.

————. *La función Delta.* Madrid: Debate, 1981.

————. *Te trataré como a una reina.* Barcelona: Seix Barral, 1983.

Montoriol i Puig, Carme. *Teresa o la vida amorosa d'una dona.* Barcelona: Llibreria Catalonia, 1932.

Oliver, Maria Antònia. *Croniques d'un mig estiu.* Barcelona: Club Editor, 1970; 2d ed. 1983.

————. *Estudi en lila.* Translated by Kathleen McNerney, *Study in Lilac.* Seattle: The Seal Press, 1987.

————. *Vegetal i Muller qui cerca espill.* Barcelona: La llar del llibre, 1982.

Ortiz Sánchez, Lourdes. *Luz de la memoria.* Madrid: Akal, 1976.

Pàmies i Bertran, Teresa. *Amor clandestí.* Barcelona: Galba, 1976.

————. *Dona de pres.* Barcelona: Proa, 1975.

————. *Memoria dels morts.* Barcelona: Planeta, 1981.

Pardo Bazán, Emilia. *Obras completas.* Madrid: Aguilar, 1947; 3d ed., first reprint 1973.

————. *Morriña—Homesickness.* New York, 1891.

Quiroga, Elena. *Algo pasa en la calle* in *Las mejores novelas contemporáneas.* vol.

12. Edited by Joaquín de Entrambasaguas. Barcelona: Planeta, 1971.
———. *Escribo tu nombre.* Barcelona-Madrid: Noguer, 1965.
———. *Presente profundo.* Barcelona: Destino, 1973.
———. *Tristura.* Barcelona-Madrid: Noguer, 1960; reissued, Barcelona: Plaza y Janés, 1984.
Rafael Marés Kurz, Carmen de [pseud. Carmen Kurtz]. *Al lado del hombre.* Barcelona: Planeta, 1973.
———. *El desconocido.* Barcelona: Planeta, 1956; 10th ed., 1976. Also in *Premios Planeta, 1955-1958.* Barcelona: Planeta, 1979.
Riera Guilera, Carme. *Epitèlis tendríssims.* Prologue by Ana Maria Sureda. Barcelona: Edicions 62, 1981.
———. *Una primavera para Doménico Guarini.* Barcelona: Marte, 1981.
Rodoreda i Gurgui, Mercè. *El carrer de les Camèlies.* In *Obres Completes,* vol 7. Barcelona: Edicions 62, 1976–78.
———. *La meva Christina i altres contres.* Translated by David Rosenthal, *My Christina and Other Stories.* Port Townsend, Wash.: Graywolf Press, 1984.
———. *La Plaça del Diamant.* Translated by Eda O'Shield, *The Pigeon Girl.* London: Deutsch, 1967; also translated by David Rosenthal, *The Time of the Doves.* New York: Taplinger, 1983.
Roig i Fransitorra, Montserrat. *La hora violeta.* Barcelona: Argos Vergara, 1980.
———. *La ópera cotidiana.* Barcelona: Planeta, 1983.
———. *Ramona, adiós.* Barcelona: Argos Vergara, 1980.
Salisachs, Mercedes. *La gangrena.* Barcelona: Planeta, 1975; Colección Popular, 1981.
———. *El volumen de la ausencia.* Barcelona: Planeta, 1983.
Serrahima, Núria. *Mala guilla.* Barcelona: Edicions 62, 1973.
———. *L'olor dels nostres cossos.* Barcelona: Edicions 62, 1982.
Soriano, Elena. *Mujer y hombre.* Trilogiá. 3 vols. Madrid: Calleja, 1955. 1. *La playa de los locos.* 2. *Espejismos.* 3. *Medea.*
Tusquets, Esther. *El amor es un juego solitario.* Barcelona: Lumen, 1979; 4th ed., 1980.
———. *El mismo mar de todos los veranos.* Barcelona: Lumen, 1978; 6th ed. 1983.
Varada tras el último naufragio. Barcelona: Lumen, 1980.
Valentí, Helena. *L'amor adult.* Barcelona: Edicions 62, 1977.

SECONDARY WORKS

1 General Works on Spanish Women Writers
Aguilar, Isabel Calvo de. *Antología biográfica de escritoras españolas.* Madrid: Biblioteca Nueva, 1954. Covers eighty-five women writers, with a one-

page bio-bibliography on each and a short anthological selection.
Conde, Carmen. *Poesía femenína española (1939–1950)*. Barcelona: Bruguera, 1967. A pioneering anthological study of women poets.
———. *Poesia femenína española (1950–1960)*. Barcelona: Bruguera, 1971. A continuation of the collection above.
Criado y Domínguez, Juan Pedro. *Literatas españolas del siglo XIX: Apuntes bibliográficos*. Madrid: Pérez Dubrull, 1889. An early, ambitious, but almost inaccessible bibliography on women writers of Spain's nineteenth century.
Estreno X:2 (Fall 1984). Devoted to Spain's women dramatists.
Fox-Lockert, Lucia. *Women Novelists in Spain and Spanish America*. Metuchen and London: Scarecrow Press, 1979. Contains essays on twenty-two women narrators, most of them dealing with a single novel. Nine are from Spain.
Galerstein, Carolyn, ed. *Women Writers of Spain: An Annotated Bio-Bibliographical Guide*. Westport, Conn.: Greenwood Press, 1986. The most complete guide available to date on women writing in Spain, emphasizing contemporary (nineteenth and twentieth centuries), but with a few earlier writers who have had recent reprintings or studies of their works.
Letras femeninas 12: 1-2 (Primavera-Otoño 1986). Devoted to Spanish women writers and the Civil War.
Manteiga, Robert, Carolyn Galerstein, and Kathleen McNerney, eds. *Feminine Concerns in Contemporary Spanish Fiction by Women*. Chapel Hill: University of North Carolina Press, 1988 [?]. A collection of critical essays emphasizing feminist fiction.
Miller, Beth. *Women in Hispanic Literature: Icons and Fallen Idols*. Berkeley, Los Angeles, and London: University of California Press, 1983. Marginally relevant, as this collection emphasizes the portraiture of female characters.
Nelken, Margarita. *Escritoras españolas*. Barcelona: Labor, 1930. Somewhat tendentious and very hard to find, this is the work of a feminist pioneer who set out to disprove the contention that there were no women writers in Spain.
Pérez, Janet, ed. *Novelistas femeninas de la postguerra española*. Madrid: Porrúa, 1984. Essays on Salisachs, Matute, Martín Gaite, Galvarriato, Quiroga, Rodoreda, Laforet, Medio, and Moix, by well-known Hispanists, with a study of the changing female protagonist by Margaret Jones.
Serrano y Sanz, Manuel. *Antología de poetisas líricas*. Madrid, 1915. A bibliographical classic on turn-of-the-century women poets, but hard to find.
———. *Apuntes para una biblioteca de escritoras españolas desde el año 1401 al 1833*. Madrid, 1903–05. The most ambitious bibliographical attempt published to date, including women writers in Spain from 1401 to 1833, but of difficult access.
Servodidio, Mirella, ed. *Reading for Difference: Feminist Perspectives on Women*

Novelists of Contemporary Spain. Anales de la literatura española contemporánea 12:1–2 (1987; pub. 1988). Contains thirteen essays plus introduction, three on general aspects or overviews, ten on individual writers or works, including: Rosa Chacel, Rosa Montero (2), Martín Gaite (*Entre visillos*), Tusquets (2), Montserrat Roig, Lidia Falcón, Concha Alós and the single girl as viewed by Rodoreda and Laforet, with more panoramic treatments of the greater freedom in democratic Spain; "L'Ecriture Féminine" and intertextuality.

Valis, Nöel, and Carole Bradley, eds. *In the Feminine Mode: Essays on Hispanic Women Writers.* Lewisburg, Pennsylvania: Bucknell University Press. 1988. Critical and interpretive essays by well-known contemporary Hispanists.

Women Writers in Translation: An Annotated Bibliography, 1945–1962. New York and London: Garland Press, 1984. Contains only twelve Spanish women writers, six from the twentieth century.

2 Women's Studies

Fagoaga, Concha. *La voz y el voto de las mujeres.* Madrid: Editorial Icaria, 1985. A history of early Spanish suffragism, 1877–1931.

Falcón, Lidia. *Los derechos civiles de la mujer.* Barcelona: Nereo, 1963. Explication by a Spanish female lawyer on the status of women's civil rights at the time of publication.

———. *Los derechos laborales de la mujer.* Madrid: Montecorvo, 1965. A legal view of women's right to work in Spain.

———. *La razón feminista.* 2 vols. Barcelona: Fontanella, 1981, 1982. A two-volume treatise studying women's social condition from the perspective of exploitation by society.

———. *Mujer y sociedad.* Barcelona: Fontanella, 1969. A militant historical and cross-cultural study of women's situation in Spain, Latin America, and several other countries.

Levine, Linda Gould, and Gloria Waldman, eds. *Feminismo ante el franquismo.* Miami: Ediciones Universal, 1982. Interviews with several of Spain's leading feminists on the situation during the Franco regime.

Martín-Gamero, Amalia. *Antología del feminismo.* Madrid. Alianza Editorial. 1975. An anthology containing extracts from the writings of many early feminists from various European nations, including a few Spaniards: Zayas y Sotomayor, Amar y Borbón, Gómez de Avellaneda, Concepción Arenal, Pardo Bazán, and others.

Mieza, Carmen. *La mujer del español.* Barcelona: Ediciones Marte, 1977. A journalistic essay on the situation of married women in Spain at the time of publication.

Nash, Mary. *Mujer, familia y trabajo en España, 1875–1936.* Barcelona: Anthropos, 1983. Heavily oriented toward the working woman in Spain in the late nineteenth and early twentieth centuries.

Nelken, Margarita. *La condición social de la mujer en España*. Madrid: CVS Ediciones reprint, 1975. Re-edition of a feminist classic by an early militant, originally written at the inception of the Republic.

3. Essays on Specific Writers

Arnau, Carme. *Introducció a la narrativa de Mercè Rodoreda: El mite de la infantesa*. Barcelona: Edicions 62, 2d ed., 1973. By the leading Catalan critic on Rodoreda, this volume surveys the novelist's treatment of childhood.

Boring, Phyllis Zatlin. *Elena Quiroga*. Boston: Twayne Publishers, 1977. The only bio-bibliographical and critical study in English of this important writer's works up through the mid-seventies.

Bretz, Mary Lee. *Concha Espina*. Boston: G. K. Hall Co., 1980. An objective survey of this writer's works, with an appraisal of her waning popularity. The most complete source in English.

Brown, D. F. *The Catholic Naturalism of Emilia Pardo Bazán*. Chapel Hill, N. C.: University of North Carolina Press, 1957. Concentrates on the novels of Pardo Bazán's naturalistic period (the 1880s and early 1890s).

Díaz, Janet. *Ana María Matute*. New York: Twayne Publishers, 1970. A bio-bibliographical and critical study of Matute's novels and stories with the exception of *La torre vigía*.

Harter, Hugh. *Gertrudis Gómez de Avellaneda*. Boston: G. K. Hall Co., 1981. The most complete study in English of this writer who was one of the nineteenth century's early feminists.

Hemingway, Maurice. *Emilia Pardo Bazán: The Making of a Novelist*. London and New York: Cambridge University Press, 1983. One of the most recent works on this writer available in English, but studies only her early period.

Johnson, Roberta. *Carmen Laforet*. Boston: Twayne Publishers, 1981. A complete study in English of Laforet who was Spain's best-known woman novelist during the early postwar years.

Jones, Margaret E. W. *Dolores Medio*. New York: Twayne Publishers, 1974. The most complete study available of Medio, although this novelist has continued to publish steadily since.

—————. *The Literary World of Ana María Matute*. (Lexington, Ky.: University Press of Kentucky, 1970. An excellent scholarly interpretation of Matute that emphasizes her portraiture of children and adolescents.

Klibbe, Lawrence. *Fernán Caballero*. New York: Twayne Publishers, 1973. The most complete study in English on this transitional mid-nineteenth-century novelist who was Spain's first great popular best-seller.

Miracle, Josep. *Victor Català*. Barcelona: Edicions 62, 1963. A life and works survey of one of the greatest Catalan prose writers. In Catalan.

O'Connor, Patricia W. *Gregorio and María Martínez Sierra*. Boston: Twayne Publishers, 1977. In her study of the collaborations of this husband-and-wife team of dramatists, O'Connor shows conclusively that most of the writing was done by María. The most complete study available of a little-known but important woman writer.

Oller i Rabassa, Joan. *Biografía de Victor Català.* Barcelona: Edicions 62, 1967. A biography of Catarina Albert [pseud. Victor Català]. In Catalan.

Pattison, Walter T. *Emilia Pardo Bazán.* New York: Twayne Publishers, 1971. A scholarly overview of the works of Spain's most important ninteenth-century woman writer, in English.

Servodidio, Mirella, ed. *From Fiction to Metafiction: Essays in Honor of Carmen Martín-Gaite.* Lincoln, Neb.: Society of Spanish & Spanish American Studies, 1983. The most complete collection of scholarly interpretations of Martín Gaite, with essays by many well-known Hispanists. At least one study of each of Martín Gaite's major novels, but several on *The Back Room.*

Starçevic, Elizabeth. *Carmen de Burgos, defensora de la mujer.* Almería: Editorial Cajal, 1976. A life-and-works survey, emphasizing the biographical accomplishments of one of the twentieth century's pioneers in women's liberation in Spain.

Index